A SHIP MODELMAKER'S MANUAL

A SHIP MODELMAKER'S MANUAL

John Bowen

CONWAY MARITIME PRESS

Frontispiece
A quiet moment during the
annual regatta for scale ship
models on the Round Pond in
Kensington Gardens, London,
organised by the Thames
Shiplovers and Shipmodellers
Society. Three models are
interesting the spectators. At
the top is a 6ft model of
Brunel's famous ship the *Great
Britain*, built by Mike Taylor of
London. It has electric
propulsion, as well as sails, and
is radio-controlled. In the centre
is a 50in model of the
whalecatcher *Rorqual*, at
$\frac{5}{16}$in = 1ft scale, by R C Jackson
of London; this model is also
electrically powered and fitted
with radio control. In the
foreground is a steam-powered
model of the steam tug
Challenger. This model is some
55in long and was built by G
Thurston of London; it, too,
has radio control. *Model
Shipwright*

First published in 1982 by
Conway Maritime Press Ltd,
2 Nelson Road, Greenwich,
London SE10 9JB.

ISBN 0 85177 235 8

Typesetting and page make-up
by Page Bros (Norwich) Ltd
Printed and bound in the
United Kingdom by Cambridge
University Press

Contents

Acknowledgements

I would like to record my appreciation of the help which I have received from Messrs Ansell Jones & Co Ltd, Clarke Chapman Marine, Kort Propulsion Co Ltd, Laurence, Scott & Electromotors Ltd, MacGregor & Co (Naval Architects) Ltd, Maxwell Hemmens Precision Steam Engines Ltd, R Perry & Co Ltd, RFD Inflatables Ltd, Stuart Turner Ltd, Taylor, Pallister & Co Ltd, Welin Davit & Engineering Co Ltd, and Unit Steam Engine Co Ltd.

I am especially grateful to my friend Brian King for contributing the section entitled 'Propulsion – The Powering of Models'; my thanks also go to Roger Chesneau and to Steve Kirby for allowing me to quote from their articles in *Model Shipwright*, and to my publisher not only for much help and advice, but also for the use of his photo library.

Lastly, I am indebted to those model shipwrights whose efforts have produced the models which I have had so much pleasure in seeing, and in photographing. Other people have contributed photographs, and I hope that they will accept the credit with the caption as an expression of my appreciation for their use. All the uncredited photographs have been taken by myself.

John Bowen

Introduction

One of the definitions given in my dictionary for 'Introduction' is 'preliminary matter prefixed to a book'. Taken literally this could offer considerable scope. It could embody a discourse upon the pleasures to be gained from building scale models of ships, whether this be from kits (as a starting point) or from scratch, with the added enjoyment, if they are working models, of sailing them. It could dwell upon the advantages to be derived from working to scale, as opposed to building models to semi- or standoff-scale – a term which has no logical meaning – with all that that implies. It could concentrate upon that other very significant part of the model shipwright's work, research, indicating its place in the order of things, its importance, and indeed its essentiality if both technical and historical accuracy are to be achieved. It could extol the benefits to be gained from membership of a ship model society, and at the same time commiserate with those many modellers who, for diverse reasons, are unable to do so.

By hypothesising in this way I have in fact identified the salient aspects of ship model building as a recreation, for that is what it is, in both meanings of the word. As with many of today's leisure occupations, it is experiencing an upsurge in interest, which is good. But what is of greater significance is that this is accompanied by a fairly widespread improvement in the standard, quality and detailing of models being built, whether they belong to the showcase, scenic, miniature or working categories.

The continuing expansion in communications, in the improvement of research facilties, in the information available in the way of books, plans and other records (despite the appalling destruction of much valuable and irreplaceable material), and in the availability of new materials and tools have all contributed to this situation. This is very encouraging and yet, in spite of what has just been said I, and others too, during our attendance at exhibitions, regattas and rallies, still come across many excellent models which are marred by faults and mistakes. These are largely of detail and not of workmanship – that is another matter entirely – and why it should be so gives rise to much speculation.

Many books have been published about ship modelling. These cover a very wide range of ship types and periods, some treating the subject in general terms, others dealing with a ship or method of construction in great detail. Hitherto the powered merchant ship, or 'steamer' as it is widely and loosely designated, has fared

less well in this respect than has the sailing ship and the warship. But times change, and while the interest in these latter two remains as great as ever, a growing number of modellers are finding, as I have long advocated, that there is a very great potential of worthwhile subjects among the smaller merchant ships and service craft.

It is to offer some guidance and help to those whose interests are turning to, or already lie, in this area that this book has been written. Much of the content has been engendered by notes and observations made at, and resulting from, visits to those exhibitions, regattas and rallies. A considerable proportion of the text has been devoted to notes on full-size and shipyard practices, including those of past years. These cover some aspects of hull construction and of fittings not normally accorded more than a passing reference, if that. For it is in just these areas that many of the faults mentioned above had been found to lie. Although this book deals primarily with 'steamers', the opportunity has been taken to include a number of fittings for sailing ships for similar reasons.

Model hull building methods have been included since they are affected by the remarks on full-size practices, and much attention has been focused on many of the more prominent shipboard structures and fittings. Doing this has led to the omission of some of those features so habitually associated with books on ship modelling – painting and finishing, radio control, notes on tools and materials, gadgetry, minor constructional techniques, etc. All of these have been covered adequately in our previous books, *Scale Model Sailing Ships* and *Scale Model Warships*, and in other publications.

A large proportion of the illustrations have been chosen quite deliberately because they are of the kind which a modeller might be able to obtain for himself during the course of his activities or researches. As well as showing what can be achieved, many indicate the way in which photographs can also contain a great deal of

Fig 1
A very fine example of a builder's model from the period when it was the practice to use a plate finish to such fittings as the winches, ventilators, masts and derricks, boat davits, etc. This model is 1/48 scale. The *Gelria* was a twin-screw passenger liner built by Alex Stephen & Sons Ltd, Glasgow, in 1913 for the Koninklijke Hollandsche Lloyd. *Museum of Transport, Glasgow*

useful information about equipment not connected with the principal subject. Commercial organisations have been particularly helpful with information about some of their specialised products.

Types of Ship Model

Ship models can be divided into two groups, static models and working models.

STATIC MODELS
Static models include the following categories:

Exhibition or showcase models. To a certain extent this classification is a hold-over from the days when the leading passenger ship companies displayed in their offices superb, large-scale models of their vessels. These models were several feet long and complete in every detail, though the method of finishing much of that detail was by plating the metalwork rather than by painting in the true colours. They came to be regarded as the yardstick of perfection in scale modelling. Nowadays examples of these models are seen mainly in museums, for they have been superseded by models built to a much smaller scale, generally of the waterline type but still beautifully detailed in most cases, and correctly painted throughout. It is significant that many of the ships now represented are cargo vessels – a true indication of the passing of the great passenger liners.

Museum models. This is another much used categorization, though today its significance is hard to define, since models of widely different scales, sizes and, regrettably in some instances, quality, are to be found in museums. It would seem that originally the term stemmed from the belief that only models of a very high

Fig 2
The scenic model. Shown here is the 50ft = 1in (1/600) scale model of the four-masted barque *Herzogin Cecilie* wrecked at Salcombe, Devon. Built by D Hunnisett, this is a good example not only of a scenic model with plenty of atmosphere, but also of a miniature model. Notice the extra 'life' given to the whole concept by the inclusion of two small boats in the foreground.

standard of accuracy, authenticity and craftsmanship were accepted for display. On this basis the application of the term 'museum standard' to a model would be indicative of its high quality in all respects.

Scenic models. These are models built mainly to a small scale and showing a ship in a sea or similar setting. If this setting, and particularly the sea, is well executed they are very attractive, being full of action and atmosphere. In all such models it is essential that the ship itself is the principal feature. Recently some very fine examples of a development springing from the scenic model concept – the diorama – have appeared. The idea is not new, but it is not one practised by many modellers. In the diorama the model, or models, merely forms a part of a whole waterside scene. They can occupy quite a large space, or equally be compact yet full of atmosphere.

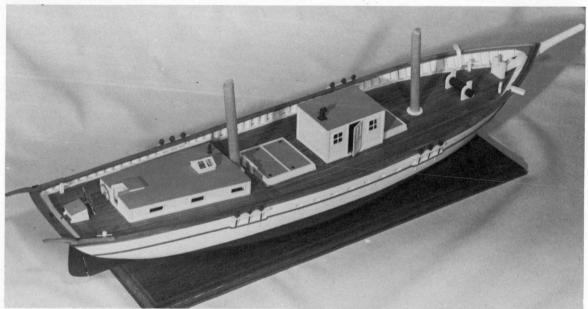

Miniature models. Of all the groups this is the one which arouses most controversy, particularly in competitive exhibitions. What constitutes a miniature? I have long held the view that this term was used originally to refer to models of steamers (and here and elsewhere I am including motor ships when using this word collectively) built to a scale of 100ft = 1in (1/1200). In the course of time the term has been broadened to include scales of up to 50ft = 1in (1/600), and nowadays all types of vessel are built to these scales. For competitive purposes the parameters have been widened still further to take in models built to scales as large as $\frac{1}{8}$in = 1ft (1/96), provided the finished model does not exceed some 8in or 9in in overall length.

Decorative models. These are another type of model frequently encountered, and the term refers mainly to those models of 'galleons', highly coloured representations, of dubious proportions, of no particular vessel, though frequently given the name of some well-known historical ship. They must not be confused with the genuine models of those vessels built as the result of lengthy and painstaking research through the records and other documentary evidence now available, and which can be said to portray the vessel as accurately as all known data allow.

Kit models. Mention must be made of the kit model, the wood variety rather than the plastic one. The quality of kits is gradually improving, from the point of view both of their historical and technical accuracy and of the quality of the materials and fittings provided. Nevertheless some research into the accuracy imparted to the vessel portrayed is advisable. It must be appreciated that the whole package of pieces has been designed with factory production requirements in mind; however, kits do provide straightaway nearly everything in the way of materials needed for a model, and many people have developed an interest in ship model building through the acquisition of such a kit. It is quite a common practice to take a kit, research the vessel thoroughly, and then use the materials provided, or rather those considered usable, as the basis for a more detailed and accurate model. So popular has this aspect of modelling become that in many competitions now there is a special category for modified kit models.

Fig 3
The miniature model. This 100ft = 1in (1/1200) scale waterline model of the Italian passenger liner *Cristoforo Colombo* was built by the author. With an overall length of just under 7in (178mm) it exemplifies what he considers to be the original true 'miniature model' concept.

Fig 4
The decorative model. 'Galleons', the customary subject for decorative models, are more usually seen as static models. In point of fact this working model of the *Elizabeth Jonas* (1598) is based on the model of an Elizabethan galleon in the Science Museum, London. The latter model was constructed to lines and structural details taken from Matthew Baker's *Fragments of Ancient English Shipwrightry*, with the rigging being based on a list of rigging of the Queen's ships in 1600. It is thus a model which comes into the category – referred to in the text – as being the result of research through such documentary and other records as are available and portraying the vessel as accurately as all known data allow. Model by A J Lench.

◄Fig 5
This model of the Great Lakes schooner *Challenge* by Delmar Searls of Oklahoma, USA, shows clearly the advantage to the beginner of choosing a simple prototype. Fittings and equipment are minimal, and if storage space is at a premium (as it was in this case) then masts and rigging can be omitted. *Delmar Searls*

Fig 6
Curlew, by M Jones of Dartford, Kent, belongs to the smaller type of Thames sailing barge known as a 'swimmie' because of the swim head (bow) in place of the customary stem head. The scale of this model is $\frac{1}{2}$in = 1ft (1/24). The presence of the two members of the crew at work adds much to the realism of the model.

Fig 7▶
The smack *Mystery*, with its clear, uncluttered decks and simple rigging, despite the comparatively large sail area, shows the value of choosing one of the smaller types of vessel as a subject for a working model. Norman Allen built this model, to a scale of $\frac{1}{16}$in = 1ft (1/192).

Fig 8
◀◀ Schooners, particularly those like the New York pilot schooner *Phantom*, make excellent sailing models. At $\frac{1}{2}$in = 1ft scale (1/24) the hull of this model by George Bland of Ruislip, Middlesex, is still only some 38in (965mm) long.

◀Fig 9
Clara May was a small trading ketch built in 1891. This radio-controlled model was built by Alastair Brown, of Cowes, Isle of Wight, to a scale of $\frac{3}{8}$in = 1ft (1/32), and shows the vessel in the later stage of its life, around 1937, with the much reduced rig which gradually followed the installation of an auxiliary engine. Even with this small sail area the model sailed well (it did not have an auxiliary). With a hull length of 30in (762mm) the all-up weight, or displacement, was only 9lb (4kg).

WORKING MODELS

For many years there was a firmly held belief that working models had to be robustly built, and that it was essential to increase the depth of the underwater body to provide the displacement necessary to accommodate the size and weight of the powerplants then available. There was an additional school of thought which considered it impractical to build a scale working model to the same high standards of detail and finish found in exhibition or

Fig 10
Models of a different type – open boats. The building of very accurate, highly detailed models of ships' boats to a large scale (1/48) by a unique method of construction was pioneered by George Draper at the end of the 1930s. Although more conventional methods of construction, rather than the Draper method of preparing wafer-thin shells of limewood and covering them with bristol board planking, have been used here by Nelson Wallis, the builder of these models, the attraction of such prototypes is well demonstrated by the boats seen in the illustration. They are a clinker-built transom stern merchant ship's boat and a clinker-built double ended ship's lifeboat. Both are to a scale of ¾in = 1ft (1/16).

Fig 11
Tugs, whether they be of the large ocean-going salvage type, harbour or ship-towing tugs, or paddle tugs, are a popular subject for modelmakers. Their fairly generous proportions in relation to the size of the vessel allow quite good displacement for the powerplant and radio control equipment. This working model of the Ardrossan Harbour Board's steam tug *Seaway* was built by P N Thomas of Glasgow to ⅜in = 1ft scale (1/32); it is fitted with electric drive and radio control. *P N Thomas*

museum-grade models. To a certain extent there may have been some element of truth in these assertions. However, in recent years the work of pioneers like Norman Ough, coupled with advances in the field of miniaturisation and the introduction of new materials and adhesives, has shown the total practicality of building and operating working models with true-to-scale underwater bodies and topsides and museum-grade finish throughout. This is not to decry the work and standards of those earlier modellers, for their results were of a very high order, particularly in the field of powerplants: today's modellers owe a very great

Fig 12
The *Minard* is a most interesting model, since the builder, Gordon McIntosh of the Glasgow Model Steamer Club, has chosen to depict one of the little, hard-working, local cargo ships which plied their trade year in year out. Rarely chosen as a subject, such vessels do in fact make excellent and interesting models. The very nature and variety of their deck loads offers plenty of scope to the builder, and yet the layout of the vessel itself is quite simple. *Minard* was built in 1925 at Bowling, on the banks of the Clyde, for Clyde Cargo Steamers Ltd, and was broken up in 1954. The scale of the model is $\frac{1}{4}$in = 1ft (1/48), the hull is of fibreglass, some 36in (915mm) long, and the displacement 8$\frac{1}{2}$lb (3.86kg); it is fitted with radio control. *P N Thomas*

Fig 13
Trawlers such as the one shown here look well on the water, and make good working models. However, the larger types do have quite a lot of detail round the deck and the casing, and for this reason some of the smaller inshore or near-water vessels, or some of the older steam trawlers or drifters (vessels with a great deal of character and atmosphere), are perhaps better subjects for the less experienced modeller interested in these vessels. The model in the photograph was built by D J Stewart. The $\frac{1}{4}$in = 1ft (1/48) scale model is of the 1937-built Hull trawler *Lady Shirley*. With an overall length of 44in (1118mm) the hull is constructed of tinplate, and the model is fitted with a steam propulsion plant.

Fig 14
A model of an ocean-going ship, whether cargo vessel or passenger liner, always makes an imposing sight when under way. This electrically driven, radio-controlled model of the Standard Fruit & SS Company's fruit-carrying steamer *Granada* (1/100 scale) was built by Colin Bishop. The model is 39in (990mm) long overall.

deal to their pioneering work. Much of what they did forms the basis of many current techniques and practices, and the tribute to their work can be seen at any regatta or rally of scale models.

When considering the construction of a working model there are a number of factors to be taken into account, starting with the availability of suitable sailing water and its condition. Weeds can ruin everything, and trees or other impedimenta upset the wind. The method of transporting the model must have a bearing on its size and its weight. Size and weight must also be borne in mind when assessing the suitability of the ground at the water's edge for launching and recovering the model, which may weigh many pounds. For average conditions a model having a length of between 3ft and 5ft would be considered a reasonable size. It gives scope for detail and can have adequate space and displacement (though much must depend on the nature of the prototype) for radio control and, in the case of powered models, the machinery. This is not to say that much smaller models cannot perform well; they do. But as well as the limitations imposed by their overall dimensions there is another drawback. In ship modelling, whilst everything on the vessel can be reduced to scale size, the elements, wind and waves, cannot. Unless there is, literally, almost a complete calm, which is of little use to the sailing enthusiast, the slightest ripple on the surface of the water will cause the model to bob and bounce all over the place in a most unrealistic manner.

In referring to unrealistic performance there is another fault which is seen all too frequently in powered models – excessive speed. The correct scale speed for a scale model can be calculated by a simple formula (see 'Definitions'). There are times when this can be exceeded slightly without detriment either to general effect or to the correct wave formation along the hull. But what is so ridiculous is to see a model of a vessel which has a service speed of, say, 16kts, or perhaps about 2½kts scale speed, sailing along at something like 8 or 9kts. Scaled up, this means that the prototype would be doing about 55–60kts!

In addition to the points just mentioned, builders of working models have to consider such matters as ballasting, false keels, rudder extensions, the ease of handling sails, the possible fitting of radio control and the functions which it will operate, and the transportable state of the model. Is the top hamper, ie masts and spars, to be permanently in place or will it all have to be adapted to stow flat?

Some of these matters – ballasting, radio control, and the facility of being able to unship masts and perhaps funnel – apply also to powered vessels. But the main decision for anyone contemplating such a model will be the choice of a prime mover. Will it be electricity, steam or internal combustion? Of these the last-named is little used except for fast racing craft. Electrical propulsion is by far and away the easiest and safest, and the range of small, powerful and lightweight motors and lightweight batteries is very extensive. Steam went out of favour for a long time, but it is making a welcome return, with some useful units coming on to the market. There is no doubt that it does make an interesting and satisfying powerplant for models of suitable prototypes.

Fig 15
Paddle steamers make interesting models, particularly since in many instances, as here, the deck layout is quite simple and there are not a great number of fittings to be made. This model, electrically powered, is of the paddle tug *Brigadier*, belonging to Steel & Bennie Ltd, Glasgow. In the photograph it is seen going hard astern.

Fig 16
Where warships are concerned the destroyer has long been one of the most popular prototypes, but as well as having a great deal of intricate detail, particularly on those built over the past 50–60 years, the somewhat shallow hull with limited draught can pose problems for the builders of working models. That these problems can be overcome very successfully is seen by the model shown here of HMS *Ashanti* by Don Brown of Chiswick, London. It is to ⅛in = 1ft (1/96) scale, electrically powered and fitted with radio control.

Fig 17
Of the smaller naval vessels the corvettes of the wartime 'Flower' class are popular with modelmakers. The characteristics of the hull give more scope, *ie* room, and the fittings and armament, though not negligible, are not too onerous. Although 269 corvettes were built for the Allies, the inevitable modifications and alterations which were made as a result of development and operational experience offer the possibility of individuality to a modeller in a class of basically similar ships. Shown here is HMS *Clematis*, by S Kirby. Realism has been given to the model both by 'weathering' the hull and funnel and by the inclusion of a number of members of the crew going about their duties. The model is electrically driven, has radio control, and is built to a scale of ⅛in = 1ft (1/96), giving a hull length of 25in (635mm) overall.

Definitions and Terminology

The following definitions of the principal dimensions of a ship, and of some of the technical terms most often encountered, apply mainly to vessels built during the last hundred or so years. See **Figs 20, 21 and 22**.

DIMENSIONS

Length overall (LOA). The extreme length of the ship.

Length between perpendiculars (BP, or PP). The horizontal length between the forward perpendicular (FP) and the after perpendicular (AP).

Forward perpendicular (FP). This is the line drawn perpendicular (*ie* at right angles) to the base line to pass through the point where the designed load line cuts the forward side of the stem. At one time the FP was taken as the line perpendicular to the base which passed through the point where the line of the upper deck cut the fore side of the stem.

After perpendicular (AP). This is the line drawn perpendicular to the base line to pass through the intersection of the designed load waterline with the after side of the rudder post. For ships which have no rudder post the after perpendicular is taken as the centre of the rudder stock.

Registered length. Used for registration purposes, this is the length from the fore side of the top of the stem to the after side of the rudder post.

Lloyd's length. Used for scantling purposes, this is the length from the fore side of the stem to the after side of the rudder post, or centre of rudder stock if there is no rudder post, on the summer load waterline.

Breadth extreme. The greatest breadth of the hull to the outside of the planking or shell plating.

Breadth moulded. This is the greatest breadth of the hull to the outside of the frames.

Depth moulded. The vertical distance from the top of the keel to the top of the beams of the uppermost continuous deck at the side amidships.

Draught. The vertical distance from a waterline to the underside of the keel at its lowest point. Mean draught is the average of the draught forward and the draught aft when these differ.

TECHNICAL TERMS

Amidships. This is taken as the mid-point of the length between perpendiculars and is indicated on plans by the symbol shown in **Fig 23**.

Buoyancy, centre of. Denoted by the letter B, this is the centroid of the underwater body of the ship. It is the position through which the total force or buoyancy acts. Its position is indicated as a height above the base line and a distance either forward or aft of midships.

Camber. The downward curvature given to a deck transversely. The generally accepted camber of the midship beam of a merchant

Fig 18
Although modern warships are the choice for the majority of modellers, many unusual and fascinating craft are to be found among the earlier vessels of the world's navies. Locating such craft has been helped very considerably by the recent publication of several reference books to the world's navies with a much wider coverage of their vessels than has been the case in the past. Plans of many of these ships are, moreover, obtainable from some of the sources mentioned later. *Keokuk*, illustrated here, is an example. Described as an armoured ship she was, in the words of Steve Kirby who researched and built this 1/60 scale electrically powered, radio-controlled working model, 'one of the many extraordinary creations to appear during the American Civil War'.

Fig 19
The recent revival of interest in steam plants has led also to an interest in the steam-driven pleasure launches of the Victorian and Edwardian eras. Since, coincidentally, much salvage, restoration and preservation work is being done with the real thing, more information is becoming available to modelmakers. The grace, beauty and appeal of these craft is well exemplified in this model of the Lake Windermere steam launch *Branksome*. It was built by D Jacques of Barrow-in-Furness to a scale of 1½in = 1ft (1/8). The engine is a Stuart Turner Double 10, driving a 3in (76mm) diameter brass propeller.

ship is one-fiftieth of the breadth of the ship; for simplicity a figure of ¼in per foot of beam is often used in practice. This does not apply necessarily to naval vessels, where figures in excess of this figure are often to be found. As with sheer, the use of the arc of a circle to form the curve has in recent years been discarded in favour of straight-line camber. In some cases this peaks on the centreline, and sometimes there is a short level section on the centre-line. Camber is customarily expressed in inches; it is also referred to as the round of beam. The method of drawing this curve is shown in **Fig 22**.

Coefficient, block. This is the ratio of the underwater volume of a vessel (*ie* its displacement expressed in cubic feet or cubic metres) floating at the load waterline to the volume of a block having the same length, breadth and draught as the ship at that waterline. The length used is normally that between perpendiculars. This ratio, written as C_B, can lie between 0.50 and 0.65 for fast ships of fine form such as ferries, liners, destroyers and some small craft; between 0.65 and 0.75 for vessels of moderate form; and between 0.75 and 0.85 for vessels of full form. Note that the units must always be the same – displacement in cubic feet, dimensions in feet, and so on. It will be seen that if the block coefficient is known, then the displacement of a model can be determined using the dimensions of the circumscribing block.

Coefficient, midship section. This is written as C_M. It is the ratio of the area of the immersed part of the midship section to that of a rectangle having the same breadth as the ship and a depth equal to the draught of the ship.

Coefficient, prismatic. This is written as C_P. It is the ratio of the volume of displacement to the volume of a solid having a length equal to the length between perpendiculars and a constant section equal to the area of the immersed midship section.

Flare. The way in which the sides of the hull curve outwards at the fore end above the waterline.

Floor, rise of. The amount by which the line of the bottom amidships rises above the base line when extended to the moulded breadth lines at either side.

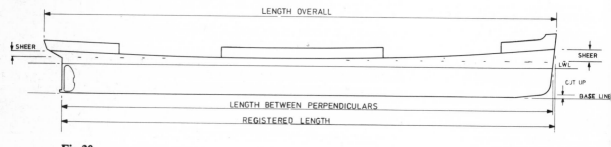

Fig 20

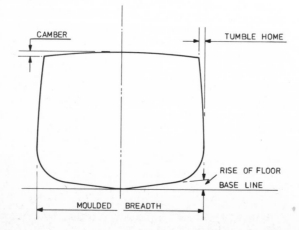

Fig 21

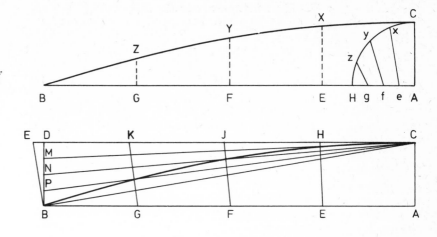

Fig 22
Method of preparing a camber or round of beam curve.

In (i), AB represents the half-breadth of the ship. At A erect a perpendicular AC, the length AC being the maximum round of beam amidships. With centre A and radius AC, strike an arc to cut AB at H. Divide AB, AH and the arc CH into the same number of equal parts. At E, F and G erect perpendiculars equal to *ex*, *fy* and *gz*. Draw a fair curve from B to C through X, Y and Z. This is the round of beam curve. Complete the full beam curve by repeating on the opposite side of AC.

In (ii), AB represents the maximum half-breadth of the ship. The perpendicular AC is the maximum round of beam. Complete the rectangle ACBD and join the diagonal CB. Draw BE perpendicular to CB to meet CD produced to E. Divide AB and CE into the same number of equal parts, and join the points EH, FJ and GK. Divide BD into the same number of equal parts at M, N and P, and join these points to C. Draw a fair curve from B to C through the points where CM cuts EH, CN cuts FJ and CP cuts GK. This is the round of beam curve.

The camber at any half-breadth can be obtained by measuring the perpendicular distance from the horizontal line to the camber curve at that half-breadth on AB. If the camber curve is being developed full-size for the model (in order to make a round of beam template), AB and AC must be to the same scale. If it is required only to *calculate* the camber at any half-breadth, then greater accuracy can be obtained by drawing AC to a larger scale than AB.

Gravity, centre of. Denoted by the letter G, this is the point through which the total weight of the ship acts. Its position is also marked by a height above base line and a distance forward or aft of midships.

Sheer. This is the curvature of the deck in a longitudinal direction when seen from the side. Usually the sheer or rise forward is twice the rise aft. The amount of sheer at any point is the difference between the height at side at that point and the height at side amidships. There is an increasing tendency these days for ships to be built either without sheer, *ie* level from stem to stern, or to be level over the major part of their length but having a straight-line sheer over comparatively short distances at bow and stern.

Speed, scale. If the service speed of the prototype ship is known, and its length, then the appropriate speed for a scale model of that ship can be calculated by means of the following formula:

$$\frac{V}{v} = \sqrt{\frac{L}{l}}$$

where L = the length of the prototype, l = the corresponding length of the model, V = the speed of the prototype, and v = the speed of the model. The two lengths must always be in the same units, *ie* feet, metres, etc, and so must the speeds, *ie* knots, miles per hour, kilometres per hour, etc.

As L/l is the same as the scale expressed as a ratio, *ie* $\frac{1}{4}$in = 1ft is 1/48, then the ratio 48, or whatever is appropriate for the model, can be substituted for L/l in the formula.

Stability. This is an involved subject, and one that is outside the scope of this book. A ship is said to be stable if, when it is floating at rest and it is inclined at a small angle from that position, it returns to that position. One of the conditions which governs this situation is that the ship's centre of gravity must be in the same vertical line as the centre of buoyancy.

Tonnage. Perhaps the most baffling statistical data both for the layman and the ship modeller. Gross, underdeck, net and registered tonnage are based on internal volume and not mass (though they are given in tons or tonnes). Deadweight tonnage is basically the mass or weight of cargo, passengers, fuel and stores which a ship can carry, and is the difference in tons or tonnes between the light and loaded conditions of the ship. Displacement tonnage is the only one which is of interest to the builder of working models. Displacement is the amount of water put aside, or displaced, by a vessel when afloat. Imagine a ship afloat in still water, then imagine that the water is solidified (without contraction or expansion) and the ship is lifted out, leaving in the solidified water a cavity which is the exact shape of its underwater body. The Law of Archimedes states that a floating body displaces its own weight of water. So the weight of the quantity of water required to fill this cavity to the brim will be equal to the weight of the ship and its contents. This weight is known as the displacement, and being a quantity it can also be expressed as a volume (cubic feet, cubic metres, etc).

The volume of displacement at any draught can be calculated using certain data taken from the lines and body plans, but it is a somewhat involved process. Those who are interested will find the necessary details of the calculations used in any book on naval architecture.

In the case of scale working models the displacement at a particular draught can be calculated from the prototype's displacement at the equivalent draught. This is a very useful exercise as it allows the modeller to know beforehand just what weight he has available for the hull, machinery, radio, fittings and so on. The calculation is as follows. Convert the ship's displacement into pounds weight. Express the scale of the model as a ratio (*eg* ¼in = 1ft scale is 1/48). Cube the ratio figure (*eg* 48 × 48 × 48) and divide the previously computed displacement in pounds by this result. The answer will be the displacement of the model at the given draught. An approximate figure for the model's displacement can be obtained by multiplying the volume (in cubic inches) of the circumscribing block at the required draught by the estimated block coefficient and dividing the result by 27.7, the quotient being the displacement in pounds (27.7 cubic inches of water weigh one pound).

Waterlines, bowlines, buttock lines, etc will be found in the description of the lines plan (see under 'Plans').

Trim. The difference between the draughts forward and aft. If the draught aft is greater than that forward the ship is said to trim by the stern. If the draught forward is greater the ship trims by the bow or head.

Tumblehome. The amount by which the sides amidships fall in from the maximum breadth at any depth.

Fig 23
Amidships symbol

CATALOGUE

The After End

There are three main forms of stern, elliptical (counter), cruiser and transom, and examples of these can be seen in the photographs. The shape of each above the waterline can vary quite considerably, depending on owner's and design requirements, and also at times the practices of the shipbuilder. Failure to follow faithfully lines of the stern given in the plans can ruin the whole character of a model.

Below the waterline the hull ends with the stern frame, a heavy forging, casting, or prefabricated unit designed to carry the rudder and to provide support for the tailshaft bearing of single- or triple-screw vessels. This is merely a development of the heavy timber sternpost found in wooden-hulled vessels (**Fig 24**). The shell plating is attached to the stern frame. **Fig 25** is a typical stern frame for a single-screw vessel having an elliptical stern, while **Fig 26** shows one of the types most often seen in ships with a cruiser stern. **Fig 27** is another design where the rudder is of the semi-balanced type, and **Fig 28** outlines the arrangement where the rudder is of the 'dagger' type without bottom support.

The classification society's rules govern the scantlings of the main parts of the frame. In single-screw vessels the forward part of the frame incorporates a boss to accommodate the tailshaft bearing, the propeller shaft stern tube being attached to the forward end of this boss. On the after side of the after member, referred to as the rudder post, are the gudgeons to take the rudder pintles. The dimensions of the gudgeon are governed by the size of the pintle, which in turn has to be in accordance with the classification rules, as has, too, the spacing of the gudgeons. The size of the aperture is determined by the dimensions of the propeller. In working scale models this may have to be increased slightly over scale size to suit the propeller being used. The same will apply to the size of the boss on the propeller post. In cross-section, posts were either rectangular or of a streamlined shape.

On a model this will be a somewhat fragile part of the hull, and whilst it can be formed with the hull it is much better to make it, or part of it, as a separate unit, to be added later once all the heavy work has been finished. So

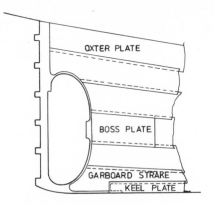

Fig 24
Arrangement of shell plating in way of stern frame of single-screw vessel.

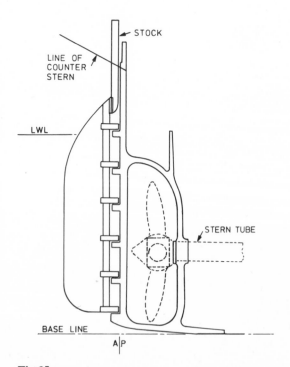

Fig 25
Typical stern frame of a single-screw vessel with a counter (elliptical) stern.

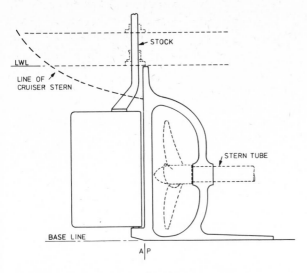

Fig 26
Typical stern frame of a single-screw vessel with a cruiser stern and double plate rudder.

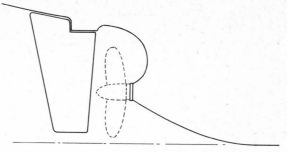

Fig 28
Stern arrangement for single-screw vessel with a 'dagger' type rudder. Note absence of any bottom support to rudder.

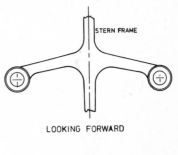

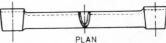

Fig 29
'Spectacle' type stern tube casting for twin-screw ship. Castings attached to stern frame.

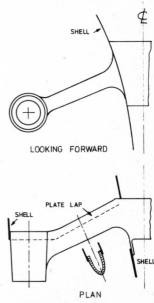

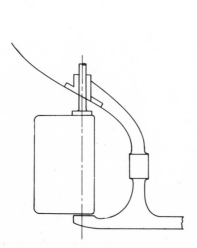

Fig 27
Stern frame arrangement for single-screw vessel with semi-balanced rudder, double plate type. Note absence of rudder post.

Fig 30
Stern tube castings for twin-screw ship. These are separate castings well attached to adjacent side frames.

Fig 31
The counter stern is seen to advantage in this
photograph of the Harrison Line vessel *Custodian*, built
in 1900, and here seen being used as a troopship
during the Boer War. The individual plates of the shell
plating are clearly visible, and notice the way the
strakes of plating sweep up under the counter. *Conway
Picture Library*

doing also has the added advantage of making
the work of shaping the hull in the way of the
shaft bossing much easier and, in the case of
working models, simplifies the job of drilling
the hole to take the propeller shaft tube. Where
working models are concerned it is advisable
to make the rudder post, sole piece, etc separately and of a material which will withstand
the inevitable bumps and bangs it will suffer
from time to time. All the gudgeons can be
included, but only the bottom pintle need be
fitted, the remainder being false, to reduce
friction on the rudder's movement.

In twin-screw vessels the arrangement is different. Where the propeller shaft emerges from
the hull the frames in way are shaped to form
bossing, the stern tube is fitted in the recess
so formed, and the after end of the propeller
shaft is supported by 'A' brackets. Alterna-

Fig 32 ▲
The whole form of a cruiser stern. Although this is a
triple-screw vessel, the stern frame and the bossing for
the centre propeller shaft are the same as for a single-
screw ship, while the bossing for the wing shafts is
similar to that of a twin screw vessel. Note the
gudgeons on the rudder post with the pintles in
position. The plating of the cruiser stern is well
defined, and is interesting in that the strakes are
possibly slightly narrower than would be the case today
– the ship was built in 1914. Note also the hawsepipe
for a stern anchor of the stockless type. *Conway Picture
Library*

Fig 33▶
An example of the present-day transom stern; on some
vessels it is very much wider at deck level. Note the
recess for the stern anchor, the mooring pipes in the
bulwark, the rudder gudgeons and the horizontal type
coupling. *By courtesy of Manchester Liners Ltd*

tively (and this is more the customary practice), the stern tubes are fitted as near to the propellers as possible, the frames again being shaped to form bossing, with the shell plating enclosing the whole shaft. The stern tube is supported at its after end by a casting or bracket, well tied into the hull structure, to which the boss plating was attached. These castings are aptly referred to as 'spectacle frames'. **Figs 29** and **30** show two such castings in outline. The first is attached to the propeller post of the stern frame, while the second is a separate casting attached to the adjacent side frames.

Being much more rigid, this bossing can be carved with the hull, though it is best to leave it slightly oversize until the hole for the propeller shaft tube has been drilled, after which it can be fined down to the correct shape. The sectional shape of the bossing, as previously mentioned, is shown on the body plan – see **Fig 129**, and **Fig 130**.

On iron and steel sailing ships the stern frame was a simple affair consisting of the rudder post and a bottom piece, being in fact rather like that shown in **Fig 25** but without the curved section carrying the propeller boss.

Anchors

In the course of time anchors have progressed from the initial stone on the end of a rope to the well-known forms in use today. Many and varied have been the designs produced to meet the altering requirements, and it is impractical to mention more than a few.

The common stocked anchor carried by many of the latter-day sailing ships and other vessels is seen in **Fig 34**. The stock is fixed, but an alternative form with movable stock is shown in **Figs 35** and **38**. For stowage purposes the forelock (locking pin) was removed from the stock, thus allowing the latter to be moved to lie alongside the shank, the large ball at the end of the short turned section of the stock preventing it from coming too far through, as did the swelling halfway along the stock for the reverse operation.

Another type of close-stowing anchor was the Martin anchor, shown in **Figs 41** and **42**. Its appeal lay in the fact that, with the stock and arms being in one plane, no parts projected very much above the shank. It was usually stowed on an anchor bed, close to the ship's side, inclined at about 20° and fitted with skids on which the anchor rested.

The Trotman anchor (**Fig 39**) was much used on the earlier transatlantic steamers and other vessels of the period until the advent of the stockless anchor. Since the arms were pivoted at the crown and the stock could be released in the same way as that of the common

Fig 34
The common stocked anchor with fixed stock, seen here in the stowed position. One end of each of the two securing chains, those through the shackle and round the crown, is connected to the quick-release gear. *Conway Picture Library*

Fig 35 ▶
Another type of common stocked anchor. In this the stock can be released by removal of the forelock (pin) just visible above its keep chain. By sliding the stock through until the short turned end lies in the hole in the shank, the length of the stock will lie alongside the shank, making stowage on deck much easier. The ship is the three-masted schooner *Kathleen & May*, now berthed in St Katharine's Dock, London, as part of the Historic Ships Collection. Note the protective doubling on the bulwark in way of the flukes.

Fig 36
The stowage of a stockless anchor. The vessel is a coaster, the *Peroto* and this photograph, taken in 1979 is useful in that it shows an interesting construction of an all-welded hull and soft-nose stem.

stocked anchor, it was very easy to stow on deck, being lifted up over the ship's side by means of an anchor davit or crane.

A stockless-type anchor is shown in **Fig 40**. Its advantage is that the shank can be drawn right into the hawsepipe, thus allowing the anchor to stow automatically and in a matter of moments, as can be seen in **Figs 115** and **245**. In **Fig 37** can be seen a form of prefabricated anchor frequently fitted on modern small coasters, particularly those from the Continent.

The size of an anchor is denoted by its weight, not by its physical dimensions. The number of anchors, type, weight and the minimum amount of cable for each which a vessel has to carry are determined from the classification society's rules. Some idea of the dimensions of a stockless anchor may be gained from the table which accompanied an article by P N Thomas in *Model Shipwright* 34 (December 1980). The principal anchors carried by a ship were the bower anchors (so called because they were found at the bow of the ship); some examples of the weight of these anchors and the size of cable used with them are shown below for a number of different vessels:

Normandie: 16 tons each, $4\frac{1}{8}$in stud link cable (=slc).
Mauretania I: 10 tons each, $3\frac{3}{4}$in slc.★
500ft cargo ship (1949): $81\frac{1}{4}$cwt, $2\frac{3}{16}$in slc.

Fig 37
A form of prefabricated anchor, seen on the Panamanian-registered coaster *Elisabeth-S* in 1979.

Fig 38
The parts of an anchor. This is the common stocked anchor, with loose stock.

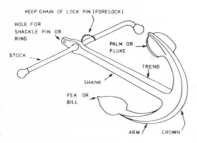

Fig 39
The Trotman anchor. The arms can swivel about the pin through the crown, and the stock is of the loose type.

SD14 cargo ship (1970s): 80cwt, $2\frac{1}{8}$ in special grade steel.
Cross channel ship (1951): $46\frac{1}{2}$cwt, 2in slc.
Coastal pass/cargo ship (250ft): 33cwt, $1\frac{11}{16}$in slc
214ft coaster (1950s): $22\frac{1}{4}$cwt, $1\frac{1}{4}$in H/T slc.
* each link was $22\frac{1}{2}$in long $\times$ $13\frac{1}{2}$in wide and weighed approx $1\frac{1}{2}$cwt.

So many variables have to be taken into account when determining the outfit of mooring equipment for a vessel, which includes also the statutory outfit of wires and hawsers, that it is not really practical to suggest guidance sizes for particular types. What the diagrams and the table do show are reasonable proportions for the items concerned so that if, for example, it is known that the vessel being modelled has a 2in anchor cable, then the size of the links can be worked out.

A study of the anchors illustrated will show that, from a modelmaker's point of view, they can be looked upon as comprising a number of individual parts – stock, shank, crown, arms and flukes – all of which can be made separately, thus simplifying construction. It is always better to make your own anchors rather than rely on the purchased article, unless you can find one which really tallies with that which the vessel carried, in respect of both size and detail. To be fair, there are some on the market which are of reasonable quality and which can, with care, be used as the basis for a scale anchor.

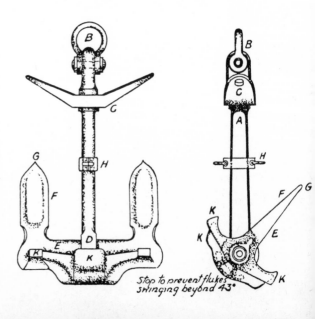

Stop to prevent flukes swinging beyond 43°

DIMENSIONS OF HALL ANCHORS.

WEIGHT OF ANCHOR (W) IN LBS.	A = .558 ∛W	B = .622 A	C = 1.539 A	D = .412 A	K = .857 A	F = 9.616 A	G = 4.903 A	H = 1.177 A	I = 2.401 A	K = 3.413 A	L = 1.823 A	M = .73 A
165	3.07	1.93	4.92	1.26	2.64	29.53	14.76	3.62	7.20	10.47	4.06	2.90
220	3.39	2.09	5.43	1.38	2.91	32.52	16.26	3.96	8.11	11.54	4.49	2.44
330	3.86	2.36	6.18	1.57	3.31	37.05	18.54	4.53	9.25	13.15	5.12	2.80
440	4.25	2.64	6.81	1.73	3.66	40.00	20.43	5.00	10.20	14.49	5.63	3.07
550	4.61	2.87	7.36	1.89	3.94	40.28	22.13	5.43	11.06	15.71	6.10	3.31
660	4.88	3.03	7.80	2.00	4.17	46.90	23.47	5.75	11.73	16.65	6.46	3.50
880	5.35	3.35	8.54	2.20	4.61	51.42	25.71	6.30	12.87	18.27	7.09	3.86
1,100	5.79	3.58	9.25	2.40	4.96	55.63	27.80	6.81	13.90	19.72	7.68	4.17
1,320	6.14	3.82	9.80	2.52	5.28	59.02	29.40	7.24	14.76	20.95	8.11	4.41
1,540	6.46	4.02	10.32	2.68	5.55	62.02	30.91	7.60	15.51	22.00	8.54	4.65
1,765	6.77	4.21	10.83	2.80	5.79	65.04	32.52	7.95	16.26	23.11	8.96	4.88
1,985	7.05	4.37	11.26	2.91	6.02	67.68	33.86	8.27	16.93	24.06	9.33	5.12
2,200	7.28	4.53	11.65	2.99	6.26	69.96	35.00	8.58	17.48	24.83	9.65	5.28
2,760	7.83	4.88	12.56	3.23	6.73	75.28	37.64	9.21	18.82	26.73	10.35	5.67
3,310	8.35	5.20	13.35	3.43	7.17	80.16	40.42	9.80	20.04	28.54	11.02	6.02
3,800	8.78	5.47	14.06	3.62	7.52	84.33	42.50	10.35	21.06	29.96	11.61	6.34
4,410	9.17	5.71	14.69	3.78	7.87	88.47	44.39	10.79	22.00	31.30	12.13	6.65
4,900	9.53	5.96	15.24	3.94	8.15	91.54	46.09	11.22	22.87	32.52	12.60	6.89
5,510	9.88	6.14	15.79	4.06	8.46	94.92	47.82	11.61	23.74	33.70	13.07	7.13
6,610	10.51	6.54	16.81	4.33	9.02	100.99	50.81	12.36	25.24	35.87	13.90	7.60
7,720	11.06	6.89	17.68	4.57	9.49	106.26	53.49	13.03	26.58	37.76	14.65	7.95
8,820	11.58	7.20	18.50	4.76	9.92	111.30	55.93	13.62	27.80	39.83	15.32	8.35
9,920	12.00	7.48	19.21	4.96	10.28	115.36	58.02	14.13	28.82	41.32	15.91	8.66
11,020	12.44	7.76	19.88	5.12	10.67	120.28	60.06	14.65	29.88	42.78	16.46	8.96
13,230	13.23	8.23	21.14	5.43	11.34	127.09	63.88	15.55	31.77	45.46	17.52	9.57

HALL ANCHOR.

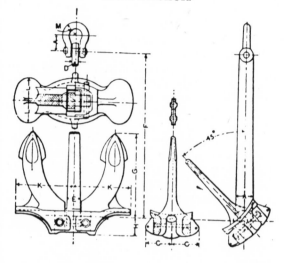

Fig 40 ▲
Hall's stockless anchor, with table of dimensions for various weights of anchor from approximately 1½cwt to 6 tons. *By courtesy of P N Thomas*

◀Fig 41
Martin's close-stowing anchor. **A** Shank. **B** Ring. **C** Stock. **D** Crown. **E** Arms. **F** Flukes. **G** Pea or bill. **H** Gravity band. **K** Tripping palms.

Fig 42 ▶
Martin's close-stowing anchor. In this anchor the stock and arms are in one plane, and as can be seen no parts project very much above the shank. The flukes turn, to about 40° either side, on a pin through the crown. This one illustrated is on the former Trinity House lightship *Nore*, now part of the Historic Ships Collection in St Katharine's Dock, London.

Anchor Cranes: Quick-Release Gear

Prior to the introduction of the stockless type, once an anchor had been raised clear of the water it was transferred to its stowed position in one of two ways. In one, lifting tackle making use of the cathead sheaves was hooked on and the anchor was brought up to the edge of the deck, as in **Fig 34**, where it was secured by chains. A long link at each end of the chain was slipped over the lugs of the quick-release gear fitted either on the side of the cathead or on the deck nearby. Details of this gear can be seen in **Figs 45** and **47**. The alternative method was to lift the anchor up over the ship's side by means of an anchor davit or anchor crane, and stow it on deck. Where the cable came over the deck-edge, removable lengths of chain were fitted between the rail stanchions in place of rods. **Figs 43** and **44** show details of typical anchor cranes; the scantlings would be suitable for the weight of anchor being handled.

Fig 45▶
Deck mounted anchor quick-release gear; disregard the wire ropes, which would not normally be there. The end links of the securing chain slip over two hook-shaped lugs on the long horizontal bar – they can be seen just a few inches along from the end bearing plates. To release the anchor the retaining pin (missing in the photograph) was removed from the double lug on the left to allow the short bar or handle to be swung over to the right. On the pivoted end of this handle is a half-cup which locks over that short central locking rod at the middle of the long bar. By swinging the handle over to the right this half-cup is turned so that its open half comes uppermost. The weight of the anchor hanging by the securing chains from the lugs on the long bar causes this to rotate through 180° as it is no longer restrained from so doing by the half-cup holding the short locking rod. The chain links slip off the lugs and the anchor falls clear.

Fig 43
Most anchor cranes were built on the lines of the one shown here.

Fig 44▶
An early-pattern anchor crane.

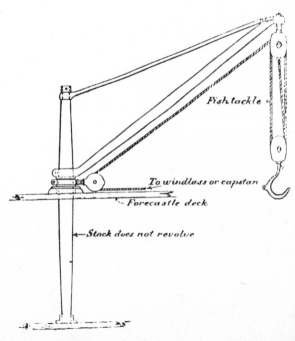

Fish tackle

To windlass or capstan

Forecastle deck

Stock does not revolve

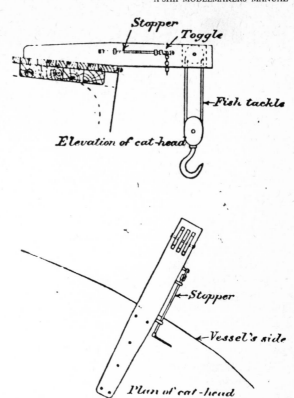

Fig 46
Arrangement of quick-release gear fitted to a cathead.

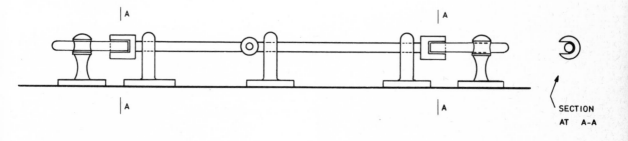

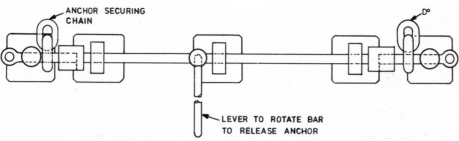

Fig 47
Quick-release gear fitted on deck.

Awning Stanchions

Vessels sailing through, or operating in, warm climates usually rig awnings over some of the open decks. These canvas awnings are spread over an arrangement of wooden ridges and rafters supported by steel stanchions.

Fig 48 shows very clearly the general set-up. Although the component parts are bolted together, and thus can be dismantled when necessary, they are generally left in place. In fact, on a number of ships the extensive array of awning supports is quite a salient feature of their general appearance.

Sometimes certain areas are covered with a semi-permanent fixed awning. At one time this was of light timber construction, but nowadays recourse is made to other materials such as aluminium or a translucent 'plastic'.

Fig 48
The details of the awning gear described in the text are clearly visible here. Note that the bolts are at, or just below, mid-depth of the timbers, and that the sides of the shoes are about three-quarters the depth of the ridge and rafter. Clear of the boats the awnings extend to the ship's side, and notice that they are also fitted over the open bridge wings.

Other useful points in this photograph are the crescent-type davits to the boats, with the operating mechanism and boat falls well visible, together with the lead of the wire fall through the deck-mounted sheaves to the boat winch. The winch has a divided drum to keep the wires from the forward and after davit of each boat separate. Just visible to the port side of the radar mast on the wheelhouse are two aerial lead-in trunks, topped by the usual heavy insulators. The ship is the cargo liner *Ben Venue*, built in 1948 for the Ben Line.

The scantlings of the fittings shown in the illustration are a good average of those normally used. Both the ridges (those pieces running fore and aft) and the rafters are about 6in × 3in, or perhaps 7in × 3½in. The ends of the rafters drop into steel shoes bolted to the ridges, or into similar shoes attached to the side of an adjacent deckhouse. Where, because of the length of run, the ridges have to be in several pieces (as here), these are joined with horizontal scarph joints, through-bolted and with a flat bar strap on the underside; the bolt-heads would be sunk below the top surface of the timber to prevent chafe on the canvas. The ridges are supported by steel stanchions, about 2–2½in in diameter and of a height to allow adequate headroom below the rafters. A flat U-shaped socket was welded to the top of each stanchion to take the ridge, which was secured by a through-bolt. Where necessary, supporting stays, of about 1in diameter steel bar, were fitted. These would have an eye formed at each end, that at the top being bolted to a flat bar lug welded to the stanchion, and the one at the other end being bolted to a double lug secured to the deck.

Binnacle

The basic design of a binnacle seems to have altered very little over the years. It is essentially a cylinder of wood construction with non-magnetic fittings, and having the compass fitted to the top. On each side are the L-shaped brackets with slotted arm to carry the correction spheres. On either side of the compass cover is a holder for the light used to illuminate the compass card. All these can be seen in **Fig 49**.

Bollards

Many modelmakers do not appreciate that the size of bollards, that is the diameter of the post, varies according to the size of the vessel and their position on board. **Fig 52**, which is the plan of the forecastle of a typical cargo ship of some 11,000 tons carrying capacity, shows three sizes of bollard – 16in, 14in and 12in. A 100ft tug and a 180ft distant-water trawler both carried 8in bollards, while on a cross-channel vessel similar to the *Maid of Orleans* they were 10in and 11in diameter. Time and time again models – good, well-built scale models – are spoilt because the maker resorted to the use of a purchased set of one-size (and out of scale) bollards. After all, as a study of the illustrations will show, they are not very difficult to make: a flat base and two posts turned in wood, metal

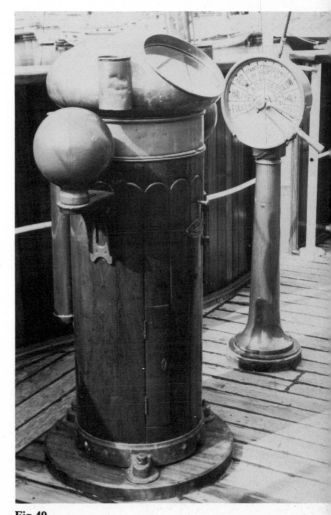

Fig 49
A typical binnacle and compass, with (right) an engine-room telegraph.

or plastic. If the top of the post is flat, the task is even simpler.

Fig 53 shows the general form of bollard found on board ship, and examples of this can be seen in **Fig 50**. **Fig 55** shows a similar type, but this time each post incorporates a snug, the size of which may vary; one such bollard can be seen in **Fig 65**. A different form of bollard, or mooring post, can be seen in **Fig 51**. These are to be found on such craft as coasters and tugs; whereas those illustrated have a small snug, more often than not they are fitted with a horizontal pin about 1½in in

diameter, lying fore and aft and projecting about 4in either side. **Fig 54** illustrates a further variation: the posts are not on a common base but secured to the deck plating by a heavy angle bar ring. Although the bollards in the diagrams are shown with a cambered top to the posts, these tops are often flat.

The dimensions given in the diagrams are those for the particular fitting illustrated, and have been included to give an idea of the proportions in relation to the key dimension; in the case of bollards this is the diameter of the post.

Fig 50
A 14in bollard of the pattern shown in **Fig 53**. The several vertical tubes with canvas covers are the coaming plates for cowl ventilators. The ship is the CPR *Beaverglen*.

Fig 51
Mooring posts fitted to the stern bulwark of a small coaster. Note the stern anchor, with the windlass and cable compressor. The *Anjola* was built in 1977, and this photograph was taken in 1979.

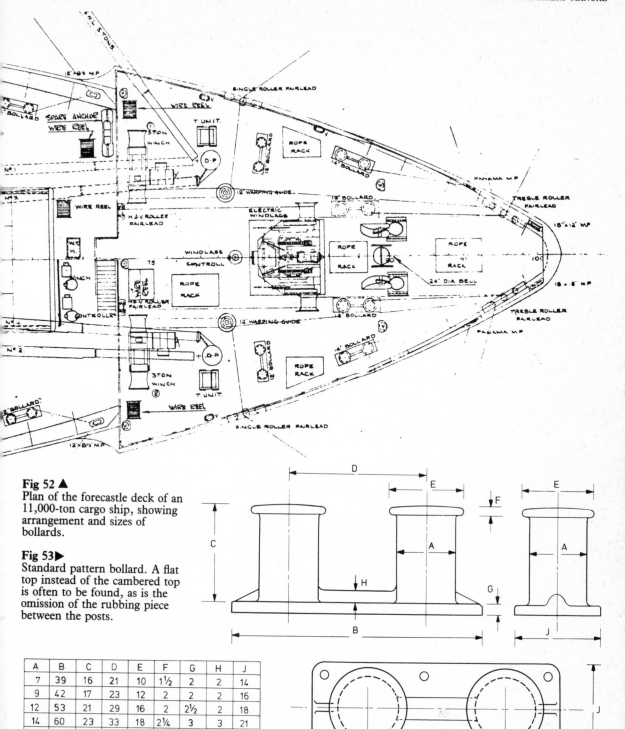

Fig 52 ▲
Plan of the forecastle deck of an 11,000-ton cargo ship, showing arrangement and sizes of bollards.

Fig 53 ▶
Standard pattern bollard. A flat top instead of the cambered top is often to be found, as is the omission of the rubbing piece between the posts.

A	B	C	D	E	F	G	H	J
7	39	16	21	10	1½	2	2	14
9	42	17	23	12	2	2	2	16
12	53	21	29	16	2	2½	2	18
14	60	23	33	18	2¼	3	3	21
16	68	25	38	20	2½	3½	3	24

SIZES IN INCHES

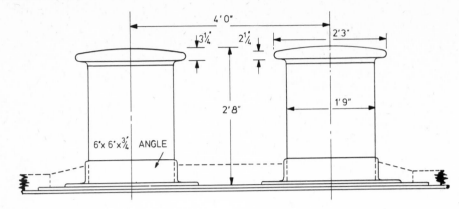

Fig 54
Single bollards secured to the deck by an angle bar ring. The level of the wood deck planking, if fitted, is shown by the broken line.

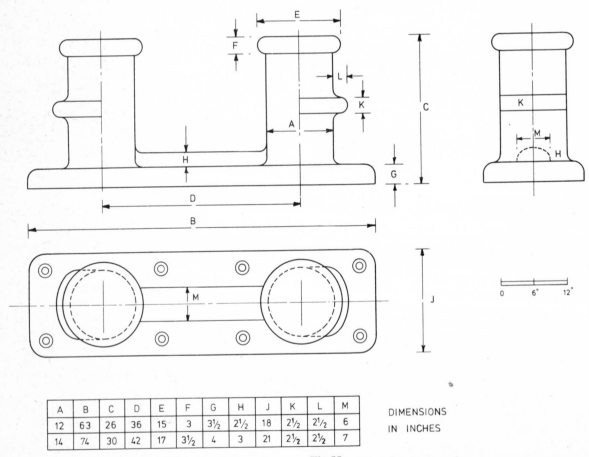

A	B	C	D	E	F	G	H	J	K	L	M
12	63	26	36	15	3	3½	2½	18	2½	2½	6
14	74	30	42	17	3½	4	3	21	2½	2½	7

DIMENSIONS

IN INCHES

Fig 55
Bollard fitted with snugs; the size of the latter can vary, some being greater in length horizontally than those shown in the diagram.

◀Fig 56
Showing the way in which the bulwark plating is swept up to the house end, and how the bulwark capping rail is carried aft to act as a stiffener and is then bracketed to the house end.

Fig 57▼
A swinging cover to a freeing port. The deck of this vessel has been covered with a layer of cement, hence the absence of the customary sheer angle. The rod and chain in the foreground are part of the steering gear; note the coupling between the two. The horizontal bar on which the port cover swings is fitted just above the centreline of the plate so that the port will swing shut of its own accord.

Bulwarks

Some notes about the construction of bulwarks on wooden vessels appear in the section dealing with plank-on-frame hulls. On steel ships the bulwark plating of the weather decks of the hull proper was attached (lapped) to the top of the sheerstrake, as shown in **Figs 58** and **59**. In recent years many vessels have been constructed with the bulwark plating for the greater part of its length fitted clear of the sheerstrake, leaving what looks like a long slot or gap between the lower edge of the bulwark plating and the top edge of the sheerstrake. This gap acts as a very long washport or freeing port. The bulwark plating is attached to stays or brackets in the usual way, and its lower edge is often flanged inboard. **Fig 61** is a cross-section through such a form of construction, and a further development can be seen in **Fig 62**.

On many large bulk carriers, tankers and other vessels of welded construction, the conventional sheer angle has been replaced by a rolled plate of appreciable radius to which the shell and deck plates are butt-welded. The lower edge of the bulwark plating is stopped short of the hull to provide an escape for any water that comes on board. The diagram shows a typical bulwark stay for this form of construction. In the other diagrams can be seen various types of bulwark stays.

The bulwark capping rail was usually a bulb angle fitted as shown, or a bulb plate welded direct to the top of the plate. Where a wood capping piece was fitted this was bolted to an angle bar, or flat bar, welded to the top of the plating.

Where the bulwark plating of a well deck ended at a deck erection, such as a forecastle

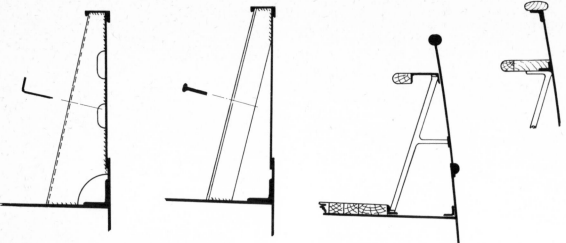

Fig 58 ▲
Section through bulwark showing plate lapped to
sheerstrake. The stay is a flanged plate.

Fig 59   ▲
Section through the bulwark showing method of fitting
a bulb plate stay.

Fig 60
Section through a bulwark with a topgallant rail,
showing alternative finish, either a wood capping or
double-convex or half-round bars.

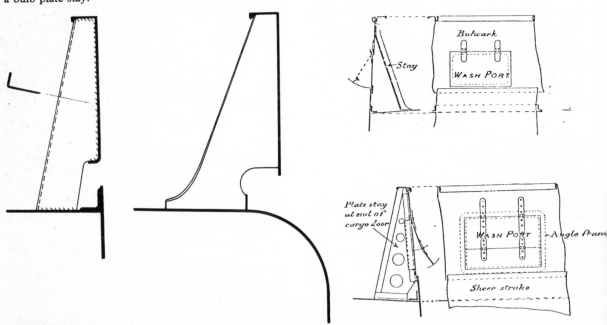

Fig 61 ▲
Section through bulwark where plating is stopped short
of top edge of the sheerstrake to form a long freeing
port. The lower edge of the bulwark plate is flanged.
The stay is a piece of flanged plate, welded to bulwark
plate and deck.

Fig 62   ▲
Section through deck-edge of a vessel with a radius
plate gunwale in lieu of the conventional sheer angle,
showing the way in which the bulwark plating is kept
well clear of the deck.

Fig 63
Arrangement of single- and double-hinged freeing or
washports.

or midship bridge structure, the plate was swept up in a gentle curve to the level of the top of the house, and was suitably bracketed to the house end, as can be seen in **Fig 56**. The same photograph also illustrates a simple type of forged stay.

The more conventional method of freeing a deck quickly of large quantities of water was through rectangular openings in the bulwarks known as freeing ports (sometimes called wash-ports), the final drainage of course taking place through the scuppers. The classification societies lay down a schedule for the total area of the freeing ports each side in a well-deck bulwark for a given length of well. The openings have to be protected by rails spaced not more than 9in apart. Many ports are fitted with hinged covers, as in **Fig 63** or with swinging ports as in **Fig 57**.

Cable Stoppers

To prevent the full strain of the anchor cable coming on to the windlass when a ship is at anchor a cable stopper, also known as a bow-stopper, is fitted between the windlass and the deck entry to the hawsepipe, as in **Fig 64**. As can be seen, the cable is held by the heavy horizontal bar lying between two links. This bar is pivoted at one end. When heaving in the anchor in heavy weather, the cable stopper automatically takes any excess of strains outside the hawsepipe owing to the rise and fall of the vessel as the chain cable lifts the bar link by link. The stopper has to be mounted on a seat angled to suit the run of the cable between hawsepipe and windlass.

Fig 65 shows a form of stopper known as a cable compressor. Here the two vertical arms, pivoted at their lower end, are tightened on to the cable by means of the threaded T-handled rod seen at the top of the arms.

Another form of stopper, more of a relieving tackle, can just be seen in **Fig 252**. This comprises a heavy steel plate having a pair of hooks or claws so shaped as to grip on to one link of cable – and very appropriately known as the 'devil's claws'. This is attached to a robust rigging screw which in turn is shackled to a lug on the windlass frame or base, as shown in **Fig 311**.

Fig 64
A cable stopper. The cable is held by the horizontal bar, which is rectangular in cross-section. This bar is pivoted at one end, and the cable is freed when the bar is raised clear of the socket. The sliding steel plate cover over the hawsepipe entry is, of course, moved clear before the windlass is worked. The metal of the cable links is about 1½in (38mm) in diameter.

◀Fig 65
A compressor-type cable stopper. The cable is locked when the pivoted arms are tightened on to the cable by turning the handle on the end of the threaded rod. Note the mooring posts with snugs in the background.

Fig 66 ▶
The main capstan of a sailing ship (name unknown), with two of the square-ended capstan bars lying nearby on the deck. Note the wood rail at the after end of the forecastle, and the treble sheaves in the bitts at the foot of the foremast. In the foreground are the inboard ends of the catheads, and beyond them one fluke of each of the two bower anchors stowed on deck. *Conway Picture Library*

Fig 67 ▼
Steam capstan as fitted to many sailing trawlers, in this case the Rye (Sussex) vessel *Three Brothers*. The pawls can be seen on the castings fitted between the main members. The thin batten standing against the capstan is a fully extended 3ft rule. The photograph was taken in the 1930s.

Capstans

Capstans play an important part in the working of a ship. On sailing ships the manually operated main capstan, fitted on the forecastle and connected to the windlass on the deck below, was used for raising the anchor(s). One such capstan can be seen in **Figs 66** and **68**, while **Fig 69** shows one of the smaller type used for sail handling. When not in use the capstan bars were stowed nearby. These bars were of timber such as ash, and there was some variation in both length and diameter. Back-run on the capstans was prevented by a series of pawls on the bottom rim of the barrel engaging a ratched ring incorporated in the base.

Fig 316 includes a large, powered, mooring capstan, while in **Fig 252** can be seen two more types of mooring capstans. The after one has its own motor, but the forward one is driven by a take-off shaft from the windlass, the unit being mounted on a raised base to accommodate the necessary gearing.

A very different type of capstan is illustrated in **Fig 67** which is of the kind fitted on many of the old sailing trawlers. Under the top cover was a small steam engine, supplied with steam passing up through the hollow spindle of the capstan from a boiler placed below deck. Drive was to the toothed ring visible below the top

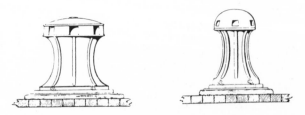

Fig 68 ▲
Main capstan as fitted on the forecastle of sailing ships. This has a single head, but sometimes a double head was fitted, as can be seen in **Fig 66**.

Fig 69 ▲
Brace or halliard capstan.

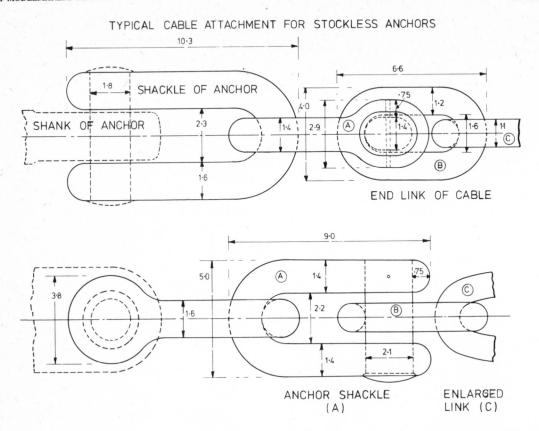

TYPICAL CABLE ATTACHMENT FOR STOCKLESS ANCHORS

SHACKLE OF ANCHOR

SHANK OF ANCHOR

END LINK OF CABLE

ANCHOR SHACKLE
(A)

ENLARGED
LINK (C)

SIZES ARE PROPORTIONAL TO CABLE DIAMETER (=1)

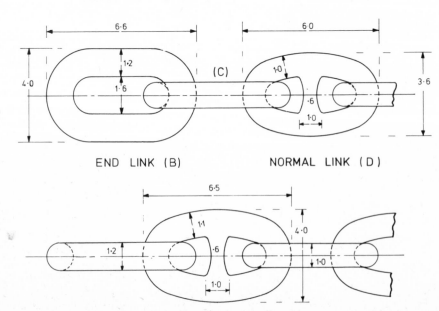

END LINK (B)

NORMAL LINK (D)

ENLARGED LINK (C)

Fig 70
Details of stud-link chain, together with proportions of attachments to stockless anchors, namely the enlarged link (C), the end link without stud (B), and the anchor shackle (A) which must not be confused with the large shackle of the anchor.

cover. The customary pawl and ratchet arrangement at the base of the capstan prevented back-run. The capstan could be worked by hand if necessary by means of crank handles fitted on to the square end of the shaft at the top of the barrel.

Chain Cable

In **Fig 70** can be seen the general method of attaching a stud-link cable to the anchor shackle. It gives the relative sizes of the component links in relation to the basic link diameter of the anchor cable.

Chain is another matter. Quite a good range of sizes is available from model shops for ordinary oval link chain, but stud-link chain is not manufactured. However, it is not difficult to make stud-link cable, even in very small sizes. Start by making a bending jig. One way to do this is to file the tip of each jaw of a pair of fine pointed-nose pliers to the inside shape of the required size of link. A less expensive way is to take an oval wire nail, file the end square, make a saw cut across the end to suit the diameter of the wire to be used, and then reduce the cross-section to that of the inside of the proposed link.

To make a link, take a length of the wire of the right diameter, make sure that the end is square, grip it in the pliers, or place it in the cut in the nail (which can be held in a vice for convenience) with the end flush with the edge, turn the wire round the jig and cut off at the point where it meets the wire again. Press the cut end home against the stud, and solder if required. If there is no strain on the cable, paint can be used to fill the joint, and also to impart a slight impression of the actual dumb-bell shape of the stud. The links should be slipped one on to the other before closing the gap.

If ordinary oval link chain is being used on a model, be sure that you can vouch for the correctness of its presence wherever it is being fitted. So many models are spoiled by the use of wrong-size and incorrect chain. It simply will not do to run any old piece of readily available chain between anchor and windlass or whatever and then, as is so often the case, compound the error by leaving it in all its pristine plated glory!

Cleats

Several different types and size of cleats are to be seen on board ship, ranging from the simple horn cleat shown in **Fig 72(a)** to the large belaying cleat in **Fig 72(b)**. Dimensions for larger and smaller cleats can be worked out from the sizes shown. Another form of horn cleat can be seen in **Fig 181**. Each horn is mounted on its own base which is riveted to the derrick post.

On wooden vessels the belaying cleats took

Fig 71▶
Wood cleat (cavil) fitted inside the bulwarks. This one has a couple of belaying 'pins' of ordinary round iron, driven through the timber.

the form of a heavy timber fitted horizontally across, and well fastened to, the bulwark stanchions, as in **Fig 71**.

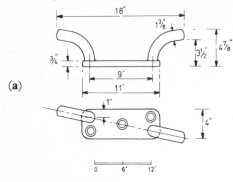

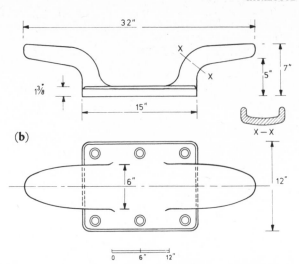

Fig 72
(**a**) Horn cleat. (**b**) Belaying cleat.

Cranes, Cargo Handling

Although small cranes for cargo-handling have been fitted on board ship for nigh on a hundred years, it is only in comparatively recent times that they have really been developed for this purpose. As far back as the last couple of decades of the nineteenth century the Royal Mail Line and the P&O Steamship Co were installing hydraulic cranes in many of their passenger liners; their big advantage was silent operation, which allowed some cargo working at night without disturbing the passengers' sleep. The P&O were still fitting this type of crane to new buildings in the mid-1920s. Small steam cranes were sometimes part of the cargo-handling equipment on coastal vessels, especially those on regular coastal cargo-passenger services.

Today's cranes are of a much more comprehensive design, powered either by electric or hydraulic motors, and with considerably more lifting capacity and outreach. To begin with they tended to be of the open type seen in **Fig 73**, an arrangement which is still much used. The natural progression was to enclose as much as possible of the mechanism and to provide an enclosed cab for the operator, as shown in **Fig 74**.

◄**Fig 73**
The 5-ton capacity cranes on board the cargo ship *Ben Loyal*, built in 1959. The control position and the machinery are fully exposed, but this does give the modelmaker an opportunity to see the constructional details.

Fig 74
Cargo-handling cranes, each having a 10-tonne
capacity, mounted in tandem. *Clarke Chapman Marine.*

Davits

As with many other pieces of deck equipment the lifeboat davit has been the subject of much development, and the postwar years have seen considerable advances, particularly in the design of gravity davits.

The radial davit is probably the one most frequently encountered by modelmakers. It has been in use on almost every type of vessel from small coasters to large passenger liners such as the first *Mauretania*. A ship's general arrangement plans will show the position, height and reach (span) of the davit with reasonable accuracy, but the diameter is often in some doubt. The maximum diameter is in the region of the uppermost support, tapering slightly to the ball at the head, and again at the lower end towards the heel. There is a formula for calculating the maximum diameter (*d*) in inches of a radial davit:

$$d^3 = \frac{L \times B \times D(H + 4S)}{C}$$

where L, B and D are the length, breadth and depth respectively of the boat, H is the height of the davit head above the uppermost support and S is the span or outreach. When all these dimensions are in feet, the diameter *d* will be in inches. C is a constant, the values of which are 144 for wrought iron davits or 174 for wrought ingot steel davits, in each case with enough men to launch the boat. For boats which will be launched with the full complement on board the corresponding values are 82 for wrought iron and 99 for steel. A rough guide, which will go some way to reducing gross errors, is that boats under 20ft long have davits 2–3in in diameter, boats about 20–25ft long, 3–4in in diameter, larger boats 4–6in in diameter, and large liners up to 8in diameter. Those on the *Mauretania* mentioned above were actually 10½in diameter, but they were steel tubes, not solid drawn.

The head of the davit is formed into a ball (see **Fig 86**), with a flat surface on top and

Fig 75 ▲
A quadrant davit in the inboard position. Note the relative position of the arm to the quadrant.

Fig 76 ▶
A close-up of the frame of a quadrant davit showing the operating screw mechanism and the teeth and rack. The operating crank handle has been reversed for stowage.

◄**Fig 77**
Crescent-type davit. Note the falls made fast to the cruciform bollard between davit and standing part of operating mechanism. The bevel gears are turned by a crank handle, the arm extends and the davit pivots outboard on the heel hitting.

Fig 78▼
Construction of heel fitting of crescent davit.

bottom and a hole to take the pin securing the horizontal spectacle eye to which the span wire and guys are shackled. The lower end of the pin has an eye to take the upper block of the boats falls. **Fig 85** shows an arrangement of radial davits; although this is for a paddle steamer, it can be considered as typical. The main difference for other vessels would lie in the size of the boat, and this would in turn affect the various scantlings.

Some of the davit designs which have stood the test of time – there were other which have been made, only to go out of production later – can be seen in the photographs. The quadrant davit was probably the earliest design after the radial davit. It has the advantage of being able to handle either a single boat or, with some

◄**Fig 79**
Lower block of falls seen in the photograph of the crescent davit.

Fig 80 ▲
The Welin 'Lum'-type davit. When the crank handle (seen here reversed for stowage) is operated the davit pivots outboard on the heel fitting.

Fig 81 ▲
The heel fitting, base and operating mechanism for both the 'Lum'-type davit, and the 'Col'-type luffing davit, the lower part of which is seen in this photograph. The upper part of the 'Col' davit is very similar to that of the overhead quadrant davit.

◄Fig 82
The general arrangement of Welin gravity-type davits is clearly seen here. For simplified construction the curved lower end of the trackways seen in this and other photographs has given way to the straight-line form shown in **Fig 90**. Note the wood framework over the boat to support the canvas protective cover. *Welin Davit & Eng Co Ltd*

Fig 83▶
An interesting arrangement to support the inboard end of one of the gravity davit trackways. The layout is very much on the lines of that shown in **Fig 90**. The drive tube between the two rope drums is quite clear, and the motor has been fitted to the forward davit – it can be seen in line with the top bar of the guard rails. Note how the canvas cover of the boat is sagging between the wood supports. What is really the equivalent of the lower block of the boat falls can be seen hanging from the tusk at the head of the davit. As the cradle reaches the limit of its travel when the boat is being lowered this block slips free of the tusk. *Welin Davit & Eng Co Ltd*

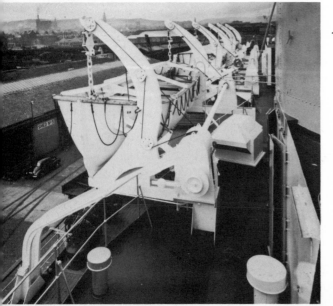

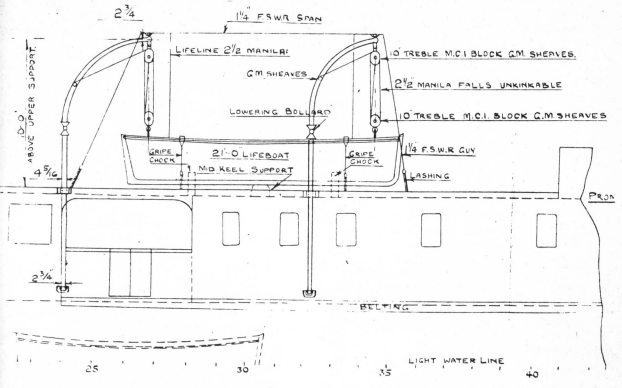

Fig 85(a) ▲
Side elevation showing arrangement of radial davits and falls for 21ft × 7ft × 2ft 9in lifeboat, Class IA for 24 persons. The vessel in the diagram is a paddle steamer.

Fig 84 ▼
Typical arrangement of 'A' bracket support for the inboard end of gravity davits where there is no adjacent structure to take a bracket. *Conway Picture Library*

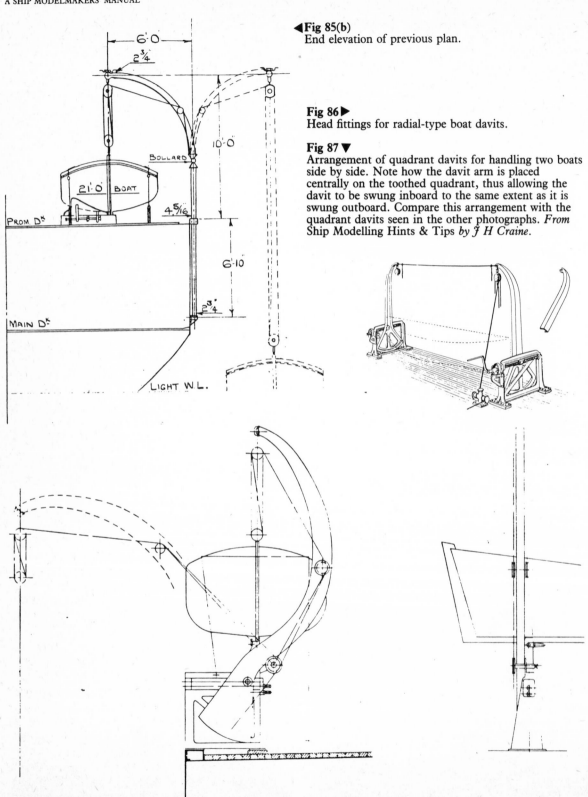

◀Fig 85(b)
End elevation of previous plan.

Fig 86▶
Head fittings for radial-type boat davits.

Fig 87▼
Arrangement of quadrant davits for handling two boats side by side. Note how the davit arm is placed centrally on the toothed quadrant, thus allowing the davit to be swung inboard to the same extent as it is swung outboard. Compare this arrangement with the quadrant davits seen in the other photographs. *From Ship Modelling Hints & Tips by J H Craine.*

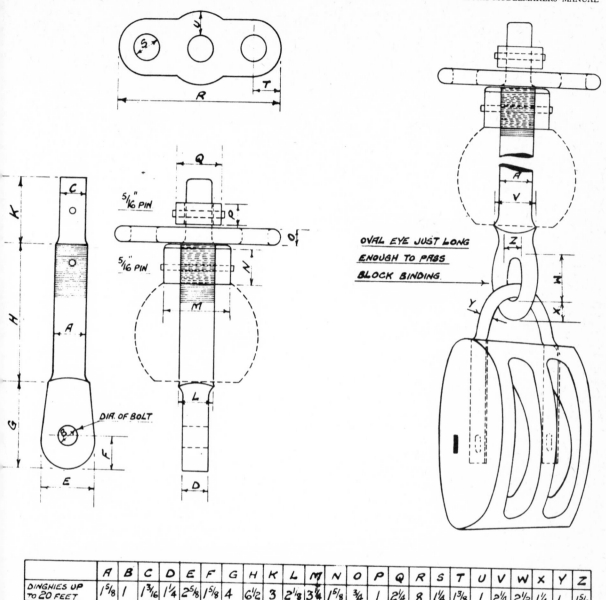

	A	B	C	D	E	F	G	H	K	L	M	N	O	P	Q	R	S	T	U	V	W	X	Y	Z
DINGHIES UP TO 20 FEET	1⁵⁄₈	1	1³⁄₁₆	1¼	2⁵⁄₈	1⁵⁄₈	4	6½	3	2⅛	3¼	1⁵⁄₈	¾	1	2¼	8	1¼	1³⁄₈	1	2¼	2½	1¼	1	1⁵⁄₈
LIFEBOATS UP TO 28 FEET	1¾	1⅛	1⁵⁄₁₆	1³⁄₈	2¾	1⁵⁄₈	4¼	6½	3	2¼	3½	1¾	¾	1	2¼	8	1¼	1³⁄₈	1	2½	2¾	1³⁄₈	1⅛	1¾

◀ **Fig 88**
The Welin quadrant overframe-type davit. This davit was first introduced in 1901, and was of cast steel construction. It is still in use, but is now fabricated of wrought mild steel. Instead of the old-style teeth, the base of the quadrant is now fitted with a series of studs which engage in holes in the bottom member of the frame. *By courtesy of the Welin Davit & Eng Co Ltd*

modifications, two boats stowed either side by side or one above the other. In its modernised form, it is still fitted to ships of all sizes, though from about the mid-1920s onwards the gravity davit has been fitted to quite a wide range of vessels.

The illustrations show the best-known form of the gravity davit. There are variations in the method of supporting the inboard end, and

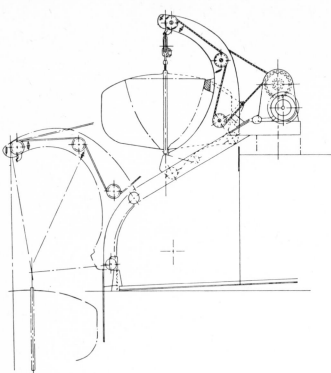

Arrangement of Welin overhead gravity davit. The side elevation is drawn looking outboard. *By courtesy of the Welin Davit & Eng Co Ltd*

Fig 90 ►
Typical elevation of gravity davit track and cradle. The method of supporting the inboard end of the track depends upon the layout of the ship at that point. The broken line at point B shows the shape of the track before the adoption of the straight-line form introduced more recently (as depicted by the continuous line), no doubt in the interests of reducing production costs. *From information supplied by the Welin Davit & Eng Co Ltd*

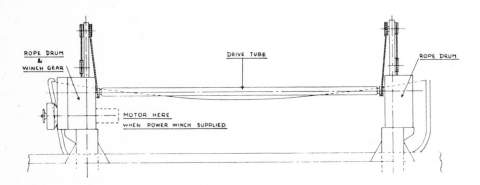

two arrangements in way of deckhouses are shown. In clear or open decks, it is held up by some form of 'A' bracket support.

As can be seen from the photographs and diagrams, the trackway for the cradle which carries the boat is composed of two heavy steel channels tied together. The cradle runs between the toes of these channels, being fitted with two pairs of rollers which run on the lower flange of the channels. What takes place when the boat is lowered can be seen in the diagram. The arrangements for the control of the boat's movement and operation of the falls by some form of winch depends on the davit manufac-

turer, the requirements of the shipowner and the layout of the ship. Some of the types of boat-winch can be seen in the photographs and diagrams.

Deck Plating

The plating of steel decks follows much the same lines as that for the shell plating. The layout of the strakes of plating and the position

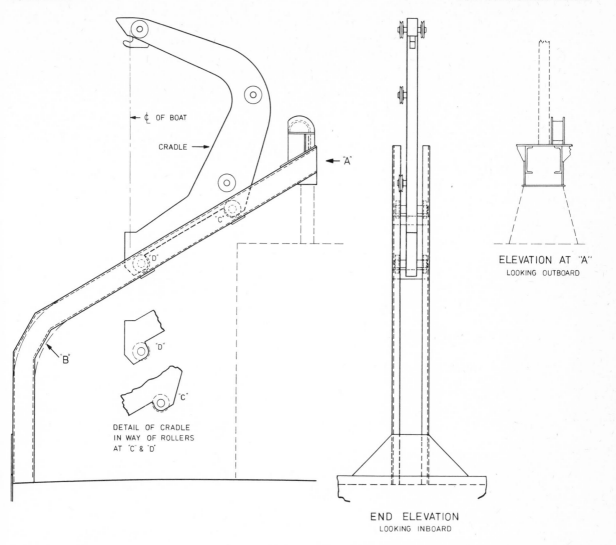

Ç OF BOAT

CRADLE

"A"

"C"

"D"

"B"

"D"

"C"

DETAIL OF CRADLE
IN WAY OF ROLLERS
AT "C" & "D"

ELEVATION AT "A"
LOOKING OUTBOARD

END ELEVATION
LOOKING INBOARD

of the individual plates, together with the method of fastening are given on the appropriate deck plating plans. In **Fig 91** the run of strakes of deck plating can be seen.

Fig 91▶
The run of the strakes of deck plating: in this ship one side of each plate was joggled, but the end laps were plain. Two other points are worth noting – the deep curtain plate to the after end of the forecastle, and the hatch coamings. The ship is the *Delius* (1937), belonging to Lamport & Holt Ltd

Fairleads

Like bollards, fairleads can vary considerably in size and in form. **Fig 96–100** illustrate a type seen on many vessels large and small. The diameter of the sheave will vary according to the size of the ship. Another example can be seen in **Fig 92** of that shown in **Fig 96**; note that in this case the fairleads are open at the top, and that they are set on canted seats fitted well clear of the waterway and top of the sheerstrake. **Fig 98** is of a similar type, but it has a solid top piece over the sheaves; three-sheave versions of this can be seen in **Fig 252** mounted on seats spanning the waterway, similar to those in the diagram. **Fig 100** is of another much-used type. Each sheave is mounted on its own base, which allows them to be fitted in pairs or threes and be so placed as to follow the curvature of the ship's side. The ordinary open fairlead is shown in **Fig 99** and an example can also be seen on the bulwark capping rail in **Fig 312**. An early type of Panama fairlead is shown in **Fig 102**, while some forms of those currently being fitted can be seen in **Fig 91**.

On many vessels pedestal fairleads are fitted to facilitate the run of ropes. These consist of a single sheave, such as that in **Fig 101**, mounted on a suitable pedestal. Examples can be seen in **Fig 252**, where the sheaves have been placed on seats attached to the breakwater, and in **Fig 329**. Another form of guide to assist the lead of wires and ropes is the multiple roller type seen in **Fig 93**.

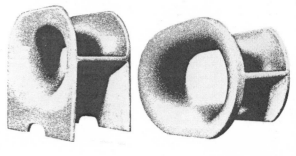

Fig 92 ▲
Two-and three-roller fairleads set on canted seats. Right forward is a Panama fairlead. To the left of the photograph is a bowstopper set on a seat angled to suit the run of the anchor cable.

Fig 93 ▼
Two patterns of roller guides. *By courtesy of Taylor, Pallister & Co Ltd*

Fig 94 ▲
Panama fairlead, deck-mounted type, conforming to latest regulations. *By courtesy of Taylor, Pallister & Co Ltd*

Fig 95   ▲
Panama fairlead for mounting on bulwark. Back of casting is made to suit flat or curved plating. Conforms to latest regulations. *By courtesy of Taylor, Pallister & Co Ltd*

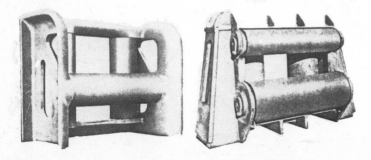

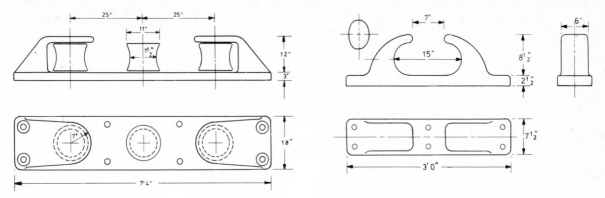

Fig 96
A three-sheave fairlead.

Fig 99
Standard pattern open fairlead.

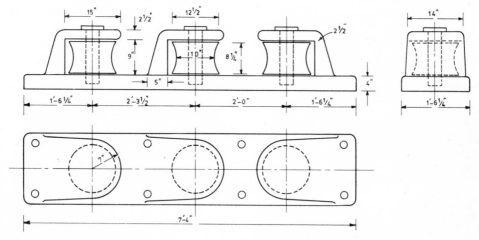

Fig 97
Another example of a three-sheave fairlead.

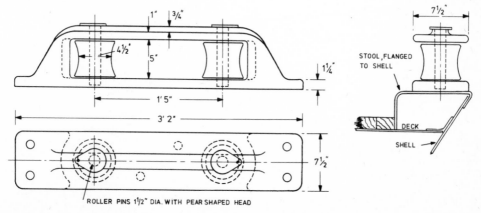

ROLLER PINS 1½" DIA. WITH PEAR SHAPED HEAD

Fig 98
Double-sheave fairlead with top bar. The end elevation
shows how a fairlead can be set on a seat spanning a
waterway.

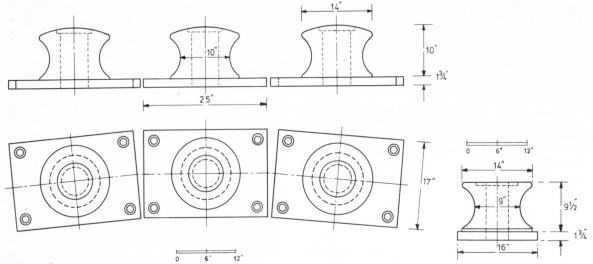

Fig 100 ▲
Triple-sheave fairlead. The sheaves are individual units mounted on baseplates; they can be arranged so as to follow the shape of the deck edge when this has considerable curvature.

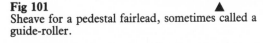

Fig 101
Sheave for a pedestal fairlead, sometimes called a guide-roller. ▲

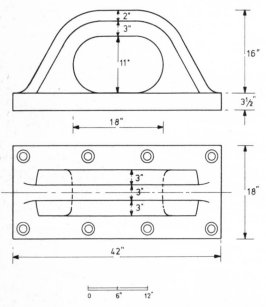

Fig 102 ▲
Typical form of one of the earlier patterns of Panama fairlead.

Fig. 103 ▶
A steam whistle. This is a simple unit, such as is found on coasters and other small craft, being operated by a direct-pull lanyard or wire leading to the wheelhouse or open bridge.

Funnels

Although the shapes of funnels are bewildering in their variety, there are a number of features which appear, not necessarily all together, on many of them. On steam-powered ships the funnel was basically a tube within a tube, the inner one providing the uptake and outlet for the boiler gases. The introduction of the diesel engine saw some departures from old principles, the most radical of which on some vessels was the plating over of the top of the funnel just below the rim, with the various exhaust uptakes just passing through the plating. It is unfortunate that many of the plans available to modelmakers do not show details of the internals of a funnel. Sometimes useful data can be found in the articles in the technical journals, and the increase in the aerial photography of ships has provided a further possible source of information.

Leaving aside the extreme designs of the past couple of decades, the illustrations show just a few of the more frequently encountered features, which are detailed in the captions.

Fig 104 ▶
A long-range shot of the funnel of a motor vessel. Points to note are the band (beading) at the top edge and again lower down, and the funnel guys, shackled to lugs riveted to the plating and set up with rigging screws shackled to eyeplates on the house top. Just below the rim are a series of lugs to take the tackles of the bosun's chairs used when repainting the funnel. The compressed air operated syren is mounted on a bracket, and there is a typical waste pipe on the after side. The presence of the D/F loop shows that the funnel has been plated over, and in point of fact this is a dummy funnel, all the exhausts on this particular ship being led up the after funnel. On older vessels the waste steam pipes, fitted externally on either the forward or after sides of the funnel, often terminated in quite prominent bell-mouths.

Fig 105 ▶
Diesel exhaust arrangement in a funnel having a plated-in top. The model is of the Federal Steam Navigation Company's motor cargo liner *Northumberland* (1955), built by D Carton. The scale is ¼in = 1ft, and the model, electrically powered, is nearly 11ft (3.35m) long.

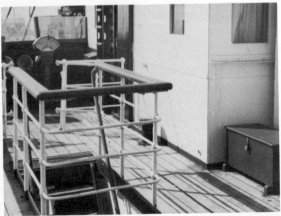

Fig 106 ▲
The taper on the stanchions can be seen in this photograph, which also includes several different railing layouts. Where there is a tube top rail, this is of greater diameter than the lower rails, while on the second open deck up there is a teak top rail. Other points of interest are the curtain plates to the decks; the bracket for a stern light on the rails with the teak top rail; the fairleads; the bars across the two portholes above the ship's name; the strakes of shell plating; and the supporting stanchions between the various decks.
Conway Picture Library

◀**Fig 107**
Rails round a ladderway opening in a deck; note the coaming to the opening. The ship is the *Winchester*, built by Denny of Dumbarton in 1947 for the Southern Railway Company.

Guard Rails

Stanchions and rails are two of the several shipboard fittings which many modelmakers find troublesome, and evidence of this is apparent at any exhibition or rally of scale ship models. So many are spoilt by the use of purchased stanchions, without attention being given to their suitability for the particular application. What is not realised by many modelmakers is that a stanchion is tapered over its length, being smaller in diameter at the top than at the bottom. Though slight, this taper is quite noticeable, as an examination of the rails in **Fig 106** will show. Furthermore, the balls in way of each rail are suitably proportioned to the rail size, a point to bear in mind since the top rail is frequently of greater diameter than the rest. Unfortunately on commercial stanchions for models there is no taper and the balls and rail size are somewhat out of proportion, whilst the method of fitting – a pointed end – means that they are often wrongly positioned in relation to the edge of the deck.

Fig 110 shows a typical shipside stanchion, the palm being riveted to the sheerstrake or side plating. The height may vary slightly, and on smaller vessels the diameters may be a little less, as in **Fig 111**. The type of foot, or palm, is based upon the location of the stanchion, and some examples are shown in the various diagrams. The fitting of stays depends upon requirements, as does the presence of removable sections. The number of rails, the spacing of the stanchions, and the type of top rail – bar or wood capping – are related to their position on the ship; examples can be seen in **Fig 106**. These are matters to which a modeller should pay attention when fitting the guard rails, as errors are obvious to those who know ships.

Fig 107 shows rails round the opening in a deck for a ladder to the deck below. This is an instance where the stanchion diameter is probably less than that of the shipside one. Typical three-ball stanchions and rails are shown in **Fig 108**; these are across the end of a boat deck on a cargo ship. The palm connection to the curtain plate is clearly seen.

From the practical point of view the problem of guard rails and stanchions really divides

Fig 108
The pattern of palm used for securing a stanchion to a coaming, or shell, plate is clearly seen here. Note also the way the steel ladder is fastened to the curtain plate, and the small two-sheave or roller-type fairlead.

Fig 109
The shipside rails of a small, raised-quarterdeck coaster, with examples of the use of flat bar for stanchions and commercial type pipe and pipe fittings for ladder handrails. This photograph of the *Vanguard* was taken in London in 1979.

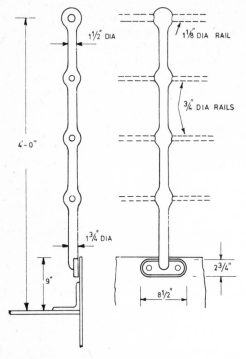

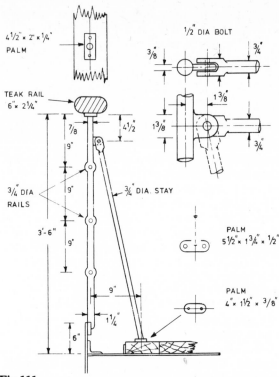

Fig 110
A standard type of shipside stanchion, riveted to the side plating. In this instance the height from the deck was 4ft, but in other cases it may be a few inches less. The top rail is of greater diameter than the lower rails.

Fig 111
Detail of a lighter type of stanchion, showing method of fitting a stay, and also a teak top rail. This stanchion is riveted to the ship's side plating.

Fig 112 ▲
Alternative types of palm or foot for stanchions.

◀**Fig 113**
Stanchion to take wire jackstay for canvas dodger on open bridge. Height may vary to suit particular ship. The one shown was for a paddle steamer.

Fig 114▼
A figure-of-eight knot round a stanchion.

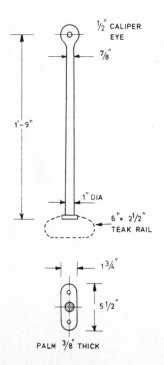

itself into two parts: how to represent them on a small scale model, and how to make them correctly on those larger scale models where this is possible. Modellers who possess a lathe ought to be able to turn stanchions of the correct size where the scale of the model allows this. The work will be simplified if a form tool can be prepared for each stanchion type.

Where turning is not possible, *ie* on very small scale models, the stanchions will have to be made from fine wire of a diameter equal to that of the top part of the stanchion, with rails of even finer wire or of a filament of thread. Attaching the rail to the stanchion is the problem. If it is just stretched along the outside of the stanchions and 'glued' thereto, it looks just that: despite the small size this is still apparent. Better results can be obtained by knotting the rail to each stanchion, if this can be done, using a figure-of-eight knot as in **Fig 114**. This last has the advantage that this type of knot brings the rail away from the outer face of the stanchion to a position more akin to that of the prototype, and the twist of material round the stanchion will form the nucleus of the ball, paint doing the rest. In the very small scales paint can be used very successfully to simulate

such items as tensioning screws in guard rails having chain in place of bars. Just build up the rail in the appropriate place with several thin coats of paint.

So far the stanchions discussed have been of the forged type, *ie* those which were produced in the shipyard blacksmith's shop. Today on many vessels, particularly the smaller ones, stanchions are of flat bar and rails of tube or similar flat bar. An interesting variation can be seen in **Fig 109**. On this raised-quarterdeck motor coaster the main shipside rail on the quarterdeck consists of strong flanged plate uprights with short lengths of flat bar welded in between for the lower rails, while the top rail is either an angle or perhaps a bulb plate with a convex bar welded along the outside. The flat bar type stanchion can be seen on the left of the picture, and what appears to be ordinary pipe elbows and tubing have been used for the ladder handrails and the top rail.

Some sailing ships (particularly the large coasting schooners of America) and some early steamships had wood rails with robust, turned stanchions. A comparatively simple example can be seen in **Fig 66**.

Hawsepipes

These are situated at the fore end on each side of the ship, or on one side if only one anchor is carried, abaft the stem. Usually made of cast iron or cast steel (but sometimes fabricated), they are the pipes which extend from the forecastle, or uppermost, deck to the ship's side, and through which the anchor cable passes. Where the pipe pierces the shell plating and the deck plating, it embodies a heavy

Fig 115
Anchor recess in hull with stockless anchor in stowed position. Other points of interest are the hinged plate cover in the bulwark in way of the fairlead, the shell plating flanged to the heavy bar stem, the protective doublings to the lower corners of the anchor recess, and the prominent riveting in the strakes of plating above the ribband. The ship is the CPR *Empress of Britain* (1931). *Conway Picture Library*

moulded flange, oval or elliptical in shape, as in **Fig 248**, while the plating in way is fitted with a doubling plate.

When ships carried anchors with stocks, which were stowed on deck, the internal size of the pipe was sufficient to accommodate the anchor cable. With the introduction of the stockless anchor the internal size was increased to allow the shank to be brought up into the pipe until the arms, flukes and crown rested snugly against the hull, as can be seen in **Fig 36**. Many vessels have a recess in the hull in way of the hawsepipe (see **Fig 115**) to allow the whole of the anchor to be stowed within the line of the hull. The pipe flange lies on the plating forming the back of the recess, and the lower edge of the shell opening is heavily reinforced.

Sometimes a vessel was fitted with a stern anchor, in which case a hawsepipe generally similar to those at the bow was fitted (see **Fig 32**), with the anchor stowed, rather vulnerably, against the stern plating. **Fig 33** shows a stern anchor fitted in a recess in the transom, and indicates very clearly the advantage of this method of stowage.

Hatches

From the modelmaker's point of view the hatches on a ship, apart from their possible use on working models as a lift-off entity for access to equipment fitted below deck, have only three main points of interest. These are the constructional details of the coamings, the type of covers fitted, and the presence or otherwise of any tarpaulins and their securing arrangements. The modern type of slab covers whether they be of the single-pull hinge-up type, the pontoon type, or the lift-up-and-slide-along-over-the-next-one type, have eased several of the constructional problems for the modelmaker but have introduced others through the presence of ancillary fittings such as stowage racks, posts for the lead wires, and the hatch side roller and chain fittings. Some of the different means of covering a hatchway can be seen in the illustrations, which also give a good guide to the constructional details of coamings.

The classification societies have strict rules about the construction of hatch gear. Only some of their requirements appear in the published rules, since so many of the applications require individual assessment and approval. Lloyd's, for instance, require that the wood covers for weather-deck hatches have a minimum finished thickness of $2\frac{3}{8}$in for an unsupported span of 5ft maximum, and $3\frac{1}{4}$in for a maximum span of 6ft 6in. The ends of all hatches have to be protected by a steel band $2\frac{1}{2}$in wide and $\frac{1}{8}$in thick. Weatherdeck coamings must have a minimum height of 24in (though

Fig 116 ▲
Single-board hatches fitted transversely and supported along the centreline by a fore and aft beam, in turn supported by a steel cross beam. The socket for the next fore and after can be seen on this beam to the right of the word 'Logan'. The vessel is the Clyde puffer *Logan*.

◄ Fig 117
Single-board hatches fitted fore and aft, and supported by a series of closely spaced cross beams. There are no fore and aft beams in an arrangement of this type. The hatches will be covered by tarpaulins.

▲ Fig 118
One of the weatherdeck hatches on the Shaw Savill cargo liner *Athenic* (1947). The height of the coamings may be judged in relation to the figure in the foreground. All the main constructional details can be seen: the coaming stays, the bulb angle horizontal support, the cleats (in this case forgings riveted to the coaming plate), the batten irons (the long pieces of flat bar lying in the cleats) and one wedge. The lug or eye in the form of an inverted 'U' on the horizontal stiffener is to take one end of the special steel bar fittings put across the hatchway after the tarpaulins are in place. The absence of a socket at the middle of the cross coaming and the locking arrangements on the side coaming ledger bar indicate that the wood hatch covers were fitted fore and aft. Note the rough, uneven appearance of the pitch in the seams of the deck planking. *Conway Picture Library*

Fig 119
The way a tarpaulin is secured over a hatch by the batten iron and wedges. In this example the hatch coaming is of wood, and the three rings can be used for any rope lashings which may be put across the hatchway for added security.

Fig 120
MacGregor single-pull hatch covers. There is a pair of rollers plus a special stowage roller on each side of each cover. For this type of cover the horizontal stiffener on the hatch coaming is fitted just below the top of the coaming, and carries the guides for the two lower rollers. Note the plate stiffeners to the hatch coamings. The way in which these covers stow when the hatch is open can be seen in **Figs 109** and **121**.

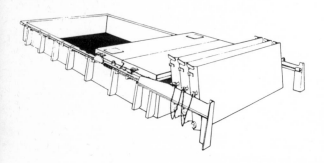

Fig 121
Diagrammatic arrangement of single-pull hatch covers being moved into the stowed position, and showing how they turn through 90° when on the stowage rails. *By courtesy of MacGregor & Co Ltd*

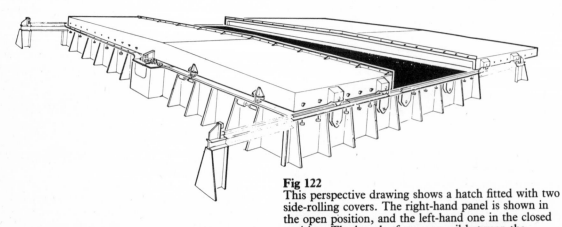

Fig 122
This perspective drawing shows a hatch fitted with two side-rolling covers. The right-hand panel is shown in the open position, and the left-hand one in the closed position. The length of stowage rail between the coaming and the separate pedestal support can be removed if required. *By courtesy of MacGregor & Co Ltd*

they are often made higher) and have to be stiffened by a horizontal bulb angle (or equivalent) 7in in depth fitted near the top edge. Supporting stays or brackets with a maximum span of 10ft have to be fitted to the coamings. The bearing surfaces, or hatch rests, which support the ends of the hatches, whether they are beams or the ledger angles fitted inside the coamings, must be at least 2½in wide. The cleats, riveted or welded to the bulb angle

stiffener, have to be pieces of strong angle bar at least 2½in wide and spaced not more than 2ft apart, the end cleats being not more than 6in from the hatch corners. Two tarpaulins have to be fitted over the hatch, and on wide hatches special lashings must be fitted for securing the covers once the tarpaulins are in place. An example of these securing arrangements can be seen in **Fig 176**.

Hull Construction

THE SOLID BLOCK HULL

One method of producing a hull is to carve it from a single piece of wood. This form of construction is suitable for the smaller static models, but it is not really advisable for large models. The basis is a block of good-quality seasoned timber, with as straight a grain and as few knots and blemishes as possible. It should be a softwood rather than a hardwood. The procedure is as follows. After truing up the block, which should be slightly larger than the overall size of the model, mark in the longitudinal centreline, and the ordinates or station lines. On the top surface mark in the outline of the deck and on each side the profile of the hull, either to the level of the top of the bulwark or to the level of the deck at the centreline, but excluding the stem, keel, and stern post where these project beyond the hull planking or plating, and the rudder (**Fig 123**). Remove the surplus wood up to, but just clear of, the line of the stem and the stern, then cut vertically round the block to the outline of the deck. If the vessel has tumblehome, then due allowance must be made for this when carrying out the last operation. Re-mark those centrelines and station lines which have been removed by the cutting processes. From the body plan prepare a set of templates in thick card, one for each half-section of the hull. Pare away the wood from the hull, constantly checking with the templates at their stations, until the correct shape is obtained, and finish off the surface with sandpaper, as shown in **Fig 124**. Make the projecting parts of the stem, keel and stern-

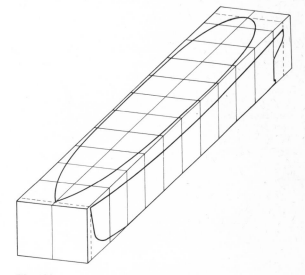

Fig 123
Trued-up wood block marked out for a solid block hull.

post from hardwood and glue and dowel them in place on the hull, which should have either a narrow flat surface or a shallow rebate (slot) where they are to be fitted. If the latter method, the rebate, is chosen, then the depth of the pieces will have to be increased accordingly.

Although the outside of the hull has been shaped, the top is still flat. If the vessel has bulwarks there are now two courses open. The surplus wood can be cut away down to the level of the underside of the bulwark capping, and then further removed inside the bulwarks down to the level of the underside of the deck planking, or of the plating if it is a bare steel deck, remembering that this surface is cambered (see **Fig 125**). Alternatively, all the wood can be removed down to the level of the underside of the deck planking or plating across the whole width of the hull (again remembering the cam-

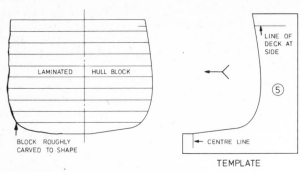

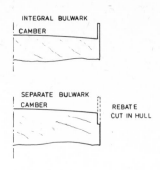

Fig 124
A typical template, with the essential datum lines marked on it, together with the station number. Alongside is a section through a partially carved 'bread-and-butter' hull block with one side finished to suit the template at that particular station.

Fig 125
Part section through deck-edge showing integral and rebated bulwarks.

ber), after which the bulwarks are added separately. This latter method has the advantage of making the cutting of the sheer and camber much easier. The strips of wood which will form the bulwarks, together with the capping rail and timbers or stays, will be added later. If the vessel has no bulwarks, or only partial bulwarks, then the second of these two courses should be adopted.

'BREAD-AND-BUTTER' HULLS

By this method of construction a block of wood is made up from a number of individual planks, all of which must be straight, true, and free from knots and blemishes. It has the advantage of saving a considerable amount of labour when shaping the hull, and it can also be more economical. Ideally the thickness of the individual planks should correspond exactly to the spacing of the waterlines on the lines plan, which is assumed to be full size for the model. If it is not possible to obtain such material, then new waterlines spaced to suit the finished thickness of such material as is available will have to be drawn, in the way described in the Plans for Ship Models section. Generally speaking plank thicknesses from $\frac{1}{2}$in to 1in are the most suitable. However, when settling on the material for the hull block, examine carefully the position of the waterlines at the top of the hull to ascertain how they are placed in relation to the sheer of the deck. If the sheer line of the deck runs across one of these waterlines it may be better to replace the two boards concerned with a single one of a thickness which will take in the whole of the sheer line.

The procedure is as follows. Temporarily fasten together all the boards and mark the longitudinal centreline all round, the shape in profile of the bow and stern, and the line of the deck. If the model is not going to be hollowed out, and the finished surface of the top board is going to form the deck, then the line to be marked in must be the line of the deck at the centre, not side, to allow for the camber to be cut. When doing so allowance must also be made for the thickness of any deck planking or plating which will be fitted later. Consideration must also be given to the matter of the bulwarks. If they are to be carved integrally, which is not really advisable, then the initial line to be marked will have to be that showing the top of the bulwark at the level of the underside of the capping rail. Cut the block to the shape of the stem, stern and deck/bulwark line, keeping the cut just clear of the lines.

Re-mark all the lines removed during the cutting processes, then take the block apart and mark on the top of each board the outline of the corresponding waterline, and on the uppermost one that of the deck. Cut away all the surplus wood on each board to within about $\frac{1}{16}$in of the line. Fasten the boards together again temporarily and carve the hull to shape, making use of templates in the same way as when carving a solid block hull. Once the work has been completed, and the hull sanded, cut any slots which may be required for keel, stem and sternpost, and the rebate for the bulwark, if applicable, once the decks have been cambered.

If the hull is not going to be hollowed out,

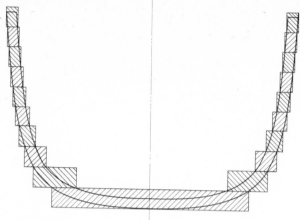

Fig 126
Section through hull of model built on the 'bread-and-butter' system, showing the arrangement of the planks, or lifts as they are frequently called, after cutting.

Fig 127
Portia Takakjian of New York at work on the hull of her model of the research vessel *Vema*, 1/96 scale. This is a good example of 'bread-and butter'- or lift (as it is called by those who refer to the planks or boards as 'lifts') type of hull construction. Notice the rebate for the bulwark. *Portia Takakjian*

then the boards could have been fastened together permanently at this time, instead of temporarily. When so doing, start by fastening and clamping two boards together. Once the glue has set add the next board, glue and clamp, then the next and so on until the block is complete. It is not advisable to try to glue and fasten together all the boards at once. Brass screws can be used in addition to glue, but dowels are preferable to screws. In either case position the fastenings well clear of any openings or holes which may have to be cut in the deck later. Those securing the uppermost board, if not to be covered with deck planking or deck plating, should be placed where they will be covered with a hatch or by a deckhouse. See **Fig 126**.

In order to produce a hollow hull, take the block apart once again. Remove as large a part as possible from the middle of each board except for the bottom one and, in the case of a non-working model, the top one. Making the hull of a static model hollow does have the advantage of reducing its weight – quite a consideration in a large model. Leave sufficient

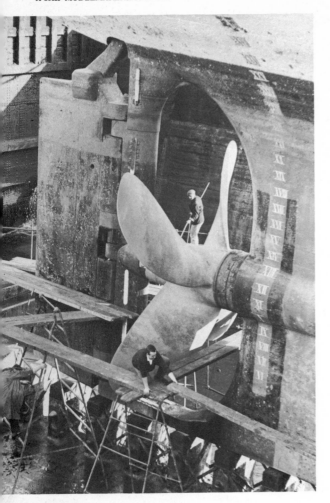

Fig 128
The boss plating of a single-screw vessel. Note the shape of the rudder post, and the streamlined blade of the rudder. This photograph also shows very well the shape of the blades of the propeller. The ship is the P&O liner *Chitral*, formerly the Belgian *Jadotville*, which the company acquired in 1961. *Conway Picture Library*

material at the ends and at each side to allow each board to be fastened to its neighbour. Some modellers prefer to do this at the same time as they cut away the excess material outside the marked waterline. In this event care must be taken not to undercut the board where there is an excessive shape on the hull. Such an error can be avoided by marking the lower waterline on the underside of the board and using this in conjunction with the upper one

as a guideline. Once all the boards have been cut in this way they can be fastened together permanently as just described.

If the model is to be a working one, the interior can be cleaned up to produce a smooth surface. It is possible to produce a hull with quite a slim wall thickness, but always leave some extra material at the stem and stern.

APPENDAGES

The foregoing notes have dealt only with the main hull of a vessel, and can be applied to the majority of ship types for the period being dealt with. The term 'appendages' is used to refer to those parts of the underwater body lying outwith the normal shape of the main hull, such as the rudder, the shaft brackets and shaft bossing. The shaft bossing is the name given to that part of the hull where the propeller shaft emerges. On a single-screw ship this shows as a slight swelling on the hull just forward of and up to the stern frame. On the body plan, when shown, it is indicated by a series of circular arcs whose centres coincide with the centreline of the propeller shaft and whose extremities are faired into the adjacent shell plating, as in **Fig 129**. On the profile it is shown as an elongated oval. The shape of the bossing must be incorporated in the templates for the hull sections in that area, but it will probably be necessary to make up a number of intermediate ones in order to get the exact shape.

In the case of twin-screw vessels the matter becomes a little more complicated. The propeller shafts emerge from the hull at a point well forward of the stern frame and some distance out from the centreline. From the point of emergence to the propeller position each is enclosed by plating which meets with and fairs into the shell plating. On the body plan the outline of the bossing is shown as a series of circular arcs based on the centreline of the propeller shaft and extended to fair in with the shell plating, as in **Fig 130**. The outline in plan view will be found on the half-breadth plan, and the line of contact with the shell will appear as an elongated oval on the profile.

When preparing the templates for this part of the hull it is better to cut a slot in the template to the maximum size of the bossing, so that on first carving the hull at this point a partially shaped 'fin' is left, the final shaping of which will be completed later, possibly after

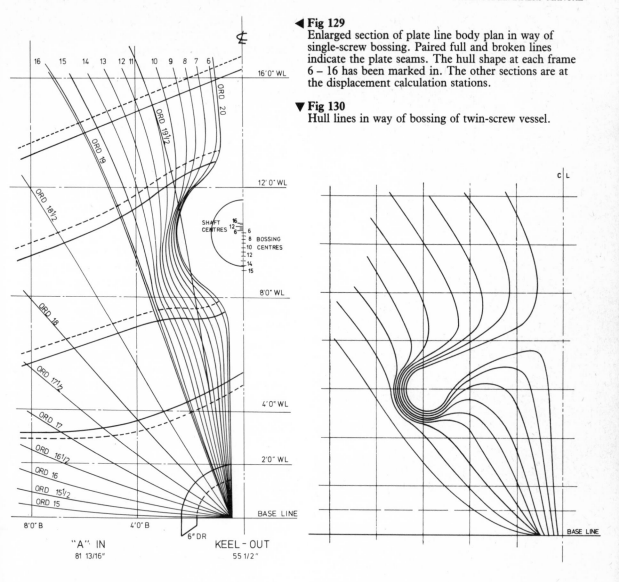

◀ **Fig 129**
Enlarged section of plate line body plan in way of single-screw bossing. Paired full and broken lines indicate the plate seams. The hull shape at each frame 6 – 16 has been marked in. The other sections are at the displacement calculation stations.

▼ **Fig 130**
Hull lines in way of bossing of twin-screw vessel.

the shaft hole has been bored. Again it will be necessary to prepare a set of intermediate templates to facilitate this work.

The bulbous bow or forefoot is a feature of many vessels, large and small, today. Hidden when the ship is fully laden, much of it is visible when the vessel is in the light condition. The shape of these bulbs varies quite considerably, and **Fig 246** shows one type. **Fig 131** gives a good idea of how a typical bulb forefoot will appear on the lines plan.

The hulls of some warships will be found to differ in a number of respects from those so far considered. Some vessels have a very pronounced tumblehome, some have anti-torpedo bulges along the side, some have a pronounced ram-type forefoot, and some have combinations of these. The design of the hull in the way of twin screws is different in that the bossing was confined to the immediate vicinity of the point of the shafts' emergence. Each shaft then ran aft, without any covering, to a large 'A' bracket fitted immediately ahead of the propeller. The arrangement for quadruple-screw vessels followed the pattern for that of twin-screw ships.

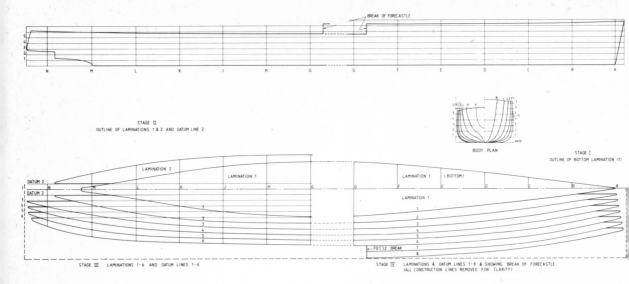

Before leaving the subject of 'bread-and-butter' hull construction it is worth mentioning a development of this form of construction evolved recently by Stephen Kirby. It requires a little more work initially, but it has the merit among other things of being very economical in the use of timber. Although details of the method have appeared in *Model Shipwright* 27 and in the book *Scale Model Warships*, a résumé of it is included, with his and with the publisher's permission, as it has much to commend it. His technique reduces the amount of timber to a minimum and also facilitates cutting out. The system is suitable for the majority of warship and merchant ship hulls. In the accompanying drawing, **Fig 132**, thirteen stations have been used, but ideally there should be more, for the more there are the greater will be the accuracy of the hull. The following is a step-by-step sequence of the method.

1 Read through this process with reference to the accompanying drawing before starting on the wood.

2 Trace out full model size of the hull profile and body plan on to a piece of paper. If a sheer draught is not available the above can be obtained from an inboard or outboard GA profile. Do not draw any horizontal lines except a baseline.

3 Select the thickness of the wood to be used and mark out the horizontal lines upwards from the baseline numbering the *lines* as you go, the line spacing being the thickness of the wood.

4 Decide how much you require each lamination to overlap the next for a good glue joint. As a guide, $\frac{1}{2}$in for large hulls and $\frac{3}{8}$in for small hulls has been found satisfactory.

5 Calculate the minimum width of wood from which to make the hull – the length will be the same as that of the hull. Width of plank = 2 [(number of laminations – 1) × overlap] + beam. In the example the number of laminations is 8. Overlap is $\frac{1}{2}$in; beam is 5in. Applying the formula,

$$\text{width} = 2[(8 - 1) \times \tfrac{1}{2}] + 5$$
$$= 2(7 \times \tfrac{1}{2}) + 5$$
$$= 7 + 5$$
$$= 12\text{in}$$

To obtain wood of this width or more, several planks will have to be glued edge to edge. If you are using wood from a timber-merchant check the flatness of the planks after planing, as at times they have a tendency to curl.

6 Mark on to the wood the centreline with the stations at 90°, putting in at least as many stations as on the drawing.

7 Plot the bottom lamination (No 1) on the wood. Using dividers, measure the width of each station on line 1 and mark off the widths as you do so on both sides of the centreline at each station. Join up the dots with a smooth curve to obtain the shape of this piece. Note that this curve starts just forward of station A

Fig 131▶
Typical lines of vessel having a bulbous forefoot.

◀Fig 132
The 'Kirby' method of marking out planks for bread-and-butter construction. *By courtesy of Stephen Kirby*

Fig 133▼
A series of planks for a 'bread-and-butter' hull produced by the 'Kirby' method. *Stephen Kirby*

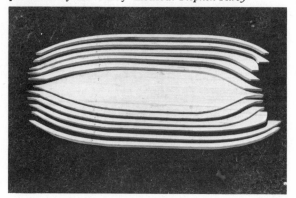

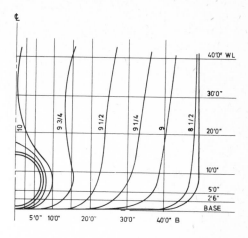

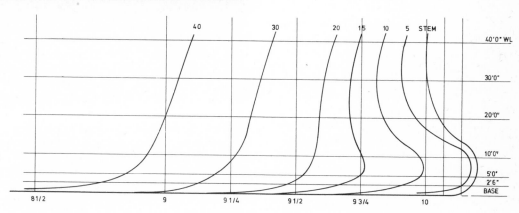

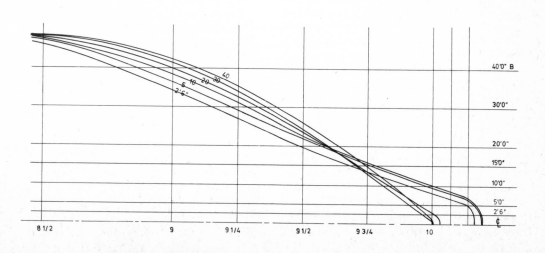

owing to the rake of the stem, and that it ends just aft of station M. See Stages I and II on the drawing. Stage I area has been left clear of other workings for clarity.

8 Next mark off a new datum line each side of the original centreline at a distance equal to the overlap selected in operation 4. In this case it is $\frac{1}{2}$in. Mark out lamination 2 using line 2 on the body plan and datum lines 2 on the wood. This is shown in Stage II on the drawing. Note that in this instance lamination 2 can be seen to finish between points M and N on the profile. Plot this point by measuring its distance from M.

9 Now mark out datum lines 3 and, using line 3 on the body plan, plot the shape of lamination 3.

10 Laminations 4–6. Note that stations G, H, J and K incorporate some tumblehome. This shows on the body plan. Care is needed here. If the tumblehome shows up on G, H, J and K it can be assumed that its total extent is from F to L. In this event the width of the actual lamination is greater on the lower surface so, when taking measurements for laminations 4, 5 and 6, the line under the lamination, that is line 3 for lamination 4 and so on, must be used, but only where tumblehome occurs. All other stations are measured in the usual way. Stage III shows all the laminations up to quarterdeck level. Observe the false datum lines 1–6.

11 Finish off the marking out of the rest of the laminations. On hulls which have a lot of sheer there may be fairly short pieces at the bow and stern. Care is required when marking out these pieces.

Stage IV shows the finished product with all station lines removed for clarity. The broken line around Stage III and Stage IV shows the plank of wood, and demonstrates how little is wasted compared with the usual way of marking the inside and outside lines of each lamination on to cardboard and arranging these on the plank for least wastage. With the method just described the waste piece of wood is at least of a usable size. The result shown in Stages II and IV will, of course, appear also in mirror image on the other side of the centreline.

12 Cut round the outside of the top lamination. When cutting the inside line on this piece, the cut will also be the first cut on the next one down, and so on. When all the cutting

has been done, the whole lot can be glued together, the one-piece bottom being a great help in the building up.

There is a tip which may be of use during the assembly: if there is the slightest difference in thickness from one side of the sheet to the other the hull will become lopsided due to the accumulated error. So lay out the laminations as they were when on the sheet and change over every alternate piece from one side to the other. This will cancel out any error due to varying thickness. It is also useful to cut out the deck(s), using the plan view on the drawing, and pin in place temporarily to avoid cutting too much off when shaping the top edge of the hull. It is also worth noting that had there been a glue line on the whole sheet of wood those joints will now be staggered and thus there will not be a weak point on the hull.

Bluff bows and sterns. These present the same problem and solution. A block of wood must be used in this instance as the system cannot cope with such shapes. The block should be rebated to accept the ends of the laminations for strength and alignment.

Transom sterns. The shape of the transom will usually be shown on the body plan. It should be made up before assembly and used to align the ends of the laminations when gluing up.

Rockered or curved keels. If this is slight then the system will stand it, but a great deal depends on the amount of curve.

Tumblehome. A certain amount of tumblehome can be accommodated, as shown in the text, but not to the extent found in some warships built around the turn of the century.

Bulges. These are best added after the rest of the hull has been shaped, as it is very difficult to carve them in one piece.

PLANK-ON-FRAME CONSTRUCTION

As the name implies this method of construction is based on the traditional way of building a ship by erecting frames on a keel, stem and stern post assembly, and fixing thereto a skin of planking. The result is a strong, light hull, and one which avoids much of the heavy work associated with the production of solid block or some types of 'bread-and-butter' hulls. Nevertheless, there still persists in some quarters the idea that there is some mystique about this form of construction, and that it is not for the tyro. This simply is not so, except

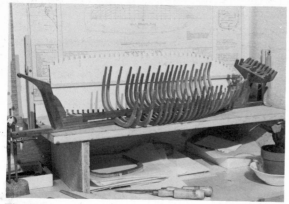

Fig 134
Plank-on-frame model of the brigantine *Leon*. In this
photograph framing is well under way. The top
timbers are scarphed to the frame, and the transom has
been made as a single unit. Note rabbet in keel and
stem. *R L Puttock*

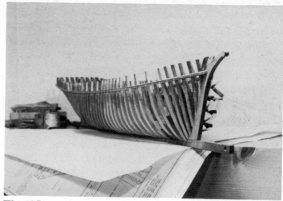

Fig 135
Framing complete. The extension to the keel will be
removed at a later stage. Note the cant frames. *R L
Puttock*

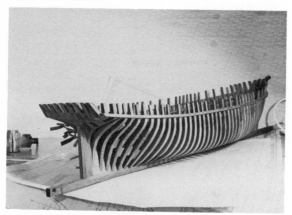

Fig 136
The after end showing stern post, after deadwood, and
framing for the square transom stern. This latter
framing has been altered slightly from the normal
practice to simplify construction. *R L Puttock*

Fig 137
Deck view showing the beams and half beams; note
the lodging knees to the half beams in way of the hatch
openings. Planking of the deck has been started. The
supports for the model during construction are clearly
to be seen. *R L Puttock*

Fig 138
The completed hull, with bulwarks fitted and the
anchor deck and the quarterdeck in place. *R L Puttock*

perhaps in the case of the Dockyard/
Admiralty/Navy Board type of model, where
a knowledge of the constructional practices of
the period is essential since much of the internal
work is visible and therefore has to be correct.

Before going further it will be as well to
appreciate that there are two distinct
approaches to plank-on-frame modelling. In
one the builder constructs his model generally
in the way the prototype was built, with at least
all the visible external detail true to scale scantlings; for example, the planks of the hull will
be of the correct length and width. All this will
still be apparent even after the finishing
medium has been applied.

In the other the 'frames' of the hull may be open or solid formers, arbitrarily spaced, with the keel, stem and the stern post being single pieces of timber suitably supported. In fact internally all 'correct' shipbuilding practices are eschewed in favour of a simple, strong core or framework on which to fix the planking, and so produce a hull having a true-to-scale external shape. The planks of the hull will, in most instances, run the full length of the model in one piece, and their width will be governed more by the material available than by considerations of scale. Since the finished hull will be sanded smooth and then painted, this approach may be considered adequate for many types of vessel, and particularly for working models.

The more conventional approach to plank-on-frame construction for vessels of the period under consideration is illustrated by **Figs 134–138**, which give a very good idea of what is involved in building a model by this method. The model is the brigantine *Leon*, being built by J Puttock of Weybridge, to plans by Harold Underhill, whose book *Plank-on-Frame Construction*, describing as it does in very complete detail the principles and practices of this form of modelling, is generally regarded as the definitive work on the subject.

At this point a few notes on some of the basics of wood ship construction may be helpful. **Fig 139**, although of an older vessel, does illustrate how a keel, stem and stern post assembly was built up of many separate pieces of timber. Over the years this came to be modified, and different countries developed their own variations of the method of supporting the end members by the mass of timber known as the deadwood, the inner timbers of which were joined to the keelson, that timber fixed to the upper surface of the floor frames to tie them and to prevent them from tripping (**Fig 140**). These variations were brought about by such things as the size of the vessel, the ideas of the shipbuilder and the scantlings and type of timber available. Frames were either single or double, and were built up from a number of individual pieces to take advantage of the grain in the timber (see **Fig 141**). The spacing of the frames was on the 'room and space' principle, where the space or gap between each frame was equal to the width or the 'sided' dimension of the frame. **Fig 142** explains the meaning of 'sided' and 'moulded' dimensions when applied to a frame.

Cant frames. Whereas the frames above were all set at right angles to the centreline of the ship, at either end, where the curvature of the vessel's sides in to the centre line became so acute that the amount of bevel on the outer face of the frames would be excessive, they were set more or less at right angles to the side planking. The spacing at the outboard end would be kept as far as possible to that of the main frames; see **Fig 143**.

Transom. Where the (lowest) deck met the stern post a heavy timber was secured to the stern post, level with the underside of the deck (*ie* level with the upper surface of the deck beams) and at right angles to the ship's fore and aft centreline; it was known as the wing transom. In **Fig 134** this can be seen, not as

Fig 139
Stem, keel and stern post construction. *From* Naval Architecture *by S J P Thearle, 1874*

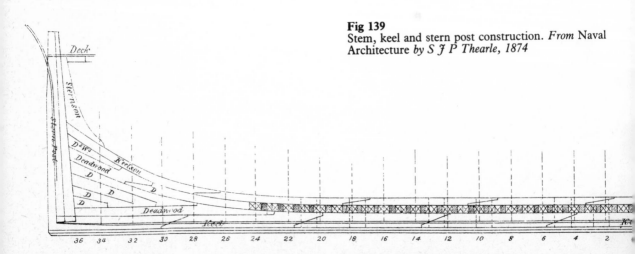

a beam in this case but as a shaped piece of timber. On the after side were fastened the shaped timbers forming the stern framing, their disposition being either as in the illustration of the vessel with a square stern, or radially, like cant frames, if the stern was round (when seen in plan view).

Rabbet line. Where the side planking met the stern post, keel and stem, the square end (or edge) of the plank was let into the timber to a depth equal to its thickness to protect it, as in **Fig 144.** A line drawn through the points where the outer edge of the plank end or edge met the stern post or other timbers was known as the rabbet line.

Bearding line. This is the name given to a line drawn through the point on the stern post, etc, where the inner surface of a plank meets the stern timbers at the start of a rabbet; refer to **Fig 144.** The rabbet to take the plank end is formed by cutting into the post from this point down to the rabbet line, the cut starting at nothing at the bearding line to a depth equal to the plank thickness at the rabbet line.

Planking. The thickness and width of planking was ultimately to be covered by classification society rules, and strict regulations were laid down concerning the shift of butts. For example, butts in adjacent strakes were not to be closer than 5ft, or 4ft if there was a strake in between; there had to be at least three strakes of planking between butts on the same frame. Towards the ends of a vessel, the taper on the planks became too great to allow the use of suitable fastenings; this was overcome by the use of stealers, as shown in **Fig 145.**

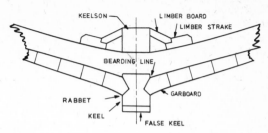

Fig 140
Section through keel, showing construction

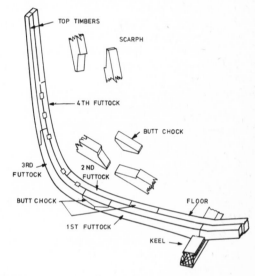

Fig 141
Built-up frame construction, showing component parts.

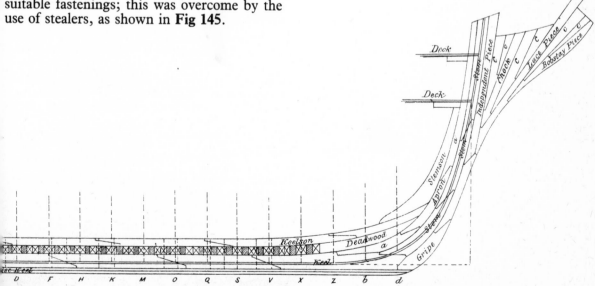

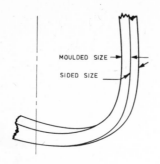

Fig 142
Diagram illustrating meanings of the terms 'sided' size and 'moulded' size.

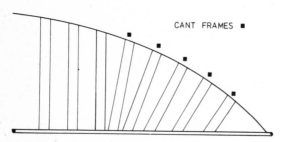

Fig 143
Arrangement of cant frames.

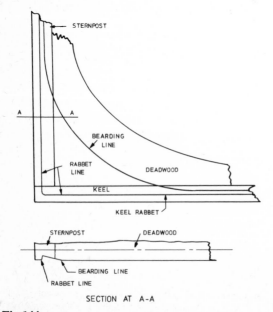

Fig 144
Relationship of bearding and rabbet lines.

Despite the varying thickness of planks required, on some larger vessels this was so arranged that the outer surface appeared to be smooth. But this was not always the case and then the outer surface of the wales, as these strakes of heavier material were called, lay proud of the rest of the hull. This is an important point to bear in mind when scale planking a scale hull. As far as possible the planking would follow the sheer of the hull unless this was excessive.

As mentioned above, where it became impossible at the ends to accommodate the number of planks used amidships due to the difference in girths, the problem was overcome by the use of stealers. Widths of planks might be about 12in, and lengths from 20ft to 30ft; so much depended upon the material available. If longer pieces of wood are used for planking a scale model, and there are advantages in so doing, particularly for wales, then false butts can be represented where appropriate, with dummy fastenings being placed each side of the butt.

Beams. These ran transversely across the ship to support the deck planking and the side frames. Where they came in way of deck openings they were butted into the carlings forming that opening (see **Fig 146**). Beams were cambered. The ends of a beam rested on the beam shelf, a heavy timber attached to the inside of the frames at the appropriate height to support the beams, and to which they were attached by strong hanging knees, as in **Fig 147**.

Deck planking. The width of deck planks was less than that of the hull planks, about 6in to 9in, and about 3in to 4in thick. They were laid parallel to the centreline, and edges and butts were caulked. As with the hull planks, butts had to be shifted; generally these ran in parallel lines across the deck, with four planks between butts on the same beam. Towards the bow and the stern, where the planks met the curve of the margin plank, the ends were cut (snaped) and butted against it. However, the planks were never cut to a point. The rule was that when the length of the snape would measure more than twice the width of the plank, then the plank had to be joggled into the margin plank; when so doing the square end of the plank after cutting had to be not less than half the width of the plank. See **Fig 148**.

Depending on the size of the model, the caulking of the deck planking can be rep-

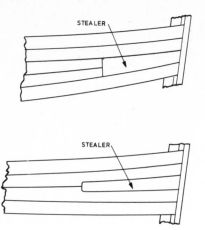

Fig 145
Two methods of arranging stealers.

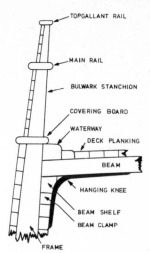

Fig 147
Section through deck-edge to show the construction.

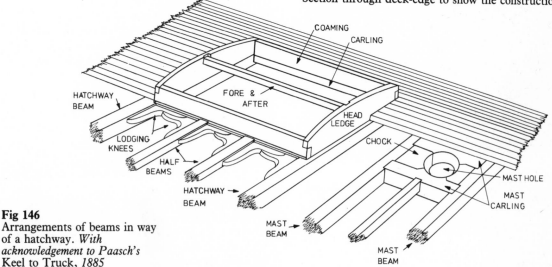

Fig 146
Arrangements of beams in way
of a hatchway. *With
acknowledgement to Paasch's*
Keel to Truck, *1885*

resented by clamping together a number of
lengths of the deck planking, gluing black
paper to one set of edges, and separating the
planks once the glue has dried with a razor
blade. When following this method use a
scraper to smooth off the decking once laid and
not sandpaper, for this will rub the black dust
from the paper into the wood. On small-scale
models the edges of the planks can be painted
black before laying, but take care not to get
the paint on the top surface.

Many modellers, rather than plank up a
deck, make it of a single width of wood and
simulate the planking by scoring in, or marking
in, the individual planks with a scriber, or a
pencil or ball-point pen. No matter how accurately this is done, it never looks right, merely

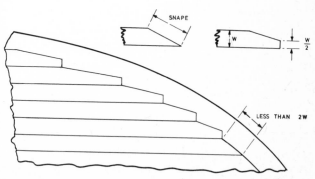

Fig 148
Joggling of deck planking into the margin plank.
W = width of deck plank. The margin plank is always
wider than the deck plank.

what it is – scored in or pencilled in. One reason, often overlooked, is that the act of using a chisel-pointed pencil, or scoring, creates a visible indent in the surface of the wood. When a deck seam, after being caulked with oakum, is payed (filled) with melted pitch the top surface of the pitch when cold was always above the level of the deck, and wider than the gap between the planks which it filled, and with wavy edges. Even when smoothed off level with the deck, whilst its edges then became parallel, there was no hollow in the surface of the pitch. These two points can be seen clearly in **Figs 118** and **149**.

On top of the beams and immediately inside the frames was a heavy timber, thicker than the deck planking and known as the waterway, and inside this was the margin plank. The top edge of the hull plank forming the sheer strake and that of the waterway were level, and the top of those frames not extended to form bulwark stanchions was to the same height. Fitted over the top edge of the sheer strake and over the heads of the frames was the covering board, also called the planksheer (**Fig 147**). Apertures were cut in the plank in way of those frame top timbers extended to form bulwark stanchions.

Bulwarks. The stanchions were planked on the outside, and fitted with a topgallant rail as necessary. **Fig 147** shows a typical cross-section through a bulwark. The inside surface was sometimes panelled.

Returning to constructional methods, **Fig 150** shows another way of framing a fully planked hull. Although once again this happens to be a model of a vessel of an earlier period, the principle can be used for others. The builder, John Blight, has cut out each pair of frames as a single entity from plywood, and has included the deck beam, correctly cambered. A departure from normal practice is the addition of a pair of diagonal stiffeners running from the turn of the bilge to the underside of the beam at the centreline. Because of the very bluff ends a solid block of wood has been worked in behind the stem and the stern post. At the time the photograph was taken, no cleaning up or bevelling had been carried out on any of the frame units.

This is a variation of the other popular and similar form of construction, plank-on-former. In this a number of solid formers, or bulkheads, are cut out and mounted on the usual keel,

Fig 149
Deck planking, showing how the pitch used for paying the seams lies in an irregular shape on the surface of the planks. On this ship the waterway outside the margin plank has been filled in with cement.

Fig 150
The hull of John Blight's model under construction, showing the deck beam and diagonal stiffeners cut integrally with each pair of frames. Note the solid block at the stern; a similar block was fitted at the bow. Distance pieces have been fitted between the after frames. The stern post, and the stem, are well supported on a solid working baseboard.

Fig 151
The stem, keel, stern and formers assembly for the hull of the steam launch *Branksome*, set up ready for planking. *D Jacques*

Fig 152
The planked hull of the *Branksome* removed from the formers, and with the timber fitted. *D Jacques*

stem and stern post assembly, any deadwoods being single pieces of timber. **Fig 151** gives a general idea of this method, and has been selected for two reasons. This particular set-up was to act as the core on which the hull of an open launch would be built, the formers being discarded once the hull was planked. The stem and keel were rabbeted, deadwood fitted aft to take the stern tube, and the counter formed of a solid block well secured to the keel assembly. The planks were fitted and glued edge to edge and at the ends, but not to the formers. Once they were all complete and the glue well set, the hull was removed from the baseboard and the formers were taken out and replaced by timbers cut from marine plywood, spaced 2in apart throughout the length of the 75in hull. The result can be seen in **Fig 152**; after it was taken two permanent bulkheads were fitted to subdivide the hull. This is in fact the hull of the Lake Windermere steam launch *Brank-*

Fig 153
The built-up after end block of the *Marie Sophie. Max Davey*

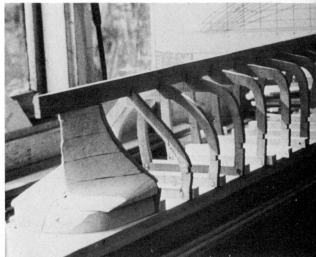

some, an illustration of which appears as **Fig 19**.

Were this to be the basis for a fully planked and decked model, some additional formers would be necessary between Nos 1, 2 and 3, and perhaps at the after end – in fact anywhere where there is considerable curvature or shape in the hull – to prevent 'flatting' of the planking between the formers. A further point to bear in mind when adopting a somewhat arbitrary spacing for the formers is that, unless the hull is going to be painted, the dowel fastenings, if used, will show up and reveal to all and sundry the non-scale spacing of the formers.

Fig 153, of the hull of Max Davey's 1/48 scale sailing model of the brig *Marie Sophie*, shows another method. The shaped parts of the stern and the bow were built up as solid blocks, in this case of obeche, and joined to the keel, stem and stern post, which were of maranti. The frames were sawn from plywood and extended above the level of the deck or bulwark rail to a common level so that they could be mounted on a solid working base-board. In this position the hull was planked,

Fig 154
A model of the tug *Willowgarth*, scale 1/48, 23in long and built by D Newton of Bootle. It is a very good example of hard chine construction. Note the details of the stern frame and skeg, typical of this form of hull, and the propeller stern tube bossing.

the material being western red cedar $\frac{3}{8}$in × $\frac{1}{8}$in. This model is now in the National Maritime Museum at Greenwich.

The 'eggbox' method. This is a simple way of making up the internal structure for a planked static model, and is one much favoured by kit manufacturers. The keel, stem and stern post are cut to form a single central member, extended up to the underside of the deck and slotted to take the formers. These formers are cut to shape up to deck level and slotted into those of the centre member. The space between the end former and the stem etc is filled with a solid block to provide a good landing for the planking. The external edge of the stem, keel, etc is usually faced with hardwood strip.

Lifeboats

The boats carried by a ship are another feature which, through lack of research or hurried construction, so frequently spoils an otherwise good model. It really is surprising how often one sees a poorly shaped, badly made and technically incorrect (in respect of both construction and period) ship's boat.

As much care must be taken in checking their accuracy and in building them as has been expended on the rest of the model. They should never be treated as a last-minute afterthought, for that is the only way many can be categorised. In competitions, rallies and regattas some judges look first at the boats on a model in the belief that so doing gives them a good indication of the quality of the rest of the model. Personally I consider this to be a somewhat ill-advised practice, and one to which I do not subscribe.

A good set of modelmaker's plans will include all the necessary details of the boats carried by the vessel depicted, and in general they will be correct for the date of the ship. But there is a point to watch. It is not unknown for boats to be replaced during a ship's lifetime, so just check that those on the plans agree with those being carried if the model is of the ship at a particular period of its life. Builders' general arrangement drawings, on the other hand, invariably indicate the boats in outline only, in both plan and profile, and from long experience it is wise to look very carefully at the shape. As these are merely arrangement draw-

ings, whilst the overall dimensions may be near enough, the shape may be less accurate, for it is not unknown for a draughtsman to make use of the handiest curve that has the approximate shape of the boat! Some shipbuilders produce a separate 'Arrangement of Boats' plan which shows the davits, ancillary equipment, lead of falls, etc in fair detail, and usually the outline of the boats with greater accuracy.

Leaving aside the matter of warships' boats, which are an interesting subject in themselves, the boats carried by merchantmen, even in the period covered by this book, have undergone many changes. For a long time the open, clinker-built wooden boat was the standard piece of emergency equipment, and prior to the *Titanic* disaster in 1912 the number carried, particularly by passenger liners, was woefully inadequate in relation to the total complement on board. Following that disaster the whole matter of lifeboat numbers and capacity was investigated and resulted in the introduction of stringent new rules and regulations covering such matters as the number of boats to be carried, their construction and outfit, maintenance, and periodic surveys by Government inspectors. In the United Kingdom information on this subject is to be found in the various publications of the Board of Trade and currently of the Department of Trade and Industry.

The advent and subsequent development of

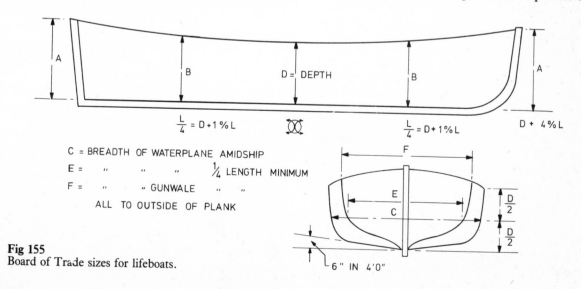

Fig 155
Board of Trade sizes for lifeboats.

An extract from a Board of Trade table of requirements for lifeboats.

Dimensions	Cubic feet	Persons	Weight complete	Weight of boat & equipment	A	B	C	E	F
30′0″ × 9′0″ × 3′ 9″	607	60	7.05 tons	2.60 tons	4′11½″	4′ 0⅝″	8′ 7¾″	6′11⅛″	7′ 5⅝″
29′0″ × 8′9″ × 3′ 7¼″	546	54	6.40 tons	2.40 tons	4′ 9⅛″	3′10¾″	8′ 4⅞″	6′ 8⅞″	7′ 3⅛″
28′0″ × 8′6″ × 3′ 6″	500	50	5.90 tons	2.20 tons	4′ 7½″	3′ 9⅜″	8′ 2⅞″	6′ 6⅛″	7′ 0⅝″
27′0″ × 8′3″ × 3′ 4⅞″	454	45	5.35 tons	2.00 tons	4′ 5¾″	3′ 8″	7′11″	6′ 4¼″	6′10¼″
26′0″ × 8′0″ × 3′ 3″	405	40	4.75 tons	1.80 tons	4′ 3½″	3′ 6⅛″	7′ 8⅛″	6′ 1⅞″	6′ 7⅝″
25′0″ × 7′9″ × 3′ 1⅞″	366	36	4.30 tons	1.65 tons	4′ 1⅞″	3′ 4⅞″	7′ 5¼″	5′11⅝″	6′ 5¼″
24′0″ × 7′6″ × 3′ 0″	324	32	3.85 tons	1.45 tons	3′11½″	3′ 2⅞″	7′ 2⅜″	5′ 9⅜″	6′ 2⅝″
23′0″ × 7′6″ × 2′10⅞″	300	30	3.55 tons	1.33 tons	3′ 9⅞″	3′ 1½″	7′ 2⅜″	5′ 9⅜″	6′ 2⅝″
22′0″ × 7′3″ × 2′ 9″	263	26	3.10 tons	1.18 tons	3′ 7½″	2′11⅝″	6′11½″	5′ 7″	6′ 0¼″
21′0″ × 7′0″ × 2′ 8½″	238	23	2.80 tons	1.11 tons	3′ 6½″	2′10⅞″	6′ 8⅝″	5′ 4⅝″	5′ 9¾″
20′0″ × 6′9″ × 2′ 7¼″	210	21	2.50 tons	0.95 tons	3′ 4⅞″	2′ 9⅝″	6′ 5¼″	5′ 2⅜″	5′ 7¼″
19′0″ × 6′6″ × 2′ 6″	182	18	2.15 tons	0.83 tons	3′ 3⅛″	2′ 8¼″	6′ 2⅞″	5′ 0″	5′ 4⅝″
18′0″ × 6′3″ × 2′ 4⅞″	162	16	1.90 tons	0.72 tons	3′ 1½″	2′ 7″	6′ 0″	4′ 9¾″	5′ 2¼″
17′0″ × 6′0″ × 2′ 4¼″	143	14	1.70 tons	0.67 tons	3′ 0⅞″	2′ 6¼″	5′ 9⅛″	4′ 7½″	4′11¾″
16′0″ × 5′9″ × 2′ 3⅝″	127	12	1.50 tons	0.56 tons	2′11½″	2′ 5½″	5′ 6¼″	4′ 5⅛″	4′ 9⅜″

the internal combustion engine saw its application to ships' boats, with some consequent changes in their design. In addition, as the years passed other materials such as aluminium, steel and fibreglass came to be used for their construction. Once more, the introduction of these new materials, coupled with the increasing size of vessels and altered types and spheres of operation, led to further changes in size, shape and construction. The accompanying drawings and illustrations can only give an insight into what is in fact quite a complex subject.

CONSTRUCTION

The method of construction, and the amount of detail to be included depends upon the scale of the model, the prototype and the method of stowage. Although there are quite a number of vessels nowadays which carry permanently uncovered boats, the practice has always been to fit them with protective canvas covers. This is ideal from the modelmakers point of view, as all the internal details were hidden, and it created the impression that construction was a simple matter. What travesties have resulted from following this idea! These covers are not always taut and smooth, as an examination of some of the boats in several of the illustrations in this book will show. Many were fitted over a framework of wood ridges and rafters (a good example of which can be seen on **Fig 82**), and the canvas would tend to sag between the supports. The covers were held in place by lashings, often attached to those familiar triangular 'tabs', the shape of which needs to be watched, for it could vary quite markedly.

Builders of miniature models usually find that the simplest way to represent covered boats is to prepare a length of wood the cross-section of which is made to the outline of the boat's transverse mid-section, including the lay of the canvas cover. One end of this stick is cut to the shape of the bow, the appropriate length for the boat parted off, and the cut end of this piece finished to the shape of the boat's stern. Open boats at these small scales, 1/1200 and a little larger, can be produced by hollowing out one of the solid boats, but it is a tricky job. One alternative which can work quite well is to cut a strip of thin paper of a width equal to the midship girth of the boat, mark on it the length of the boat, put a spot of glue at these points, fold the paper lengthwise but do not crease it, and pinch the sides together at the marked spots. The result is a 'boat' shape which can be eased into the correct outline, after which the ends can be trimmed to shape and the internals made out of paper and put in place.

For other small-scale models the open boat shells can be produced by the plug moulding

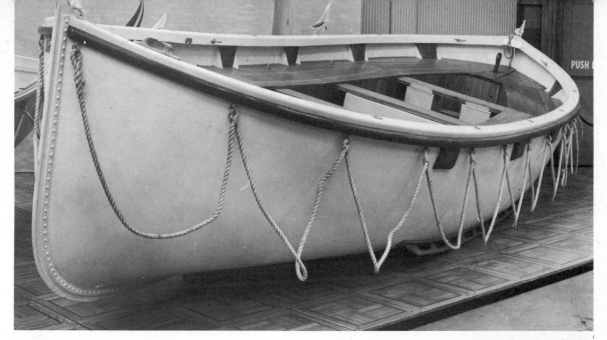

Fig 156
A typical double-ended fibreglass pulling lifeboat,
length 26ft. *Conway Picture Library*

Fig 157
The stem of a clinker-built lifeboat, showing how the
scarphing away of the last few inches of the overlap of
the strakes gives a flush finish to the ends of the
planks. Note the iron band to the face of the stem.

Fig 158
The after end of a transom-stern, clinker-built wood
lifeboat showing construction of rudder and details of
gudgeons and pintles. This particular boat also did
duty as a workboat, hence the presence of the heavy
rubbing band and the mooring bitt.

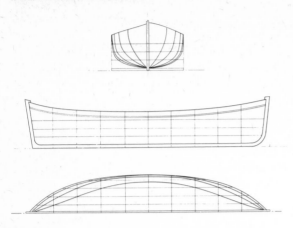

Fig 159
Lines and sections for a 30ft double-ended lifeboat of wood construction.

method (see Ventilators and **Fig 302**), the thwarts, etc being made of plastic card. But for many models other than miniatures and the like, the most usual way is to carve them from solid wood. There are two ways of doing this. The first is by carving a solid block of wood to shape, in the same way as for a block hull, *ie* mark in and cut the sheer line, followed by the outline in plan view and then the profile. After mounting this block upside down on a suitable working base (one which can be held in a vice) carve the outside to shape. When finished, make a saw cut along the bottom centreline and at each end – if a double-ended boat; otherwise at the bow only – to receive the keel, stem and stern posts, which will be made of thin wood glued into these cuts and trimmed to shape. Remove the boat from the base and hollow out the inside – easy to say, but somewhat awkward to do on small boats. If the original had buoyancy tanks along each side and at the ends, then hollow out only to the level of their tops, and of course to the bottom boards elsewhere. Thin wood can be used for the thwarts and bottom boards, also for the rudder. Equipment will include oars, mast, yard and lugsail, boathooks, water-breaker, and many smaller items, though these are normally stowed out of sight.

By far the better method of construction, and one which can be used for many types of open boats, is that which is generally referred to as the 'Draper' way. In this the hull is made

up of two pieces of wood, one forming the port half of the boat and the other the starboard side – as though the boat had been cut in two down the longitudinal centreline – with a third piece having the thickness of the keel, stem and stern posts and large enough to accommodate all three members, sandwiched in between. Each block is carved to the outside shape of the appropriate side, using templates to check the work. When completed the next step is to hollow out each block to form a thin shell. After removing as much surplus wood as possible with chisels and gouges, the job is finished off with rotary files. These can be obtained in a variety of shapes and cuts from a supplier of engineers' tools, while smaller sizes of a similar tool, for use in battery/mains-operated hand drills, can be found in leading modellers' shops. Most of the work can be accomplished with ball heads of different diameters and having a fairly fine cut, but pear-shaped ones also have their uses.

The file is fitted into the chuck of a bench drill or some similar set-up. With the drill fixed, the wood can be held firmly in both hands and moved as necessary against the rotating file. With care and practice wafer thin shells can be produced in this way, and by holding the work up to the light the thickness

Fig 160
Body plan, arrangement and constructional details for a light alloy double-ended lifeboat having dimensions 26ft × 8ft 6in × 3ft 6in.

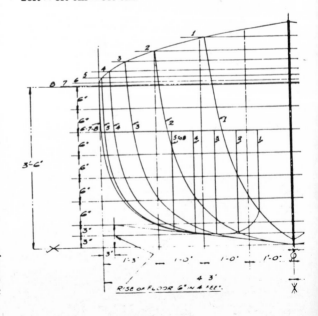

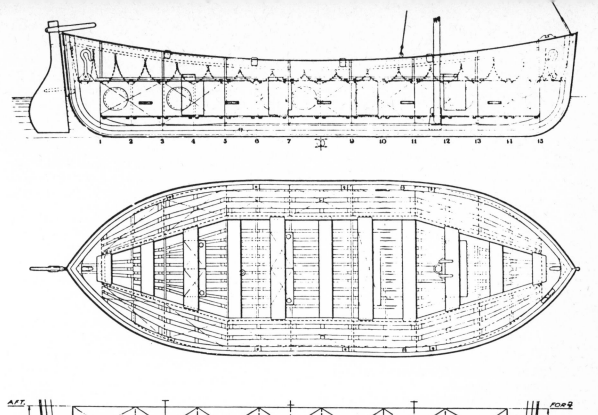

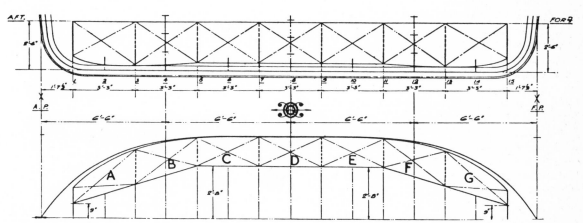

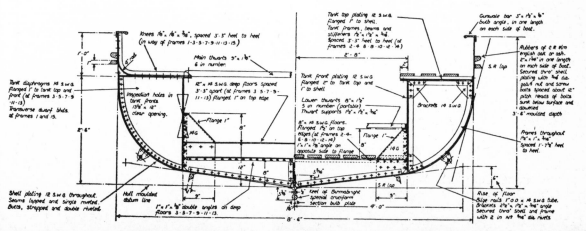

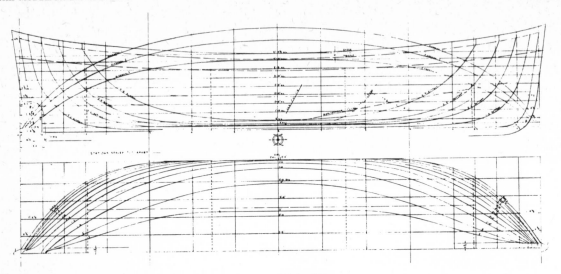

Fig 161 ▲
Lines for a 31ft × 10ft 6in × 4ft 5in double-ended
lifeboat of fibreglass construction. The moulded depth
is 4ft 4½in, and the sheer at each end is 1ft 4½in. It is
suitable for either motor or hand propulsion.

▼Fig 162
General arrangement of a double-ended steel lifeboat
29ft × 9ft 3in × 3ft 10½in. This is a pulling (rowing)
boat.

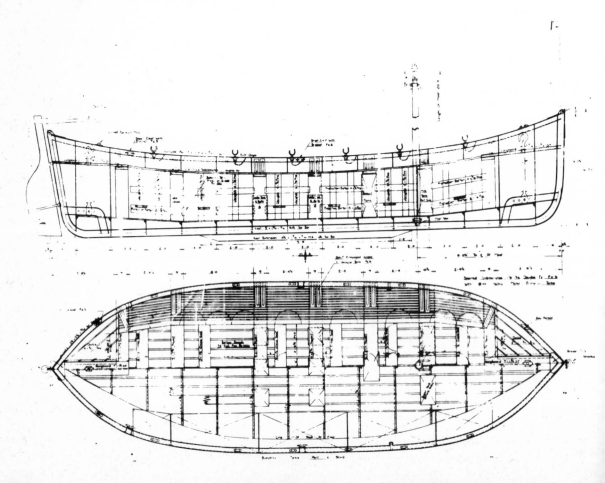

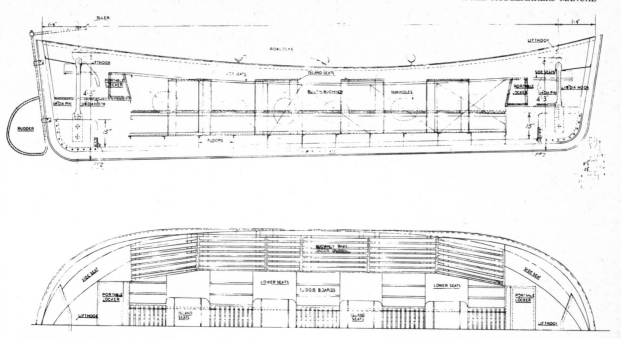

Fig 163
General arrangement of a light alloy pulling lifeboat,
26ft × 8ft 9in × 3ft 8in.

can be gauged. Perhaps the best wood to use for this purpose is lime. In the case of transom-stern boats it is best to ignore the transom altogether at this stage and cut it away entirely, thus facilitating the work of carving. Once the two shells have been completed, they can be glued to the central member, which must be cut to shape before so doing, but leaving the outside edge a little proud of the line in case of accidents.

The majority of wood lifeboats were clinker-built, and the planking will have to be reproduced both inside the boat and outside. The most suitable material for this is bristol board, or some similar thin card. Since the girth of the boat at mid-length is greater than at the stem and the stern, it will be clear that each plank will be narrower at the ends than at the centre if the number per side are to fit into the space available.

For all but the most extreme forms all the planks can be cut with the aid of a single template. First take the girth from side of keel to top edge of boat at mid-length, at the stem and at the stern, and at one or more equally spaced positions in between, by laying a strip of paper round one side of the hull at each of

these positions in turn and marking off on it the position of the side of the keel and the top edge of the shell. Check these against the similar positions on the other side of the hull to make sure that both are the same. Divide this marked length on each piece of paper into a number of equal spaces to correspond with the number of planks per side. Having done so, place each strip in turn back on its position on the hull and with a fine needle prick right through the shell at each of the marked points, thus marking the position of the edge of each plank.

To make the template, take a piece of durable material slightly longer than the longest plank, and about an inch or so wide, and on it draw a line parallel to one side and distant from it not less than the maximum width of a plank. Mark the positions of the stem, stern, mid-length and intermediate positions at which girths were taken, and at each of the points mark the appropriate width of the plank – taken from its paper strip – above the just drawn line. Draw a fair curve through these points, extending it slightly beyond the stem and stern marks. Since the planks are overlapped, draw another line below and parallel to the first line and distant from it by the amount of the overlap. On this line and just outside the bow and stern marks drill a very

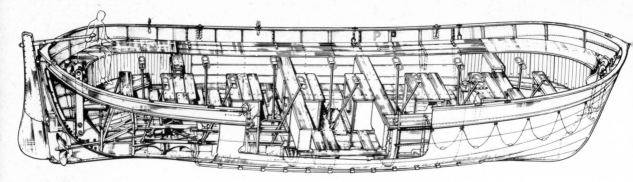

Fig 164
Diagrammatic view of a 36ft × 12ft 6in × 4ft 9in aluminium lifeboat showing the arrangement of the hand propulsion gear.

Fig 165
Arrangement of boats when carried outboard under radial davits. Note the griping spar with the padded bolsters. The facts that the boats are without canvas covers and that the familiar white and red bands of the Harrison Line funnel colours have been painted out (the ship is the *Collegian*) would indicate that this photograph was taken under wartime conditions. Other points to notice are the arrangement of the awning rafters over and forward of the navigating bridge, and the rectangular trunk of the wireless aerial lead-in.
Conway Picture Library

fine hole. If metal such as brass has been used for the template, a needle end with its point projecting just below the underside of the template, can be soldered in this hole. Now trim off the top of the template to the curved line.

To use the template, place it on the material selected for the planks and cut through it along the curved edge. If no needle points have been added to the template, prick through the two locating holes with a fine needle. Remove the template, place a straight-edge against these two pricked holes and part of the plank; mark the position of the mid-length ordinate and also the bow and stern ordinates. By repeating this process all the planks for each side can be cut.

In a clinker-built boat the planks can be seen from both sides. On the outside an upper plank overlaps the one below, and on the inside it is the other way round. The inside should be planked first, starting from the top. With the straight-edge uppermost, take the first plank and trim the end to the stem mark so as to align the mid-length mark on it with that on the shell, and chamfer the end to fit the angle between the stem and the shell. If it is a double-ended boat the other end of the plank will have to be trimmed and chamfered to fit against the stern post. In the case of transom-stern boats let the planks extend clear of the shell for trimming later. Fit this first plank so that the straight edge is uppermost and in line with the first row of pricked holes, and glue in place. Fit the corresponding inside plank on the opposite side. Since in so doing the next row of pricked holes on each side of the boat has been covered, prick them through again from the outside, and through the inside plank. Fit the next plank in the same way to these fresh marks, and repeat the process. When both sides internally have been finished,

Fig 166 ▲
Stowage of lifeboats on deck under radial davits, showing chocking arrangement. Note also the torpedo ventilators on the side of the house, and the shoes at the end of the awning rafters. The ship is the *Delius,* owned by Lamport & Holt Ltd

◄Fig 167
The after chock of a lifeboat stowed on skids. This shows clearly the method of hinging the upper part of a chock so that it will fall clear swung outboard.

if it is a transom boat trim off the plank ends level with the shell and fit and glue a transom in place, its edge being in line with the outside surface of the shell.

The outside planking is fitted in much the same way, starting with the bottom plank. This time the straight edge becomes the lower edge of the plank. There is an additional job to be done from now on at the bow end – and at the stern end if it is a double-ended boat – of each plank. As well as chamfering the plank end to a feather-edge to fit the angle between stem and shell, the inside face of the overlap must be scarphed away gradually over the last scale 6–9in so that the amount of visible thickness of the lower edge of the plank decreases until at the stem the outer face of the planks will be quite smooth. The effect of doing this can be seen in **Fig 157**. When this has been done the plank is glued in place with the lower (straight) edge of the plank placed in line with the bottom row of pricked holes. In so doing the plank will be found to have covered the

next row of holes, so these must be pricked through from the inside to provide the external alignment marks for the lower edge of the next plank. This will have to be repeated for each plank. As with the inside, follow by fitting the corresponding plank on the other side each time. In a transom-stern boat the full thickness of the overlap is maintained, the ends of the planks being cut off flush with the after face of the transom. If all is well, the last plank fitted should line up with the top of the shell. Finally glue the gunwale in place along the top edges, and after cleaning up add the rubbing band, if one is fitted, and the bilge rails.

At this point the boat can be given a thin coat of paint, taking care not to clog up the plank edges. When dry fit the timbers, starting from midships and working towards the ends. If suitable wood, such as apple, is used, each timber can be 'sprung in' in one piece, the ends being held under the gunwales. At bow and stern, in way of any deadwoods, they will have to be in two pieces. Follow this with the breasthook, stern hook, thwart clamps and stringers, and finish-paint the interior. After this add the bottom boards, thwarts, thwart knees and any other necessary internals appropriate to the boat being modelled, not forgetting such items as davit fall attachments, and paint where required. In the case of those boats fitted with hand-operated self-propelling gear, equipment on the lines of that shown in **Fig 164** will have to be added.

Externally, if the stem, stern post and keel have been left full they should be trimmed to shape, the stem being slightly chamfered off to the forward edge, though not to a sharp pointed edge. Finish-paint the whole of the outside, but remember than the rubbing strip if there is one is normally unpainted. Make the rudder and tiller, make the gudgeons and pintles and fit them, then paint and hang

the rudder, if appropriate; sometimes they are unshipped and stowed inboard. The same applies to the rowlocks and thole pins. If grab lines are fitted they should be put along each side.

The 'Draper' method has been covered in broad outline at some length since it can be used for the construction of open boats of many types. It is described more fully in the book *Modelling Open Boats*, details of which will be found in the Bibliography.

Where boats are being made solid because of the presence of canvas covers, the clinker planking can be represented by strips of gummed paper on the smaller scale boats, or by bristol board or thin card on the larger scale ones. Where possible many of the steps just described will have to be followed to obtain good results.

Lifeboat Stowage Arrangements

Boats stowed on deck, or on skids or sparred decks, are seated on wood chocks, two per boat, the top being shaped to the contour of the bottom of the boat, as can be seen in **Fig 166**. The boats are held down by means of a pair of hookplates each side which fit over the gunwale and are connected to eyeplates on deck by a short length of chain and a quick-release slip hook. To facilitate launching, the upper part of each chock is made to hinge over out of the way. Such an arrangement can be seen in **Fig 167**.

On some ships a boat under radial davits would be carried slung outboard. To secure it a griping spar is fitted horizontally across, and lashed to, the two davits at a point just above the turn of the boat's bilge. Two padded bolsters are fitted to the spar to cushion the boat, which is securely held against it by gripes of rope or of canvas webbing. These run outboard

of the boat from the head of the davit down to an eyeplate on deck, to which they are secured by a quick-release slip hook. **Fig 165** gives a good idea of this arrangement. For boats slung under gravity davits the keel rests on a step incorporated in the cradle, with additional padded chocks fitted as necessary. The boats are held in place by gripe wires fitted with quick-release gear.

On sailing ships the boats were stowed, sometimes upside down, on heavy skids running athwartships, usually over the top of a deckhouse, and to which they were firmly lashed. A pair of radial davits were fitted on each side of the ship adjacent to the ends of at least one set of such skids. On many small vessels the boat was either carried under a pair of davits or as often as not was stowed on a hatchway, being put over the side by means of a tackle to a nearby yard, boom or derrick.

Lifebuoys

The standard regulation lifebuoy has an outside diameter of 30in and an inside diameter of

18in; in cross-section the buoy is oval, 6in × 4in. Originally lifebuoys were made of

Fig 168 ▲
The 'Perrybuoy' standard lifebuoy, showing the way in which the line is attached, and also a typical stowage bracket.

◀**Fig 169**
The older type of regulation lifebuoy, made of cork and canvas-covered, showing the method of attaching the line. Other points to note in this photograph are the starboard steaming light screen, the battens lashed to the shrouds, and the cleading of the bridge bulwark. At the bottom right can be seen the steering chain passing over a guide sheave.

cork which was covered with canvas and painted white. The grab lines, of about 1¼in circumference rope, were secured to the buoy by four 4in wide bands of canvas stitched to the buoy. Modern buoys, such as the 'Perrybuoy', have an outer cover of moulded PVC with an inner core of polyurethane foam. The grab lines, of synthetic rope, pass through four lug points, being knotted at each. Lifebuoys are usually coloured red and white quarters, or bright orange.

The method of stowage and the necessary fittings depend upon the lifebuoys' position on the ship. On rails and inside bulwarks the type of frame seen in **Fig 168** is used. For emergency purposes which require swift action, a lifebuoy is often carried in a quick-release chute fitted outside the after bulwark of the bridge wing; these buoys also have a self-igniting light or flare attached to them.

Liferafts

The inflatable liferaft is now an established, indeed required, part of a vessel's safety and emergency equipment. In certain circumstances numbers of these rafts may be carried in place of some of the required outfit of life-boats. They can be stowed singly on deck in a handy cradle, or carried, several at a time, on some form of trackway for quick release (see **Fig 170**).

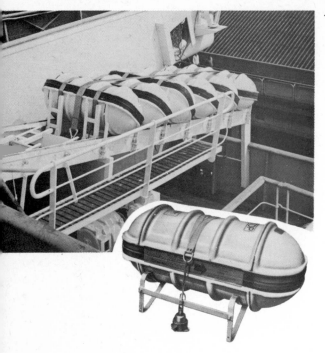

◀Fig 170
Inflatable liferafts stowed on a quick-release trackway and (inset) a similar inflatable in a cradle suitable for fitting on deck or on a deckhouse. *By courtesy of RFD Inflatables Ltd*

Fig 171▼
Oil-pattern port lamp and screen. The after face of the chock is 3ft from the centre of the lamp wick. Note how the base has been cut back to give low viewpoint visibility from ahead.

Lights

This is another area in which many models lose points because the builder has fitted oil-type steaming lights instead of the electric pattern. The visible difference between the two lies in the shape of the top. Oil lamps have a top similar to that shown in **Figs 171** and **174(a)**, whereas the electric lamp has a flat top – only a small detail one might feel, but it is an important one.

The port and starboard lamps, and the mast-head lamps, are fitted with dioptric lenses ('glasses'), as seen in the above-mentioned illustrations, and not plain glasses, though the latter were fitted in stern lamps.

A vessel under way, or being towed, has to display a red port light and a green starboard light, each so constructed that it will show an unbroken light from right ahead to two points abaft the beam on its own side of the ship, *ie* over an arc of 10 points of the compass. Each lamp is fitted with a lamp board or screen on the inboard side to prevent the light being seen from the other side of the ship. In addition a chock is fitted at the forward end of the screen

to prevent the light being seen beyond the centreline of the vessel when viewed from ahead. The flat base of the screen is cut back to the line of the outboard edge of the chock to allow the light to be seen from a low viewpoint.

A vessel under way also has to display a bright white light on the foremast which will show an unbroken light over 10 points of the compass on either side of the centreline. A second, similar light, with the same range of visibility, is usually carried further aft. It has to be higher than the forward one, (15ft is in fact the official distance), and both must be in line with the keel. There are various regulations governing the positioning of lights when no suitable masts are available, for vessels towing other craft, and so on.

Most vessels also carry a fixed stern light which has to be a white light visible astern over 6 points of the compass on either side of the centreline.

On sailing vessels the sidelight screens were either attached to the shrouds or carried on

PORT LAMP

(a)

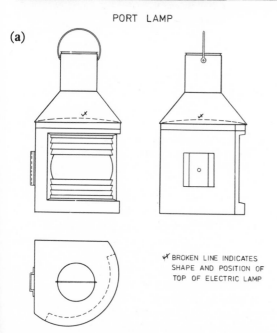

✗ BROKEN LINE INDICATES
SHAPE AND POSITION OF
TOP OF ELECTRIC LAMP

◀**Fig 172**
An oil-type anchor lamp with dioptric lens.

▼**Fig 173**
Masthead lamp and bracket. The lamp is an electric one – note the flat top – and the lens is of the dioptric type. Immediately below the platform is a compressed air operated syren, with the operating lanyard just visible to the right of the control valve. *S Lowry*

(b)

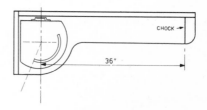

CHOCK

36"

SIDELIGHT SCREEN (STARBOARD SIDE)

(c)

MASTHEAD LAMP

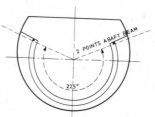

2 POINTS ABAFT BEAM

225°

Fig 174
(a) shows a port steaming lamp arranged for oil-burning. It is fitted with a dioptric lens. This lamp is 12in high to the base of the cone, and the flat part of the side and back is 10in long. Electric lamps do not require the cone and part above it, and the top is therefore finished to the slightly domed shape indicated on the sketch by the broken line. The electric lamp would also be fitted with a dioptric lens. A starboard lamp is the same but to the opposite hand.
(b) represents a typical wood screen for sidelights. A metal tongue is fitted to the back of the screen to secure the lamp in place. The back of the screen is the same height as an oil lamp is to the base of the cone part of the top.
(c) shows a diagram of the base of a masthead lamp showing the required degree of visibility.

stanchions fitted in line with the ship's side. Quite a number of the later sailing ships and the early steamers were fitted with conical light- or lamphouses, usually at the after outboard corner of the forecastle, with the necessary screen projecting forward from it (see **Fig 283**). These houses were of sufficient height to allow the lamp trimmer to go inside to fill and trim the lamp, and of course they provided good protection for the lights from the weather. Nowadays the port and starboard lights are built into the ends of the bridge wings, though still with the necessary screen and chock, and masthead lamps are fitted on the masts. On many vessels the arrangement for the lamps on the bridge wings is such that two lamps can be fitted, one above the other. This allows an oil lamp – a full set of these have to be carried in case of emergency – to be put in place rapidly and without removing the electric lamp. On small craft and service vessels the light screens were sometimes fitted on top of the wheelhouse, as on the drifter *Ocean Raleigh* (**Fig 243**), or mounted on swinging stanchions

which allowed them to be moved out of the way when not required.

Masthead lamps of the oil type had to be brought down for filling and trimming. They were carried in a simple cage, which did not interfere with the light, hoisted by a halliard; this cage ran on a pair of fixed guide-wires. Many masthead lamps will be found to have a pair of fixed rings top and bottom each side to take guide-wires; these were for use when there was no cage.

Fig 172 is of an oil anchor lamp with a dioptric lens. Used when a ship was at anchor it was hung from the forestay by a halliard attached to the top ring, with another line attached to the lower ring to prevent it swinging about. It showed an all-round (360°) white light.

Until comparatively recently sidelight screens and the exterior of the port and starboard lamps were painted either red or green as appropriate. Nowadays they are painted matt black. This is a point to remember about these fittings.

Masts, Derricks and Rigging Details

Once sail gave way to steam and the increasing reliability of the machinery allowed the shipowners to do away with the yards and sails which they had retained in case of breakdown, the rigging of ships (in this context referring more to the outfit of masts and cargo handling equipment than the cordage) took on a new aspect. Tall, tapering pole masts replaced the heavy built masts designed to carry square rig. Cargo handling was carried out by derricks mounted either on the mast, or on derrick tables or masthouses, an adequate arrangement for the hold layout on most vessels at that time. However, the increase in the number of holds led to the introduction of additional derricks carried on tall ventilators or special derrick posts (sometimes referred to as samson posts). The handling of indivisible heavy loads necessitated the installation of derricks with increased lifting capacity, the normal cargo handling derricks having a safe working load of between 2 and 10 tons. Over the years these

heavy lift arrangements developed very considerably, leading eventually to the introduction of such special equipment as the Stulcken mast/derrick arrangement, which could be fitted to general-service cargo vessels. The natural follow-up has been the construction of vessels whose sole purpose is the lifting and carrying of exceptionally heavy loads, the whole operation being carried out with the ship's own gear. This is not new, for such work was carried out prior to the last war by a few special ships; what is different about the present generation of heavy lift ships is the exceptional capacity of the lifting gear and the design of the vessels and the arrangements to take these huge loads.

The type of rigging which the majority of modellers will encounter will be much simpler – the slender pole masts of a paddler, the short stumpy masts and derricks of a coaster, the functional mast of a tug or trawler, or the simple mast and spar arrangement of a sailing coaster. Examples of most of these can be seen

Fig 175 ▲
Points to notice on this photograph of the Cunard
Line's cargo ship *Andania* (1960) are the derrick heel
and block attachments; the construction of the
unstayed mast; the slab covers to Nos 4 and 5 hatches
(but the tarpaulins, batten irons and wedges on No 6
hatch on the poop); the flat bar stanchions of the guard
rails; and the emergency steering gear to starboard of
the winchman's shelter on the poop. *Laurence Scott &
Electromotors Ltd*

Fig 176 ▶
The foremast of the King Line cargo ship *King Charles*
(1957), showing the stayed foremast, with the heavy
derrick in its stowed position; note the heel fitting and
its seat. The cargo winch has a topping winch attached
to it, the lead of the topping lift being run through
snatch blocks shackled to eyeplates on the top of the
masthouse and the side of the mast. The hatch is a
good example of the use of tarpaulins, battens and
wedges, with the required additional securing
arrangements put on across the hatches after the
tarpaulins are in place. *Laurence Scott & Electromotors
Ltd*

◀ **Fig 177**
The general arrangement for the Stulcken heavy lift derrick. This one has a capacity of 105 tons, while the four lighter ones have a safe working load (swl) of 10 tons. The constructional details for the whole system are clearly visible in this photograph. The ship is the *Al Mubarakiah*, built for the United Arab Shipping Company by Govan Shipbuilders in 1974. *Clarke Chapman Marine*

in the illustrations at the beginning of the book.

Fig 175 gives a good idea of the layout of conventional cargo handling equipment. The mast is robust up to the crosstrees, and is unstayed. There is a much lighter topmast. The derricks are mounted on a mast table, with others on derrick posts. The rigging of the derricks follows normal practices.

All, or almost all, the essential information about the standing and running rigging on a vessel will be found on the rigging plan, and a part of such a plan is reproduced as **Fig 207**. Other diagrams show typical mast and derrick fittings, details of blocks of various types, and of rigging screws, eyeplates and shackles.

Fig 178 ▼
Part of a 'streamlined' mast, showing the hollow construction, internal stiffening, and the platform carrying the radar scanner and two compressed air operated syrens. Just visible at the top are the two acutely angled outriggers carrying the signal halliards.

Fig 179 ▼
Detail of heel fitting, mast bands and gooseneck for a wooden derrick and mast.

Fig 182 ▶
General arrangement of rigging of cargo derricks. The rigging plan for a particular ship will show the features applicable to that vessel.

◀Fig 180
Detail of derrick heel fitting on a derrick post. In this the baseplate is welded to the post, while the diagram shows the arrangement for riveted construction.

Fig 181 ▲
Derrick heel fittings on a derrick post. Although provision has been made for a lead block to be mounted on the same fitting, in this instance it has not been done, the lead being taken instead through a block shackled to an eyeplate on the post. Note the type of cleats fitted to the derrick post. This ship, the *Beaverdell*, was fitted with steel hatch covers of Macanking design, which traversed athwartships, being supported on rails or guides on deck. One such support and rail can be seen to the left in the photograph.

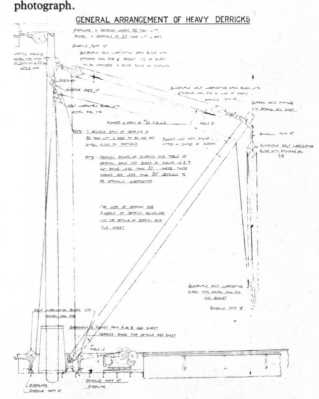

Whereas the early vessels had conventional pole masts of various forms, recent years have seen the advent, particularly on cruise liners, of 'streamlined', built-up masts. Although appearance may seem to be the overriding consideration, the governing factor has been the provision of an adequate support for the many items of essential navigational equipment. The ability to combine the two aspects has led, in some instances, to some very extreme designs!

Masts were tapered towards the truck, the greatest diameter being at the deck, that at the hounds being 85 per cent of the deck diameter in the case of masts carrying cargo derricks. Where masts were raked, it was often the prac-

GENERAL ARRANGEMENT OF CARGO DERRICKS

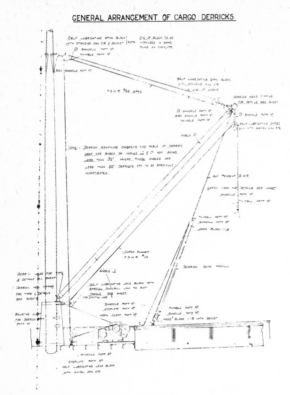

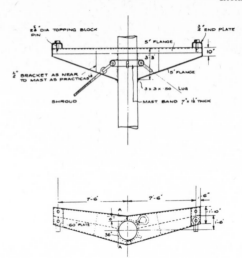

Fig 184
Typical arrangement and construction for welded crosstrees. The arms may be angled, as here, or straight, and the dimensions will vary from ship to ship.

Fig 183
General arrangement of rigging of a heavy derrick. As with the other derrick arrangement, the rigging plan will show the details for a particular ship, and these will depend upon local requirements as well as the lifting capacity of the derrick. Details of alternative types of heel fitting will be found in the diagrams.

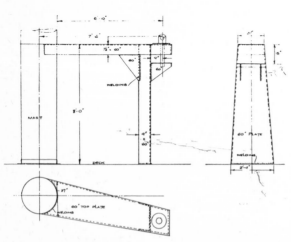

Fig 185
Construction of a typical derrick table. As with crosstrees, the side members may be straight or angled, and the dimensions will be to suit the outfit of derricks.

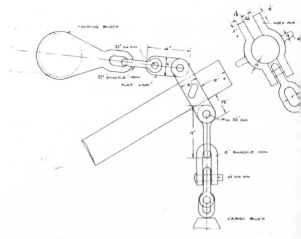

Fig 186
Derrick-head fittings. Compare the details shown here with those in the other diagram.

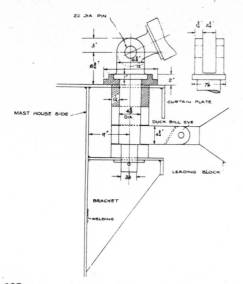

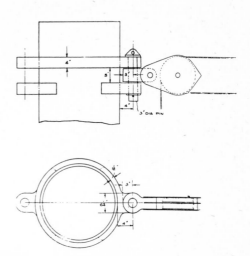

Fig 187
Heel fitting for derricks mounted on masthouses. The dimensions on this sketch are suitable for a derrick having an swl of 15 tons.

Fig 188
Fittings for topping lift blocks on derrick posts.

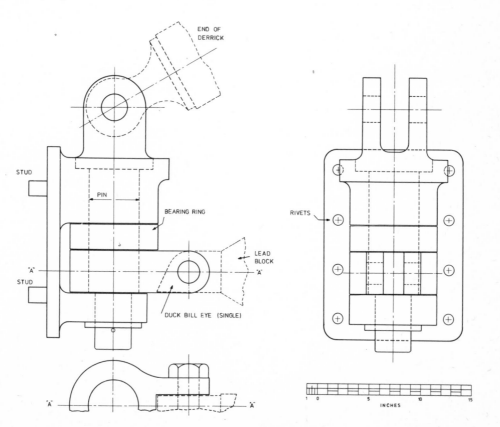

Fig 189
Heel fitting for derricks mounted on derrick posts.

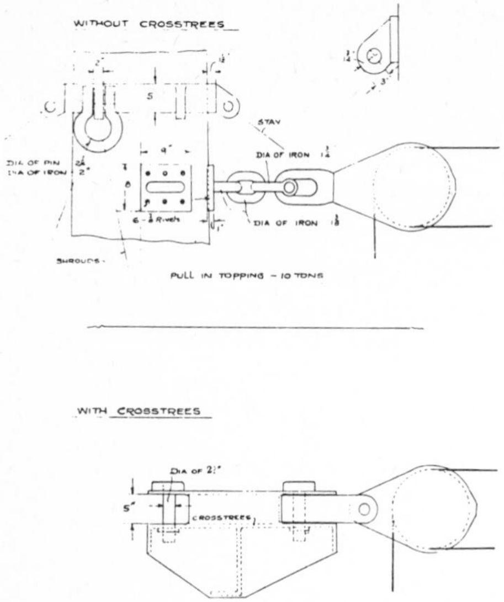

Fig 190▲
Mast fittings for topping lift blocks on masts with and without crosstrees.

Fig 191▼
Head fittings for derricks. In this type the single bar passing through the derrick forms the eyes for the two shackles.

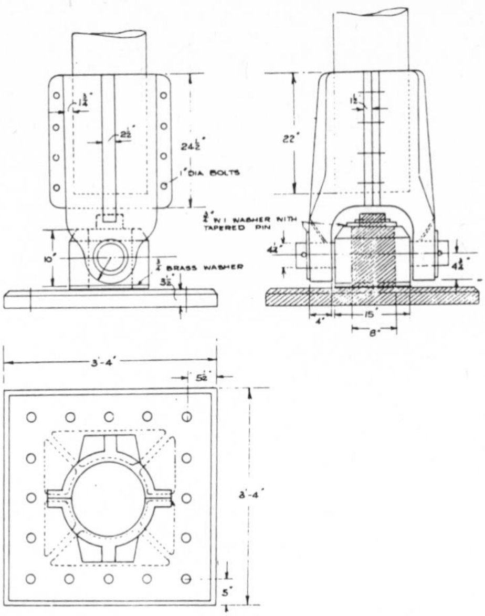

Fig 192
Cast steel heel socket suitable for a 55-ton swl heavy derrick.

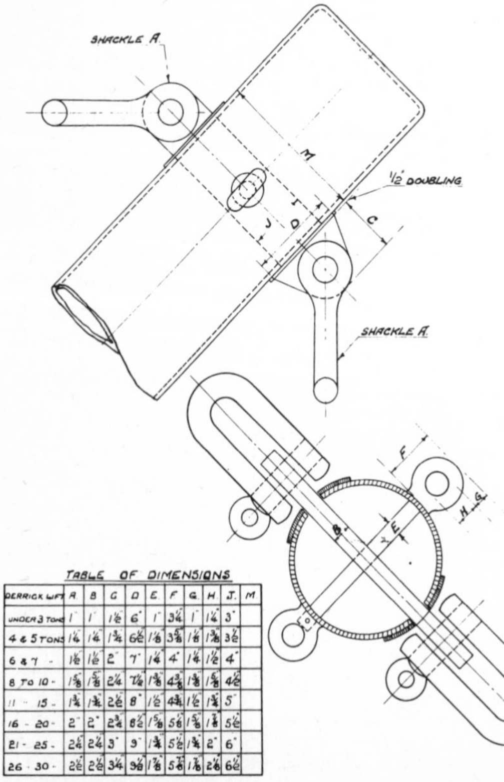

TABLE OF DIMENSIONS

DERRICK LIFT	A.	B	C	D	E.	F	G.	H.	J.	M
UNDER 3 TONS	1"	1"	1½"	6"	1"	3¼"	1"	1¼"	3"	
4 & 5 TONS	1¼"	1¼"	1¾"	6½"	1⅛"	3⅝"	1⅛"	1⅜"	3½"	
6 & 7 "	1½"	1½"	2"	7"	1¼"	4"	1¼"	1½"	4"	
8 TO 10 "	1⅝"	1⅝"	2¼"	7½"	1⅜"	4⅜"	1⅜"	1⅝"	4½"	
11 " 15 "	1¾"	1¾"	2½"	8"	1½"	4¾"	1½"	1¾"	5"	
16 – 20 "	2"	2"	2¾"	8½"	1⅝"	5⅛"	1⅝"	1⅞"	5½"	
21 – 25 "	2¼"	2¼"	3"	9"	1¾"	5½"	1¾"	2"	6"	
26 – 30 "	2½"	2½"	3¼"	9½"	1⅞"	5⅞"	1⅞"	2⅛"	6½"	

tice to increase slightly in succession the rake of each mast abaft the foremast. On derricks the taper, if present, was in either direction from mid-length. On tubular steel derricks this is achieved by the use of several pieces of tube of diminishing diameters, each of the tubes fitting into the end of its neighbour, thus giving that stepped appearance seen on many derricks.

Crosstrees can vary quite considerably in both size and design and, except in extreme cases where they are used in conjunction with special derrick systems such as Velle, Thomson, Halle, etc, they are but a development of the basic design shown in the illustration. In the same way the attachment of the various blocks to the masts, crosstrees, derrick tables, derrick posts and derricks is of, or is similar to, the forms shown in the diagrams. Typical rigging arrangements for a standard and an average heavy lift derrick have been included to give an idea of the methods used. More detailed arrangements will be found on the rigging plans. But a word of warning: even

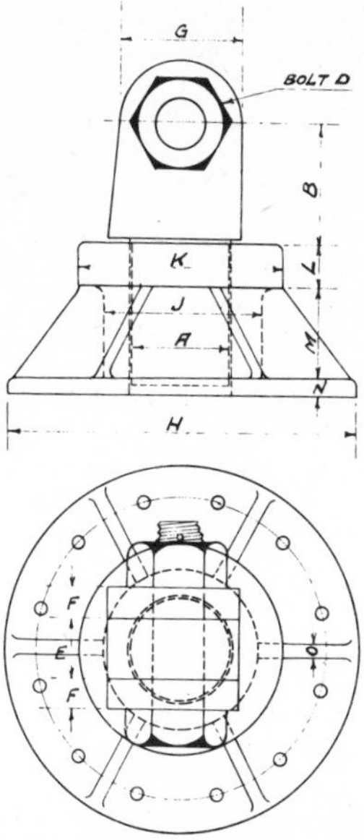

DERRICK LIFT	A	B	C	D	E	F	G	H	J	K	L	M	N	O	Nº & SIZE OF RIVETS
10 TO 15 TONS	4⅞"	6"	2"	2½"	3"	1½"	6¼	15"	9"	12"	2"	5"	1⅛	1"	8 - 1"
16 " 20 "	5½"	6½"	$2\frac{5}{16}$"	2¾"	3½	1⅝	6⅞	15½"	9½	12½"	2¼"	5½	1¼	1¼	12 - 1
21 " 25 "	6"	7"	2½"	3"	3¾	1¾"	7½"	16"	10"	13"	2½	6	1⅜	1½"	12 - 1"
26 " 30 "	6½	7½	2¾"	3¼"	4"	2"	8⅛	17"	11"	14"	2¾	6½	1½	1¾	12 - 1"
31 " 40 "	8"	8½	3"	3¾"	4½"	2½"	9⅜"	20"	13"	16"	3"	7"	1¾	2"	12 - 1⅛"
41 " 50 "	9"	9½"	3¼"	4¼"	5"	3"	10⅝"	23"	15"	18"	3½"	7½	2	2¼"	12 - 1¼"

Fig 193
Gooseneck and socket for heavy derrick.

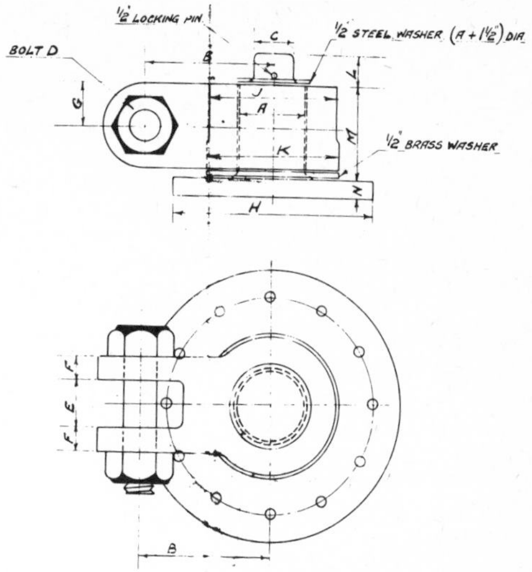

DERRICK LIFT	A	B	C	D	E	F	G	H	J	K	L	M	N	Nº & SIZE OF RIVETS
10 TO 15 TONS	4⅞"	11½"	3½"	½	3"	1½"	6¼"	16"	9"	10"	2½"	6¾"	1⅛"	8 - 1"
16 " 20 "	5½"	12½"	"	[illegible]	3½"	1⅝"	6⅞"	17"	10"	11"	"	7⅜"	1¼"	12 - 1"
21 " 25 "	6"	13½"	"	[illegible]	3¾"	1¾"	7½"	18"	11"	12"	"	8"	1⅜"	12 - 1"
26 " 30 "	6½"	14½"	"	¼	4"	2"	8⅛"	19"	12"	13"	"	8¾"	1½"	12 - 1"
31 " 40 "	7¼"	16½"	"	¾	5"	2½"	9⅜"	21"	13"	14"	"	9⅞"	1¾"	12 - 1⅛"
41 " 50 "	8"	18½"	"	[illegible]	6"	3"	10⅝"	23"	14"	15"	"	11⅛"	2"	12 - 1¼"

Fig 194
Offset type of gooseneck and socket for heavy derrick.

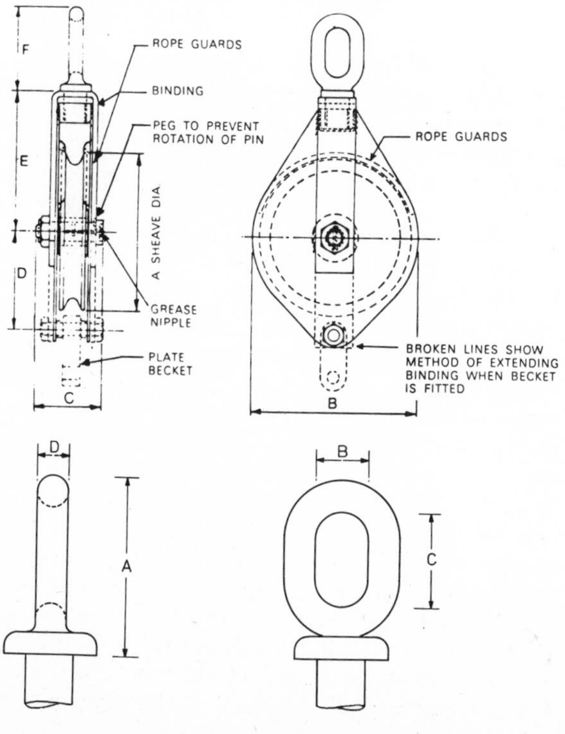

◀Fig 195
Cargo, heel or lead block (inset: enlargement of oval eye)

Outside Dia of Sheave	Dia at Bottom of Groove	To suit Wire Circ	SWL Tons	B	C	D	E	F
8	6⅞	1¼–1½	1	9	$3\frac{7}{16}$	5¾	6⅝	4¼
10	8½	2–2½	3	11	$4\frac{15}{16}$	7⅛	9⅛	7¼
12	10¼	2½–3	5	14	6	7⅞	11¼	7
14	12¼	3–3½	5	16	6	8⅞	12¼	7
16	13½	3½–4	8	17⅞	7½	9¾	14½	11
18	15¼	4–4½	10	19	9⅝	11	16½	12⅛

All dimensions in inches

Sizes for oval eyes of blocks

A(F)	B	C	D
4¼	1¼	2¼	¾
7¼	1¾	3⅞	$1\frac{3}{16}$
7	$2\frac{1}{16}$	$4\frac{1}{16}$	$1\frac{5}{16}$
11½	3	6½	2
12½	3	6¾	2¼

All dimensions in inches

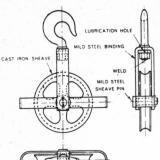

Fig 196
Gin block

Dia of Sheave	To suit Wire Circ	SWL Tons
6	$2\frac{1}{4}$	0.15
8	3	0.15
10	3	0.25
12	$3\frac{1}{2}$	0.25

All dimensions in inches

Fig 197
Examples of different types of wood and steel blocks.
1 Wood single block with swivel eye and becket.
2 Wood single block with fixed bow and becket.
3 Wood single block with swivel hook and becket.
4 Wood treble block with swivel oval eye and becket.
5 Wood double block with swivel oval eye and becket.
6 American-pattern wood tackle block.
7 Double block with swivel oval eye and becket link.
8 Treble block with swivel oval eye.
9 Fish tackle single block; sheaves are either 6in or 8in in diameter.
10 Fish tackle double block; sheave sizes as above.
11 Gilsen block for trawlers; the diameter of the sheave can range from 6in to 14in, depending on requirements.
12 Gallows hanging block for trawlers.

Fig 198
Sizes of solid thimbles for wire rope

Circ of Wire	Dia of Wire	B	C	E	F	M	Q
1	$\frac{5}{16}$	$1\frac{3}{8}$	$\frac{7}{16}$	$1\frac{7}{8}$	$\frac{5}{16}$	$\frac{1}{2}$	1
$1\frac{1}{2}$	$\frac{7}{16}$	$2\frac{1}{16}$	$\frac{11}{16}$	$2\frac{3}{4}$	$\frac{1}{2}$	$\frac{3}{4}$	$1\frac{1}{2}$
2	$\frac{5}{8}$	$2\frac{3}{4}$	$\frac{7}{8}$	$3\frac{3}{4}$	$\frac{5}{8}$	1	2
$2\frac{1}{2}$	$\frac{13}{16}$	$3\frac{3}{8}$	$1\frac{1}{8}$	$4\frac{5}{8}$	$\frac{7}{8}$	$1\frac{1}{4}$	$2\frac{1}{2}$
3	$\frac{15}{16}$	$4\frac{1}{8}$	$1\frac{5}{16}$	$5\frac{1}{2}$	1	$1\frac{1}{2}$	3
$3\frac{1}{2}$	$1\frac{1}{8}$	$4\frac{7}{8}$	$1\frac{9}{16}$	$6\frac{1}{2}$	$1\frac{3}{16}$	$1\frac{3}{4}$	$3\frac{1}{2}$
4	$1\frac{1}{4}$	$5\frac{1}{2}$	$1\frac{3}{4}$	$7\frac{1}{2}$	$1\frac{5}{16}$	2	4
5	$1\frac{1}{2}$	$6\frac{3}{4}$	$2\frac{1}{4}$	$9\frac{1}{4}$	$1\frac{5}{8}$	$2\frac{1}{2}$	5
6	$1\frac{7}{8}$	$8\frac{1}{4}$	$2\frac{5}{8}$	11	2	3	6
7	$2\frac{1}{4}$	$9\frac{3}{4}$	$3\frac{1}{8}$	13	$2\frac{3}{8}$	$3\frac{1}{2}$	7
8	$2\frac{1}{2}$	11	$3\frac{1}{2}$	$14\frac{3}{4}$	$2\frac{5}{8}$	4	8

All dimensions in inches

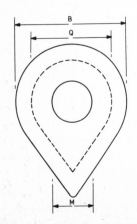

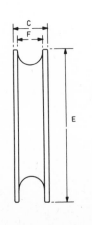

Fig 199
Sizes of ordinary thimbles for wire rope

Circ of Wire	Dia of Wire	A	B	C	D	E	F	G	J	K	Q
1	$\frac{5}{16}$	$\frac{7}{8}$	$1\frac{1}{2}$	$\frac{1}{2}$	$1\frac{5}{16}$	$2\frac{1}{8}$	$\frac{5}{16}$	$\frac{5}{32}$	$2\frac{1}{2}$	$\frac{5}{32}$	$1\frac{3}{16}$
$1\frac{1}{2}$	$\frac{7}{16}$	$1\frac{1}{8}$	$2\frac{1}{8}$	$\frac{11}{16}$	$1\frac{5}{8}$	$2\frac{7}{8}$	$\frac{1}{2}$	$\frac{5}{16}$	3	$\frac{3}{16}$	$1\frac{1}{2}$
2	$\frac{5}{8}$	$1\frac{5}{8}$	$2\frac{15}{16}$	$\frac{7}{8}$	$2\frac{5}{16}$	$3\frac{7}{8}$	$\frac{5}{8}$	$\frac{11}{32}$	$4\frac{1}{2}$	$\frac{5}{16}$	$2\frac{1}{4}$
$2\frac{1}{2}$	$\frac{13}{16}$	2	$3\frac{5}{8}$	$1\frac{1}{8}$	$2\frac{7}{8}$	$4\frac{7}{8}$	$\frac{13}{16}$	$\frac{7}{16}$	6	$\frac{3}{8}$	$2\frac{3}{4}$
3	$\frac{15}{16}$	$2\frac{1}{2}$	$4\frac{5}{16}$	$1\frac{5}{16}$	$3\frac{3}{8}$	$5\frac{3}{4}$	1	$\frac{1}{2}$	7	$\frac{13}{32}$	$3\frac{5}{16}$
$3\frac{1}{2}$	$1\frac{1}{8}$	3	$5\frac{1}{4}$	$1\frac{1}{2}$	$4\frac{3}{8}$	7	$1\frac{1}{8}$	$\frac{5}{8}$	9	$\frac{1}{2}$	4
4	$1\frac{1}{4}$	$3\frac{3}{4}$	6	$1\frac{5}{8}$	$5\frac{1}{4}$	$7\frac{3}{4}$	$1\frac{5}{16}$	$\frac{5}{8}$	10	$\frac{1}{2}$	$4\frac{3}{4}$
5	$1\frac{1}{2}$	$4\frac{1}{2}$	$7\frac{3}{4}$	$2\frac{1}{8}$	$6\frac{1}{2}$	10	$1\frac{5}{8}$	$\frac{15}{16}$	13	$\frac{11}{16}$	$5\frac{7}{8}$
6	$1\frac{7}{8}$	$5\frac{1}{4}$	$9\frac{3}{4}$	$2\frac{5}{8}$	$7\frac{1}{2}$	$12\frac{1}{2}$	$2\frac{3}{8}$	$1\frac{1}{8}$	15	$1\frac{1}{8}$	$7\frac{1}{2}$
7	$2\frac{1}{4}$	$5\frac{3}{4}$	$10\frac{5}{8}$	3	$8\frac{1}{2}$	14	$2\frac{5}{8}$	$1\frac{1}{4}$	17	$1\frac{3}{16}$	$8\frac{1}{8}$
8	$2\frac{1}{2}$	$6\frac{1}{4}$	$12\frac{1}{4}$	$3\frac{3}{4}$	$9\frac{1}{2}$	$16\frac{1}{4}$	$2\frac{3}{4}$	$1\frac{3}{4}$	18	$1\frac{1}{4}$	$8\frac{3}{4}$

All dimensions in inches

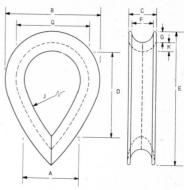

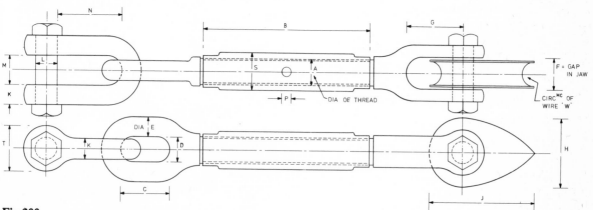

Fig 200
Detail of standard rigging screw for wire rope. See accompanying table for sizes, which are based on the diameter of the thread (screw).

Dia of Screw A	B	C	D	E	F	G	H	J	K	L	M	N	P	S	T	Circ of Wire W
$\frac{1}{2}$	9	1	$\frac{7}{16}$	$\frac{7}{16}$	$\frac{7}{16}$	$1\frac{1}{4}$	$1\frac{5}{8}$	$2\frac{3}{8}$	$\frac{3}{8}$	$\frac{3}{8}$	$\frac{5}{8}$	$1\frac{1}{2}$	$\frac{3}{8}$	1	1	1
1	14	$2\frac{1}{4}$	1	$\frac{3}{4}$	$1\frac{1}{8}$	$2\frac{1}{4}$	$2\frac{3}{4}$	$3\frac{3}{4}$	$\frac{3}{4}$	$\frac{7}{8}$	$1\frac{3}{4}$	$2\frac{5}{8}$	$\frac{1}{2}$	$1\frac{5}{8}$	$1\frac{3}{4}$	2
$1\frac{1}{2}$	16	$2\frac{15}{16}$	$1\frac{1}{2}$	1	$1\frac{5}{8}$	4	$4\frac{1}{2}$	$6\frac{1}{8}$	$1\frac{1}{8}$	$1\frac{1}{4}$	$1\frac{5}{8}$	$3\frac{3}{8}$	$\frac{5}{8}$	$2\frac{5}{8}$	$2\frac{1}{2}$	$3\frac{1}{4}$
2	16	4	$1\frac{3}{4}$	$1\frac{1}{8}$	$2\frac{3}{16}$	5	$5\frac{1}{2}$	$7\frac{1}{4}$	$1\frac{1}{2}$	$1\frac{5}{8}$	$2\frac{1}{4}$	5	$\frac{3}{4}$	$2\frac{3}{4}$	$3\frac{1}{2}$	$4\frac{1}{4}$
$2\frac{1}{2}$	16	$4\frac{3}{4}$	$2\frac{3}{8}$	$1\frac{7}{8}$	3	$5\frac{1}{2}$	$6\frac{1}{2}$	$10\frac{1}{4}$	$1\frac{7}{8}$	2	$2\frac{3}{4}$	$6\frac{1}{4}$	$\frac{7}{8}$	$3\frac{1}{4}$	$4\frac{1}{4}$	6
3	18	8	$3\frac{3}{4}$	$2\frac{1}{2}$	$4\frac{1}{2}$	$7\frac{1}{2}$	$10\frac{7}{8}$	$14\frac{1}{4}$	$2\frac{1}{4}$	$2\frac{1}{2}$	$3\frac{3}{4}$	7	1	$4\frac{1}{2}$	$5\frac{5}{8}$	$7\frac{1}{2}$
$3\frac{1}{2}$	20	9	$4\frac{1}{2}$	$2\frac{3}{4}$	$4\frac{5}{8}$	$7\frac{1}{2}$	$10\frac{7}{8}$	$14\frac{3}{4}$	$2\frac{3}{4}$	3	$3\frac{3}{4}$	$8\frac{1}{4}$	$1\frac{1}{8}$	$5\frac{1}{4}$	$6\frac{1}{4}$	$7\frac{1}{2}$

All dimensions in inches

these could differ from that finally fitted at the ship, since arrangements were often made during fitting out to accommodate the requirements of the master and his chief officer, especially in matter relating to the placing of some fittings and the leads of gear. Not all shipyards produced 'as fitted' rigging arrangements.

Mooring Pipes

These are heavy castings, with oval or circular openings, set in the bulwarks, as in **Figs 201** and **202**. A smaller version, having a different ring cross-section and often found on vessels such as tugs, coasters and paddle steamers, is shown in **Fig 203**. Knowing the size of the aperture, the other dimensions can be proportioned from those given.

Fig 201 ▶
A good example of a mooring pipe, seen from the inboard side (an idea of the outboard detail can be seen in **Fig 33**). A steel doubling plate has been fitted to the bulwark in way to compensate for the opening cut therein. Note the two-roller fairlead on the bulwark capping rail, which is a bulb angle with the bulwark plate fitted inside the standing flange of this angle. The bulwark stay is a length of bulb plate riveted to the vertical angle bar stiffener on the bulwark, and it is attached to the deck by a lug. An interesting departure from accepted practices can be seen in the very limited squared-off ends to the snape of the deck planks into the margin plank.

Fig 202 ▼
Two patterns of mooring pipe, one with an oval opening, the other with a circular opening.

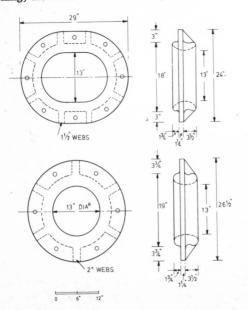

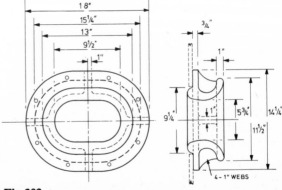

Fig 203
Small oval mooring pipe, suitable for coasters, paddle steamers and similar small craft.

Plans for Ship Models

There are several different types of plans which may come the way of a ship modeller. To begin with there are the plans prepared by the ship-builder which are, or were, of three main types. First the design plans, based on the owner's stated requirements and frequently modified at this stage from the original layout. From the finally approved drawings were prepared the second group, the working plans for the yard. As well as a general arrangement of the internal layout, these also comprised all the steelwork and other numerous plans required for the construction of a ship. Finally, though not in all instances, a further set of plans would be prepared called the 'as fitted' drawings. These showed the ship as completed, and they could differ quite markedly from the original design and working plans. I am aware that with today's practices in shipbuilding of computerised design, optical lofting, prefabrication and flow line construction, the required plans will differ somewhat from those just described. But as a high proportion of models built are of the older type of vessel, I make no apology for referring to their plans in some detail.

If 'as fitted' plans are not available, then recourse must be had to the working general arrangement plans, or to the design plans. Generally these can be adequate provided that they are checked against any available photographs of the ship. There is a point which must be borne in mind when so doing. Ships often underwent alterations and modifications during their lifetime, so it is essential when making such checks against photographs to know, or at least to have some approximate idea of, the date when the photograph was taken.

Modellers interested in warships fare better in this respect than those who prefer merchant ships or sailing ships. The Admiralty keeps a record of all work carried out on a vessel throughout its life, and this information is usually available (in the case of British vessels some 30 years after their demise) in the record known as the Ship's Cover, many of which are held by the National Maritime Museum at Greenwich.

Next come the plans prepared specially for the ship modeller, and here some care is needed because of their varying quality and accuracy.

It is unfortunate that the purchase of a set of these plans cannot in some instances be a guarantee that the resulting model will be an authentic scale reproduction of the original ship; some research to establish their accuracy is advisable before starting work. Nonetheless these plans do play a very important part in providing modelmakers with the means of pursuing their hobby, and must on no account be disregarded because of the foregoing comment.

A third type of plan is that which appears in the maritime technical journals. Articles therein are often accompanied by sets of plans (in some cases really excellent sets) which, though to a small scale, embody great detail. Builders of nineteenth and twentieth century steamers will fare best in this field, as will anyone interested in the construction of scale models of yachts of all types.

The layout of a ship is shown by the general arrangement (or GA) plan. This comprises an external elevation of the ship together with a plan of each deck; these may be on one sheet, or on separate sheets. Sometimes the fittings are well detailed, sometimes they appear only in bare outline. The rigging plan, as its name implies, shows the rigging of the masts, spars, derricks and other gear, and should include the sizes of the various materials used. In the case of sailing ships a sail plan is also required. The shape of the hull is given by the lines plan, which should include a body plan. Just what these comprise will be considered later.

After this the field broadens, though many modellers find the foregoing adequate for their needs. However, some additional plans are worth mentioning now and several of them will be dealt with in more detail in due course. For an iron- or steel-hulled vessel a shell expansion plan and a plate line body plan are required if the strakes of plating are going to be added to the hull; this is essential if authenticity is to be maintained, as can be seen in some of the photographs. In the case of hulls of all-welded construction, although the shell plating is to all intents and purposes smooth, there is a new problem for the modelmaker, the 'ripple' appearance of the plating between the frames, a feature shown to advantage in **Fig 246**. In the same way a deck plating plan is required

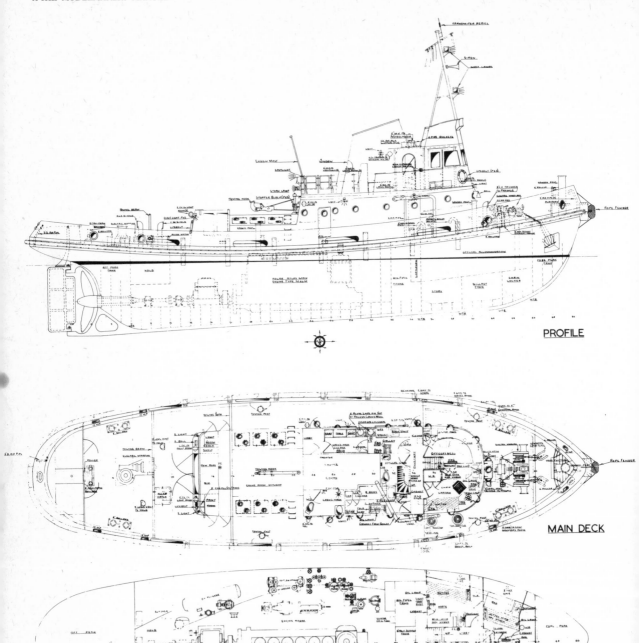

PROFILE

MAIN DECK

LOWER DECK

Fig 204
A typical example of the type of general arrangement
plan prepared by shipbuilders. (Large plans such as
these reproduce badly when reduced for printing
purposes, but give the reader an idea of the degree of
detail.)

for vessels with bare steel decks. A midship section plan contains a lot of useful data about the hull structure. Other constructional plans contain details of the deckhouses, bulwarks, hatch coamings, stem, stern frame, rudder, and so on.

There is one more plan which is worth attention, the capacity plan. Intended for shippers and the like, it shows the capacity of a ship's cargo spaces. But many are akin to a general arrangement plan and are useful in establishing a vessel's main structural details in the event of no other plans being available.

THE LINES PLAN

The first essential plan needed for building a model is the lines plan, sometimes known as the sheer draught. On this plan is shown the shape of the ship's hull as seen from three different directions – from the side, from above, and from each end. How the information contained on this plan is used is explained in the Hull Construction section. First it is necessary to understand what it shows and the purpose of this content.

Consider the lines plan shown in **Fig 206** and look at the elevation, or profile. This gives the outline of the hull as seen from the side. The line bounding the figure shows the line of the bottom of the ship, the shape of the forefoot

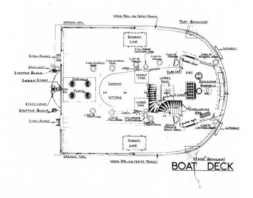

BOAT DECK

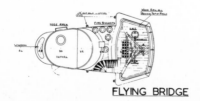

FLYING BRIDGE

and stem, the shape of the stern and the sheer of the deck.

Superimposed on this plan are a number of key lines. The base line in this case is the same as the bottom of the keel, and is extended at either end merely as a working line. Drawn parallel to the base line, and at a height above it equal to the designed load draught of the ship, is a line representing the load waterline (LWL). Through the point where this line crosses the fore side of the stem, and again where it crosses the after side of the stern post, a perpendicular to the base is erected and extended to deck level. Sometimes these two perpendiculars are identified by a numeral and sometimes they are marked FP and AP, in which latter event the FP's position can occasionally be at variance with that designated earlier. All very confusing!

For the purposes of a displacement calculation the space between these two perpendiculars has to be divided into a number of equal parts; these points, and the verticals there erected, are called ordinates, or station lines. The actual spacing of these ordinates is arranged to meet the requirements of the particular formula being used, the commonest of which is known as Simpson's First Rule. This rule requires an even number of equal spaces, hence an odd number of ordinates, between the end perpendiculars, usually ten or twenty. Other lines plans may show verticals corresponding to the spacing of the frames, and at times both may appear on the one plan. Occasionally these verticals may have been put in where considered suitable rather than at definite intervals – a practice found on some of the lines drawings in the sets prepared specially for modelmakers.

Above the base line and running parallel to it are a number of horizontal lines known as waterlines. These are normally spaced equally in multiples of feet, and are carried up to deck level. They, too, are numbered, from the base up, the base line usually being 0 (zero).

The view of the hull as seen from above, and normally placed below the elevation, is called the half-breadth plan. This shows one half of the ship only, from the longitudinal centreline outwards. As the plan has been drawn in the conventional manner, with the bow to the right-hand side, it shows the port (left) side of the hull. The ordinates, or the frame lines if appropriate, thereon have been drawn as lines

Fig 205
A plan of the *Tszru* specially prepared for modelmakers from the original drawings of the ship, *ie* lines, general arrangement and rig. The details of the fittings have been worked up from the information contained on these plans, or have been based on contemporary practice.

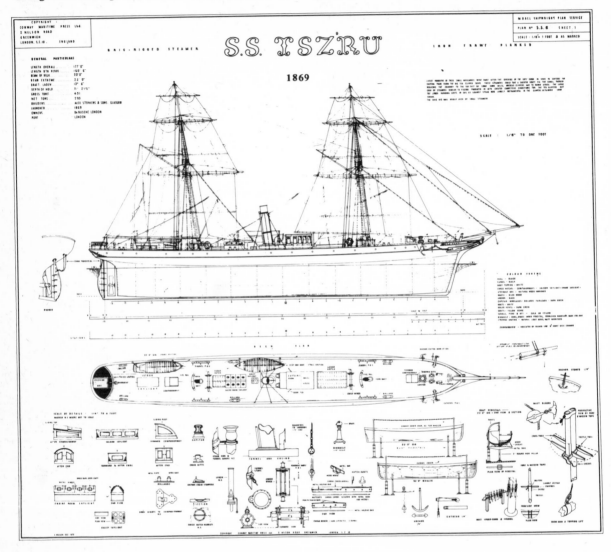

perpendicular to the longitudinal centreline and in line with their counterparts on the elevation. Running parallel to the longitudinal centreline, and spaced at equal intervals therefrom, again usually in multiples of feet, are a series of straight lines known as bowlines and buttock lines, depending on whether they lie forward or aft of midships. Also on this view are a number of curved lines running from end to end. Provided the vessel has no tumblehome, the outermost of these lines shows the outline of the uppermost continuous deck; if the ship has a forecastle, poop, etc, it could well show these as well. The remaining lines show the outline of the hull as if it had been sliced through horizontally at each of the waterlines shown on the profile; they are numbered to correspond with those on the profile.

Returning to the profile, the curved lines seen thereon running from bow to stern are the bowlines and buttock lines mentioned earlier. They show the shape of the hull as if it had been sliced vertically from end to end along each of those lines on the half-breadth plan

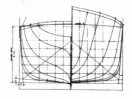

Fig 206
Lines and body plan for small tug. The dimensions were 77ft 6in BP × 19ft 6in × 10ft 4½in moulded depth.

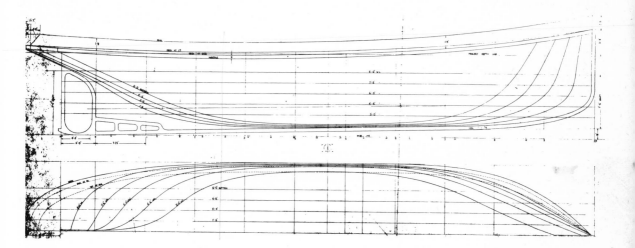

which run parallel to the centreline.

Next, the body plan. The basic framework consists of the base line and a central vertical line representing the longitudinal centreline of the ship (see **Fig 206**). The horizontal lines are the same waterlines seen on the elevation, and the vertical lines parallel to, and on each side of, the centreline are the bowlines and the buttock lines found on the half-breadth plan. The various curved lines represent the cross-sectional shape of the ship, as seen from the end, supposing that the hull had been cut transversely at each of the ordinates, or frame lines, shown on the elevation. Those lines to the right of the centreline show the half-sections from the bow to the midship ordinate, and those on the left of the centreline the half-sections from the midship ordinate to the stern. Once again convention has established the practice of putting the forebody half-sections to the right of the centreline on the body plan, and the after body half-sections to its left.

Each cross-section ends at deck level and the line running through the top of each half-section represents the edge of the deck in the elevation. It is a relatively simple operation to determine the shape of an intermediate cross-section or waterline. Having decided the place at which, say, a new cross-section is required, erect a perpendicular at this point on the elevation and again on the half-breadth plan. On the half-breadth plan mark off on the edge of a strip of paper the distance from the centreline to the point where this new perpendicular cuts the innermost, or lowest, waterline, transfer this distance to the same waterline on the body plan, measuring from the centreline, and mark in this point. Repeat the process for each waterline in turn, and then for the deck line. As a cross check, on the elevation measure the distance on this new perpendicular from the base to the point where it cuts each of the bowlines or buttock lines. Mark these heights on each of the appropriate lines on the body plan. Do the same for the vertical height of the deck above the base and transfer it to the body plan, where it should coincide with that previously marked as the half-breadth of the deck. Having put in all these points, draw a fair curve to pass through all of them, and this will be the shape of the new half-section.

A new waterline is added in a similar way. A knowledge of how to do this is particularly useful if a hull is being built on the 'bread-

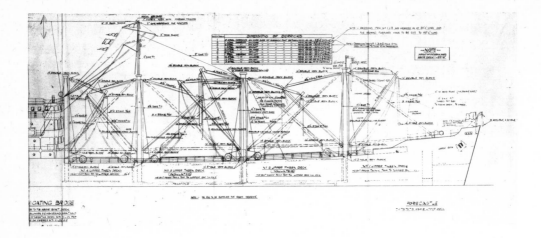

Fig 207
Part of the rigging plan for a cargo ship, giving some idea of the amount of information a good version of such a plan can contain.

and-butter' system, and the thickness of the planks being used for the hull does not coincide with the spacing of the waterlines. New waterlines can be drawn at a distance apart to suit the plank thickness. When transferred to the timber this facilitates the cutting of the boards to the shape of each waterline. On the body plan draw horizontal lines parallel to the base line and at a distance apart equal to the thickness of the planks. Starting with the lowest of these new waterlines measure the distance (paper strip method again) from the centreline to the point where the line cuts each of the sections on the body plan. Transfer these distances to the appropriate ordinates on the half-breadth plan. On the elevation mark in the position of the new waterlines. Lift off the distance from the point where each bowline and buttock line cuts the new waterlines to the nearest ordinate and transfer this measurement to the appropriate bowlines and buttock lines on the half-breadth plan. Draw a fair curve through all the points. If this vessel has a raked stem then the point at which each of these new waterlines cuts the foreside of the stem will be seen in the elevation. Transfer the distance of each of these points from the forward ordinate on the elevation to the centreline of the half-breadth plan. The sweep of the new waterlines in plan view must meet the centreline at that point, due allowance of course being made for the size of the stem bar or shape of the soft nose or rolled plate stem. At the after end a similar allowance must be made for the stern

frame or shape of the stern.

The foregoing describes a lines plan in its simplest form. Often it will be found to contain much more information, such as details of any decorative work (on the older vessels), the position of other lower decks, and the shape and extent of the propeller shaft bossing for single- and multiple-screw vessels. Bossing has not been included in the above notes as it has been covered earlier. (**Figs 128–130**).

These remarks have been based on those plans which are, possibly, available for the actual ship, *ie* shipbuilders' plans, modelmakers' plans prepared from builder's drawings or, in some instances, from information gathered at an accurate survey of the vessel itself by someone experienced in so doing. However, there is an additional type of plan which should be mentioned. A number of commercial organisations include in their plan sets for modelmakers one or more sheets showing a method for building the hull, especially in the case of wooden craft. Sometimes the information given follows the full-size practices of the period; sometimes it gives a method of fitting a series of internal formers, rather like bulkheads, to which the planking or shell can be attached. These latter are often drawn out full-size for the model concerned as individual sketches.

112

THE GENERAL ARRANGEMENT PLAN

As the name implies this shows the layout of the ship deck by deck. A good GA plan – and quality varies enormously both in the amount of detail shown and the way it is presented – will show the shape of the deckhouses and the position of all but the smallest fittings. It should indicate among other things the nature of any deck coverings, the size of bollards and ventilators, the dimensions of guard rails, and the position of all doors, portholes, windows and other openings. The elevation of the ship should show lifeboats, masts, derricks, ventilators, rails, windows, portholes and so on. If done correctly this view should indicate any difference in the placement of portholes and windows on the port or starboard side. A GA plan will often have an additional elevation, known as a sectional elevation, which shows the internal layout of the vessel. This can be particularly useful for information about 'tween deck and deckhouse heights.

THE RIGGING PLAN

This is an external elevation, often with many extraneous details omitted for clarity, which shows the masts, derrick posts, derricks, etc in full, with all the standing and running rigging and blocks, together with the types and sizes of all rigging. To a certain extent these plans are diagrammatic so far as the lead of running gear to belaying points is concerned. Those shown are quite adequate, but it was a

Fig 208
A paint line profile plan, showing how useful such a plan can be for any ship which has anything more than the simplest of paint schemes. The ship is the paddle steamer *Juno* (1937).

common practice for many of these points to be decided at ship in conjunction with the vessel's officers. **Fig 207** is part of the rigging plan of a cargo ship. In the case of sailing ships a sail plan will also be required.

PAINT LINE PROFILE

If available, this is a very useful plan, for it shows the extent of the different hull colours, the position of the ribband if there is one, the heights of the boot topping, the position and size of the ship's name and port of registry and, in some cases, many entries about the colour of deck fittings and other equipment. See **Fig 208**.

SHELL EXPANSION

This is a diagrammatic layout of the strakes of plating which form the shell of the ship. Whilst it indicates the relative position of each strake and every plate, it does not show their correct shape. It gives their size and thickness, and the relative position of seams, butts and end laps together with their size and – in the case of riveted vessels – the nature of the riveting (see **Fig 209**).

The way in which this plan was drawn is as follows. First the outline of the keel, stem, forefoot, stern frame and stern, up to the weather deck, were drawn to scale and the position of the frames marked along the keel. At each frame position a line was drawn perpendicular to the base line, its length being equal to the transverse girth (on one side of the ship only) from the longitudinal centreline on the keel round to the edge of the weather deck. A line was then drawn through the extremities of these lines from bow to stern. On this rather curiously shaped plan were marked in the

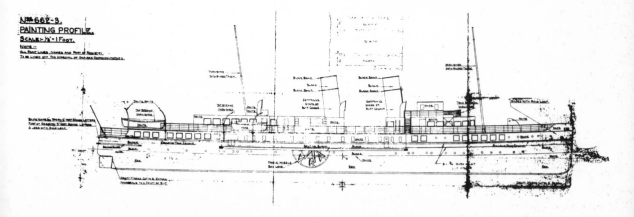

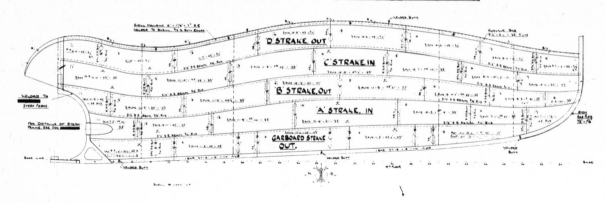

SHIP №
PLATE LINE BODY PLAN

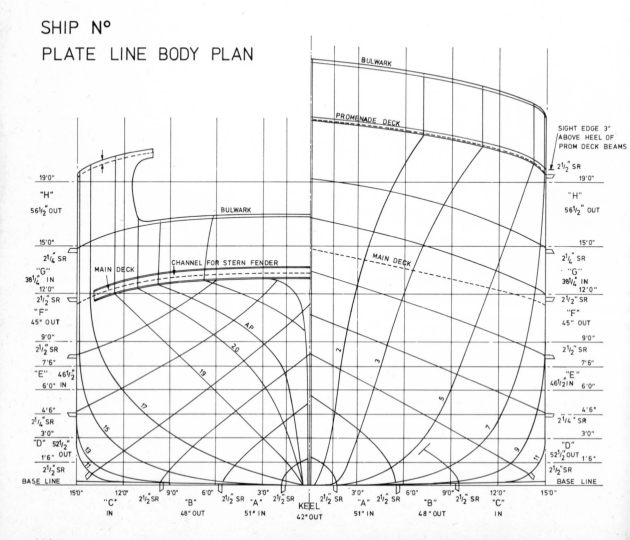

◀**Fig 209**
The shell expansion plan. This one is for a small tug,
but it embodies all the features found in such plans.

Fig 210
A typical plate line body plan; this one is of a cross-
channel paddle steamer, hence the lack of bossing. The
maximum width of each strake is shown, and also its
position, *ie* 'in' or 'out'. The 2½in SR means that the
seam (overlap) of those two particular plates is 2½in
wide and has a single row of rivets (a double-riveted
seam, *ie* one having two rows of rivets, would be
marked DR). The mark alongside the 2½in SR
indicates the width of the seam, and the longer of the
two parallel lines shows the sight edge of the plating.
The sight edge is the outer, or visible, edge of the
◀strake of plating.

Fig 211▼
Typical midship section showing structural details.

width and extent of each strake of plating, the
position of plate end laps or butts, the plate
seams, the thickness of the plating and, by
means of various symbols, the nature of the
riveting or welding of butts, laps and seams.
The plan would also show a considerable
amount of information about the adjacent
internal structure of the hull. It must be
remembered that a shell expansion plan is basically diagrammatic; it shows the run of the
plating and the position, but not the actual
finished shape, of each individual plate.

PLATE LINE BODY PLAN
This is the body plan of a ship on which is
superimposed the run of the strakes of the shell

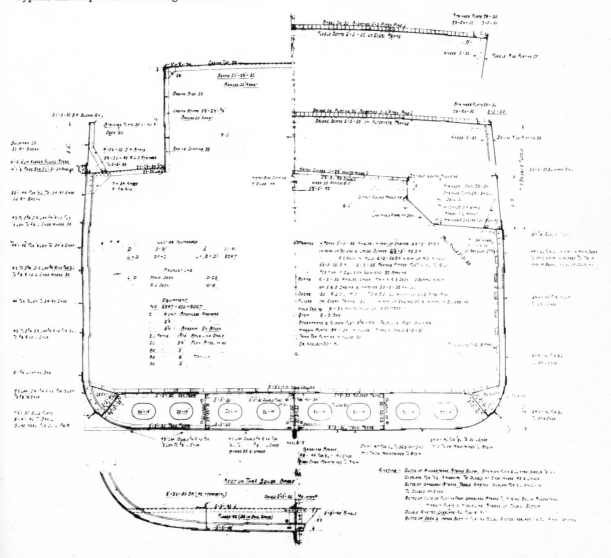

plating. It does not show the end butts or laps of the plates, though it does indicate the end of a strake of plating. It usually includes information about the size and riveting of the plating. Except for the one omission mentioned above, it can be a very useful plan for the modeller adding plating to a hull or for one building a 'tinplate' hull. See **Fig 210**.

THE MIDSHIP SECTION
As its name indicates this shows a transverse section through a vessel at mid-length. It is primarily a structural plan, and contains much data about the steelwork scantlings of the hull. From the modelmaker's point of view a good midship section plan will contain much useful information about deckhouse widths, the size of curtain plates, the nature of deck coverings, the height of guard rails and bulwarks, the 'tween deck heights, the camber of decks, the

amount of tumblehome, and at times such matters as the height above deck of the centre of portholes. See **Fig 211**.

MODELMAKERS PLANS
The plans prepared specially for modelmakers (but keeping in mind the comment made earlier) have a number of advantages over the shipyard-type plans in that invariably they omit much extraneous and often confusing detail which is of no use to the modeller, include well-detailed cross-sections, give detail drawings of fittings, and sometimes amplify these and particular parts of the structure by means of three-dimensional sketches. They have the added feature of being drawn to scale and full size for a model of reasonable proportions, thus eliminating the necessity to scale up (or down) as is the case when using shipyard plans or those from the technical journals. See **Fig 205**.

Fig 212
Typical hinged opening portholes. These are fitted to an engine room skylight. The whole top cover can be removed for access by taking out the hexagon headed bolts in the flange. Note the use of steel flat bar for the guard rail stanchions. The vessel is the Australian tug *Sydney Cove. S Lowry*

Portholes

These are sometimes referred to also as portlights or sidelights (which can be rather confusing). Those in **Fig 212** are typical of the general design. They are of the opening type, and have been fitted here on the outside of a small casing to form a skylight to the compartment below. When fitted in a deckhouse, or on the ship's hull, what is visible here will be on the inside; all that can be seen from the outside is the brass rim surrounding the glass, and projecting just beyond the surface of the plating of the house or hull. When reference is made to the size of a porthole, the figure quoted refers to the diameter of the clear glass.

Fig 213▶
Unit Steam Engines' adaption of their single-cylinder oscillating engine to provide a powerplant for a paddle steamer. For propeller-shaft drive the engine is bolted in the upright position to the end of the baseplate, the shaft, gearwheels and their supports being removed. The boiler is fired by solid fuel. *Unit Steam Engines Ltd*

Propulsion: the Powering of Models (by Brian King)

STEAM ENGINES

The simplest of steam plants is a plain single-acting oscillating engine fed by a boiler fired by a methylated spirit burner, rather on the lines of the Bowman models known before and after World War II, which gave endless pleasure to so many of us as boys. I never possessed one but a close friend did, and I well remember the day it suddenly came across the pond at about twice its normal speed because the methylated spirit burner had flooded (always a hazard with that type of burner), setting the hull alight and thus providing extra fuel and heat to one hard-pressed boiler!

Oscillating engines can be made multi-cylinder, having three cylinders set round a common crank pin at 120°. These will be self-starting. Unit Steam Engines (41 Church Street, Twickenham, Middlesex, UK) make a single-cylinder oscillating engine unit which can be coupled together in series to increase power and to provide self-starting capability, a necessity if radio control is contemplated. As well as providing more power, multi-cylinder also requires more steam, and this will be covered in the section on boilers. It is also possible to make oscillating engines double-acting. This company has made an interesting addition to their range of products. It consists of one of their single-cylinder oscillating engines mounted horizontally on the end of the casing of the boiler and geared to a transverse horizontal shaft. The boiler is of the pot type

fuelled by solid pellets. This simple and effective unit is suitable for models of paddle steamers having a hull length of 30 to 36in (0.79–0.91m).

Slide-valve engines. The single-cylinder slide-valve engine is often referred to as a launch-type engine. The cylinder is fixed, and the steam supply is controlled by a slide valve operated by an eccentric on the crankshaft. The Stuart No 10 is a typical example. These engines are usually double-acting, *ie* the steam pressure acts on both sides of the piston, unlike internal combustion engines which are always single-acting. This involves sealing the piston rod and pivoting the connecting rod to its lower end, the crosshead, instead of pivoting the connecting rod as in an internal combustion engine.

Single-cylinder launch engines are not self-starting, but this can be overcome by using two cylinders, as in the Stuart Double 10, which is virtually two single-cylinder engines fitted together with cranks set at 90° to give starting torque at any position of the crankshaft.

Twin-cylinder enclosed-type engines. In most designs these have a piston valve lying horizontally in an overhead steam chest, the valve being operated by a banjo eccentric rod. They usually run at a higher speed than the previous type, and all have their mechanism enclosed, unlike launch engines where it is all exposed. The Stuart Sun is of this type; it has a bore and stroke of ¾in, and is suitable for a model about 4ft 6in (1.37m) long.

Double and triple expansion engines. These are in line with full-size practice. Early in the development of steam power it was realised that the use of steam only once was wasteful, since the steam being exhausted still retained a considerable amount of usable expansive energy. The idea of re-using this steam, at a lower pressure of course and in a cylinder of larger diameter, was tried and found to produce a very worthwhile saving in fuel. In those early days high fuel consumption was the Achilles' heel of the steamer. Eventually three stages of

Fig 214
The Stuart Turner ST steam plant. The single-cylinder oscillating engine has a bore and stroke of $\frac{7}{16}$in, and the boiler is solid-drawn copper, brazed, fitted with superheater and safety valve and fired by a spirit lamp. Working pressure is 30lb. *Stuart Turner Ltd*

Fig 215
A double-acting single-cylinder steam engine from Maxwell Hemmens Precision Steam Models. It has a bore and stroke of $\frac{3}{4}$in and a working pressure of 60psi. This particular example is fitted with link reversing gear. *Maxwell Hemmens Ltd*

expansion were used, hence the triple expansion engine in which three cylinders of successive larger diameters were used to abstract as much energy as possible from the steam. The high-pressure cylinder, having the smallest diameter of the three, was placed closest to the boiler, with the larger cylinders aft in succession.

Raw castings and sets of machined castings for most of the above types of engine are marketed by a number of firms. As well as Unit Steam Engines already mentioned, Maxwell Hemmens Precision Steam Models, (Gunby Road, Bubwith, Selby, North Yorkshire, UK) manufacture and import a number of interesting items of steam plant, while Stuart Turner Ltd, Henley-on-Thames, Oxon RG9 2AD, England, are probably the best-known manufacturers and suppliers of steam engines and accessories for the modelmaker. Complete and fully tested engines and boilers are, of course, also available. Japanese manufacturers have entered the field recently with similar sorts of equipment.

The steam turbine. This ultimate use of steam has long interested the ship modeller, and some of the very early books on ship modelling have contained designs for very simple single-stage turbines, though looking at these one has some doubts as to their power and capability.

Full-size turbine design is very complex. With the flow shape made to utilise the expansive energy of the steam as it passes through the turbine, and the highly complex shape of the blades, both fixed and rotating, it is apparent that little can be done by even the most ambitious modelmaker. A turbine has to run at high speed, which introduces the added problem of gearing being necessary to reduce the speed sufficiently to suit the propeller. Nevertheless for those who are already experienced in the practical engineering side of modelmaking, the subject is still worthy of experimentation – the more so perhaps as there are at least a couple of simple turbines now on the market. Maxwell Hemmens are agents for a geared turbine made by Metafot of West Germany, 30,000rpm geared down to 3000rpm; a suitable boiler is also available. The Wada Works of Yokohama have a turbine and boiler unit which works on quite moderate steam pressures. One advantage of the turbine over the direct-acting piston engine is that if the engine stalls the steam can still escape.

All steam engines produce a problem if radio control is required, since in their normal construction they do not lend themselves easily to the functions of the usual radio-control servo. The way in which this can be overcome is to fit some form of reversing mechanism, such as the Stephenson link reversing gear much used on steam engines, which the servo can be made to operate. If the travel of a normal servo is insufficient to operate the gear completely, then a pivoted lever can be introduced to increase the servo's travel, albeit so doing will also create a certain loss of mechanical force.

Boilers. The very simplest consist of a cylinder or tube of copper with the flanged ends soft-soldered in place. The fittings normally comprise a filler, a safety valve of a simple type (an essential piece of equipment) and a take-off steam pipe connecting it to the engine. The whole assembly is mounted horizontally on a sheet metal support, the sides of which are pierced with a number of ventilation holes. The boiler is fired by a simple methylated spirit burner. This design is quite satisfactory for low pressure of up to about 25psi, but purists no doubt would prefer silver-soldered (hard-soldered) joints even at this pressure.

Variations to this simple scene are the use of brass for the boiler and possibly a 'D' cross-section, the flat of the D being the underside and the configuration vertical rather than horizontal. Brass as a material for boilers is not to be recommended though, as its strength tends to be an unknown quantity, varying so much according to its composition. To touch upon metallurgy for a moment, the brass commonly supplied is known as 'common' or 'basis' brass and its composition is not guaranteed. It may be entirely alpha phase or alpha/beta phase; just which it is depends upon the proportions of zinc and copper in the alloy. Only if 'cartridge' brass (70 per cent copper and 30 per cent zinc) is bought is there any real guarantee of its properties.

If the configuration is altered from circular – the perfect shape to resist pressure, as the pressure is equal all round and merely tends to make the shape larger but still circular – then the shape of the boiler may alter; it will alter if the pressure is high enough, when internal staying will be necessary. This means that internal ties are used to prevent the flat bottom of the 'D' section mentioned above bellying downwards (see **Fig 222**). Even in

Fig 216
The machinery layout of the 1/48 scale model of the paddle steamer *Albion* by Brian King. The motor, fitted transversely, is a Marx Decaperm Special fitted with a Pile gearbox carrying a ¾in sprocket on the output shaft. Drive to the paddle-shaft was by chain from this sprocket to a 2in diameter chain wheel on the shaft. The layout, from left to right, is: accumulators, receiver, receiver DEAC, proportional speed controller, motor and gearbox, filter, rudder servo. *Brian King*

Fig 217
The interior layout of the 1/60 scale model of the US armoured ship *Keokuk* (1863) by Steve Kirby. It was a twin-screw vessel, and on the model an electric motor is fitted to each shaft, one of which can be seen in the left-hand or after 'compartment'. Left to right in the centre-section are the steering servo, twin electronic speed controls (under the white cover), and the drive battery, which extends forward into the left-hand side of the forward section. In that section forward of this battery is the charging and switching panel and then the receiver at top right, with its battery at bottom right.

◀**Fig 218**
The wood-clad boiler and the polished bell-mouth funnel of these Edwardian steam launches, with all the 'works' open to view, make these craft very attractive prototypes for working models. This is the machinery of the steam launch *Lady of Aire*, built by B R Ward, a member of the Bradford MBC. The engine is a Stuart Double-Ten, fitted with Stephenson's link gear. The centre-flue boiler is gas-fired. The hull is of clinker construction, copper-fastened throughout.

Fig 219▶
The complete steam plant for a 6ft model of a cargo ship. The engine has two double-acting cylinders $\frac{5}{8}$in bore × $\frac{7}{8}$in stroke. The boiler has an internal flue crossed by water tubes and is fired by a modified paraffin blow-lamp. The burner was removed from the top of the lamp to its position in line with the boiler flue. It can be preheated by a bottled gas torch. *M Adams*

Fig 220▶
The modified burner unit of the paraffin lamp. Paraffin under air pressure is fed to the burner by a stainless steel pipe. *M Adams*

◀**Fig 221**
The latest development of the Kort nozzle, the Kort rudder. Whereas in the case of the fixed nozzle the ring would be so made as to fit on to the shell and to the stern frame, and be without the central blade, in the rudder version it is secured to the rudder stock, with a bottom pintle in the socket of the heel casting. The whole unit turns to an angle of about 25° to either side of the centreline. *Kort Propulsion Co Ltd*

Fig 222▼
Outline arrangement of pot-type boilers.

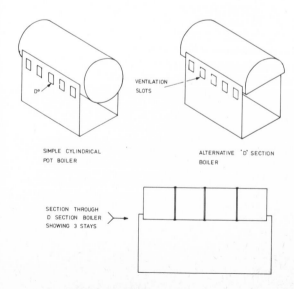

SIMPLE CYLINDRICAL POT BOILER

VENTILATION SLOTS

ALTERNATIVE 'D' SECTION BOILER

SECTION THROUGH D SECTION BOILER SHOWING 3 STAYS

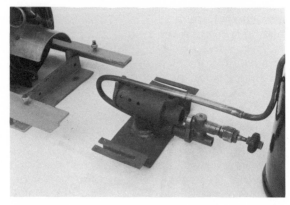

through the boiler, this flue normally being somewhat lower than the true axial axis, as in **Fig 223**. This type of boiler is usually fired with a blow-lamp of some sort.

This can be improved by putting cross-tubes carrying water in the flue, which makes it a water-tube boiler. This technique effectively increases the heating area enormously and makes a very efficient boiler. Alternatively the boiler can be arranged as a fire-tube boiler, *ie* the tubes contain fire, or rather hot gases, rather than water. Whichever is adopted the heating area is increased. Locomotive boilers are of the fire-tube type. See **Fig 224**.

The power of steam can be increased by superheating. In very simple terms this means that wet steam, *ie* the steam coming from the boiler, is re-heated to dry it. This is normally done by taking the steam pipe back into the flame before delivering it to the engine. All locomotive boilers provided superheated steam by using special superheater tubes in the fire box flue. Remember the little boiler with a pigtail outlet pipe being heated by a Bunsen in the school laboratory, and how with another Bunsen under the pig-tail the emergent steam burnt a hole in a piece of paper – well, that's superheating.

Boiler fittings. The last-named boilers are very sophisticated types and will require several fittings. They will be made of copper, hard-soldered together, stayed where necessary, and fitted with safety valve(s), gauge glasses, pressure gauges and suitable take-off piping and fittings for the steam pipe and probably a water pump as well.

Very simple boilers usually have no means of indicating the water level inside. This means that frequent topping-up is required, but on a trial and error basis as the amount remaining in the boiler is unknown. More advanced boilers will have water gauge glasses, usually fitted on one of the end faces. A point to note about safety: although these will be hydraulically tested with the boiler in the normal way (more about testing later), it has been known for them to fail at much lower pressures whilst in service. Perhaps they have sustained a knock or something. A breaking gauge glass is likely to shower the area with broken glass and boiling water all propelled by the steam pressure in the boiler. It is advisable to protect this glass with a transparent cover if at all possible; another idea is to provide cocks at both ends of the

circular-section boilers the ends are usually stayed if designed to work at anything above the lowest pressure. The screwed bushes for the ties are usually flanged with the flanges on the outside, thus preventing the soldering having to take the tension stresses. Similarly, such fittings as safety valves should be flanged on the *inside* for the same reason.

Standing the boiler on end, although often done on launches and the like, where it may become a feature in an otherwise open boat, tends to raise the centre of gravity (CG). In most vessels this is not desirable; furthermore there just is not the space available under most kinds of superstructure.

Another problem with simple drum or pot boilers is that the heating area, and thus the steam-raising capability, is limited, hence the complication of the 'D' shape as opposed to the simple circular shape in the earliest examples we looked at. One way of increasing the heating area is found in the centre-flue boiler. This consists of a circular tube-shaped boiler with another circular shaped hole axially

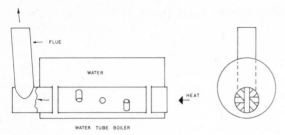

Fig 223
Arrangement of water-tube boiler.

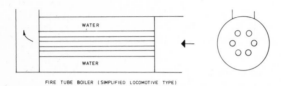

Fig 224
Arrangement of fire-tube boiler (simplified loco type).

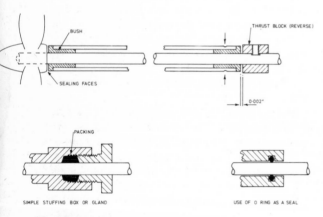

Fig 225
Arrangement of typical stern tube showing details of different methods of sealing tube.

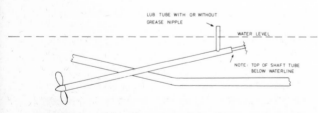

Fig 226
Diagrammatic arrangement of stern tube showing method of lubrication.

gauge glass so that it can be isolated. Stuart Turner illustrate such a gauge glass arrangement in their catalogue, in this case showing two isolating cocks and a further cock to operate the gauge. Fitting a pressure gauge is a good idea – perhaps not necessary to the normal running of the boiler, but essential when testing.

Boiler testing. Boilers need to be tested hydraulically to at least twice their working pressure – three times would be even better – giving a factor of safety of two or three, whichever is the case. Boilers are not tested pneumatically since any compressed gas once released by any failure will in effect explode and shower the area with debris. Hydraulic testing, provided the system has been bled of all air (a similar process to bleeding the brakes of a car) has no such danger because liquid is incompressible, so that even the smallest leak will remove the pressure, and hence danger, immediately and no explosion will occur.

To test a boiler it has to be filled with water, sealed, fitted with a pressure gauge of known accuracy, and be attached to some sort of pump to apply pressure. This pressure can be applied slowly in stages up to the test value whilst the boiler is monitored for leaks and any distortion, such as ends bowing out, and so on. Provided there is no air in the system this process is safe, but if air is left in then there is still some danger of explosive failure.

If insurance of any kind is to be taken out then the boiler will have to be tested to satisfy the people with whom it is to be insured. Rules for the testing of boilers which should satisfy most insurance houses were published in 1977 in *Model Engineer*. In the marine field, the Model Power Boat Association has proposed a set of rules which have been based on the methods adopted by the Southern and Northern Federation of Model Engineers.

Simple boilers have no means of water replacement except by blowing off the steam to allow more water to be poured in. The alternative is an arrangement whereby water can be pumped in manually or automatically by means of an engine-driven pump. The pump, of course, must be capable of exceeding the boiler pressure in order to get water into the boiler. There are many designs for such pumps, and there is always argument among the *cognoscenti* about the correct way to valve them.

The use of an injector is another method of adding feed water, but it is not used to any great extent in the marine model field, probably because pond water is not as clean as it might be and could interfere with its operation.

Burners. The simplest form of burner available is the methylated spirit type. The design can be varied to suit individual application, but in essence it consists of a tinplate or brass container with a suitable screw-cap filler, and having one or more wicks protruding from the top. The other essential feature is a handle with which to move it about. As methylated spirit burns with a pale blue flame which is almost impossible to see in bright light, always assume that the burner is alight unless you yourself have put it out. Following this rule will prevent such accidents as trying to refill a lighted burner, or setting light to your own, or someone else's clothing.

However, there are two disadavantages to this type of burner. It has a tendency to flood for some reason best known to itself, and invariably this occurs when the model is out in the middle of the water. The spirit pours out of the burner, spreads over the bottom of the boat and burns. One sure sign that this has happened is a sudden marked increase in the model's performance, which is just as well, as the sooner it reaches the side the sooner the blaze can be put out. To avoid this trouble the spirit container is usually filled with material such as glass fibre strands, although ordinary cotton wool wadding was used in some of the earlier types – this was the same material as was used for the wicks. Even so, experience has shown that the trouble can still take place. Another way in which the flooding problem can be avoided altogether is by the use of solid fuel pellets. These have a limited burning time, so the running time will have to be related to the burning time. These pellets only require a tray, with a handle of course. The second disadvantage is that the energy output, in terms of heat of course, is relatively low, so for large boilers something more elaborate is required.

When more heat was needed the petrol blowlamp was the type of burner selected – a somewhat fearsome object due once again to the presence of a very volatile liquid of extremely high energy content, and one not to be trifled with, particularly when under pressure. There is at least one firm today, the Ambassador Light Engineering Co (44 Park Avenue, Barnolds-wick, Colne, Lancashire, UK), who supply paraffin blowlamps not unlike those prewar Bassett-Lowke petrol lamps with pump, pressure gauge and either single or double burners.

The availability of bottled gas has made possible the introduction of a good alternative to the above petrol and paraffin lamps, and it is now possible to tailor-make from commercial heaters suitable gas-fired lamps for use in marine boilers. Possibly the main problem is that the container has to be remote from the burner, if for no other reason that there is no space available under the boiler. The only other point is to arrange the piping so that the jet itself does not receive any liquid; the connection point should be from the top of the container, even if it has to go down to the burner under the boiler. This is typical of all blowlamps in that they do not 'prime', that is, squirt liquid. This sort of burner does not require a pump since the gas is under pressure to keep it in liquid form. It vaporises as it is bled off so no vaporising coils are necessary, making the whole thing a simpler proposition.

A reminder. In making the decision to use steam as a means of propulsion for a model, it is very necessary to appreciate that of all the forms of propulsion for a model it can be the most dangerous if certain elementary precautions, some of which have already been mentioned, are not observed.

Unlike a fluid under pressure, where any leak will dissipate the pressure, the expansive power of steam will cause an explosion if given half a chance. This may not involve a major calamity such as a boiler explosion, but a simple thing like a breaking water gauge glass can cause damage. Escaping steam can also scald.

Thus it behoves anyone using steam to take all due precautions not only for their own protection, but also for that of any bystanders.

ELECTRIC MOTORS

I suppose to the real 'steam' man there is no alternative to steam, particularly if the prototype was steam-driven. But if one can bypass prejudice the ideal method of driving scale models is by electric power; steam with its heat and air supply requirements will always cause problems.

Electric power is clean, easily controlled (especially by radio control), quiet (very important on many waters these days with so many environmental pressure groups about), relatively economic and has no starting troubles. Since World War II model electric motors have benefited from the improvement in magnet material in respect of both power and permanence of the magnetic field, and so are now almost exclusively of the permanent magnet variety. I do not propose to discuss the very high power motors developed for the speed fraternity as these are capable of such high power and hence current requirements that the vessel becomes simply a power-driven battery box, which is not the scale requirement at all. In the scale field a reasonable battery life is required, say 1 to 3 hours, together with more or less scale speed. There is no point in overdriving scale models so that tugs hare around like destroyers, a phenomenon which is all too familiar.

Selecting the size of motor(s) can be done basically in two ways. Perhaps the simplest, particularly if you are a club member is to see what the opposition use, if you know that the performance of that particular model is satisfactory. It is important in such cases that the shapes of the underwater part of the hulls are very similar, as hulls with different block coefficients, even if of the same length, will obviously require different amounts of power to drive them: think of the relative shapes of, say, a 'super tanker' and a destroyer, although of course the required speed will also be different. Such comparisons will also indicate the size, number of blades and pitch of the matching propeller(s).

The other way is more scientific although in the final analysis only an approximation as there are too many variables in the equation for anything like complete accuracy. Unfortunately most motor manufacturers are very loath to put any technical specifications on their motors, but the main figure required for these calculations is the stall torque. If this is not given it can be found by fitting an arm at right angles to the shaft (a piece of rod soldered to a boss grub-screwed to the shaft will do). If a spring balance is then applied at a known distance along the rod from the motor spindle the spring balance reading with the motor switched on can then be found. The stall torque will then be equal to the spring balance reading multiplied by the distance, *eg* if the spring balance reading is 6oz and the distance 2in then the stall torque will be $2 \times 6 = 12$in oz (or mm newtons if you insist on working in SI units).

Now the resistance of the model to being driven, that is the power required to drive it, will be roughly proportional to the length/beam ratio, which will also compensate for differences in draught as the length/ratio/displacement are to a large extent connected. Curves can therefore be drawn to show the relationship between stall/torque and length for several length/beam ratios.

The majority of electric motors appear to be most efficient when running near their maximum revolutions, say 2000–3000 rpm, discounting those special racing motors of course. To allow the motor to reach this economic speed a small propeller can be fitted but unfortunately, although the motor may be happy under these conditions, the small propeller is not likely to be very efficient. A larger propeller should therefore be fitted and the motor geared down to suit.

As an example, the Marx Luder Decaperm, a most popular and dependable motor, has two shafts, one direct drive and the other geared down, the ratio being $2.75 : 1$. If the geared shaft is used with a propeller of reasonable size the current consumption will also be reasonable and this can be measured by an ammeter *in series* with the supply. If the same propeller is driven by the ungeared shaft the current will be found to have risen to an unacceptably high figure that would give a very short battery life, that is before the battery needs a recharge.

The battery life can be determined as follows. Say, for instance, the battery's capacity is given as 4 amp hrs. If the current drain is 1 amp then the expected life will be roughly 4 hours. If the drain was $1\frac{1}{2}$ amp then the life would be 4 amp hrs/1.5 amp = 2.6 hours. These figures are usually obtained with the model tethered in the bath. The current figures may not be quite correct with the model not free to move, but will be near enough to get reasonable approximations.

Similarly if the tethering is done by a spring balance various propellers and combinations of propellers, motors, etc can be tried out for efficiency and compared with current drain figures. These tests are known as bollard pull tests. The only problem is to get steady static conditions to read the spring balance, as the spring in the balance opposing the drive of the model tends to set up 'surging', with the model moving backwards and forwards; but it can be done and it gives a lot of information quickly.

I have even made a spare fibreglass hull to test out the relative efficiency between twin and quadruple propeller layouts before finally committing myself to the model proper.

One further point about motors is that they always need suppressing from the point of radio frequency interference. The larger the motor the easier this usually is. When you think of it, it is a lot to ask when you put your receiver right next door, in effect, to a most prolific source of radio noise – a DC motor commutator – but we do it. If a commercial electronic proportional speed controller is fitted, as it probably will be, these usually contain a suppressor and filter unit of great efficiency and the modeller will require to do nothing else.

DC electric motors of the permanent magnetic type are easy to control. The direction of rotation can be altered by changing the polarity (that is, swapping the negative and positive leads over) and the speed reduced by dropping the applied voltage. This used to be done by the simple but crude expedient of putting a variable resistor across the supply and burning off the excess voltage as heat. Modern electronic speed controls, which can be worked by a normal R/C servo, waste very little power and provide automatic reversing facilities, but some of them reduce the top speed. If this effect is severe they can be switched out of circuit at maximum revs. At least one commercial speed controller has a full throttle switch to switch out the controller at maximum throttle. If two motors are fitted to a twin-screw vessel and each motor has its own proportional speed controller, you have in effect complete prototype realism, exactly the same control as the captain of the original: fully independent speed control of both motors from full ahead through stop to full astern. If controllers are not fitted then switching with microswitches and servos can be employed. Interaction with the rudder is often employed,

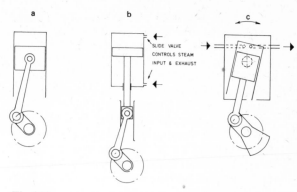

Fig 228
Pistons
(a) Piston arrangement for an internal combusion (IC) engine (single-acting). (b) Steam engine with cross-slide (double-acting). The steam input and exhaust are controlled by slide valve. As all the side thrust generated by the angular action of the connecting rod is taken by the cross-head slides, the piston can be very shallow in comparison with those in a and c. (c) Simple oscillating steam engine (single-acting). The piston rod is fixed to the piston, thus oscillating the cylinder, whose single port connects with inlet and exhaust ports on the backplate.

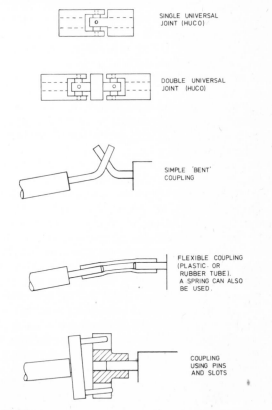

Fig 229
Outline details of different arrangements of propeller shaft couplings.

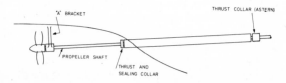

Fig 227
Sealing arrangement for stern tube used in conjunction with 'open' type propeller shafts.

switching off the inboard motor in sharp turns for example.

The final use of electric motors is the combined units, looking rather like an outboard or Z-drive. These provide a motor and a propeller so they are self-contained. For some special applications they are ideal.

Electric power supplies. These basically fall into three classes: (a) dry batteries (primary cells); (b) lead/acid accumulators (secondary cells); and (c) nickel-cadmium cells (and the like). The problem with dry batteries is that the output (in amps) is a lot less than that of a roughly similarly sized lead/acid battery. This means that, relatively speaking, more dry cells are required to keep a reasonable battery life. In practice three dry batteries will give much more than three times the life of one battery, so that this fact alone raises the expense; and of course they are not rechargeable. The use of dry batteries is therefore perfectly viable but likely to be very expensive, particularly if much sailing is undertaken.

Probably the next in popularity and simplicity is the lead/acid accumulator. The range obtainable is wide, from small, mainly Japanese types, to those not strictly built for the model field such as motor-cycle batteries. They are heavy, of course, but can usually act as some of the ballast. Charging conditions are not difficult or too sensitive, although the manufacturer's charging rate should not be exceeded unduly. Plenty of chargers are available, from car-type chargers to specially made types for model work. The main thing to avoid is leaving the batteries uncharged for any length of time because if you do they will develop a disease known as sulphating, which is terminal. This is the formation of zinc sulphate, a white substance which builds up on the plates and effectively destroys them. They should therefore be recharged immediately on discharge, and if not used be recharged once a month to maintain their condition. Other than topping up with distilled water and keeping the terminals clean there is not a lot to do. However, be careful that the electrolyte does not get contaminated otherwise early failure may be your batteries' lot. Really it is a question of following the manufacturer's recommendations strictly, when little trouble should come your way.

Perhaps the most well-known make of nickel-cadmium cell (nicad) is the DEAC, named after its German manufacturer. Nicads are used almost exclusively for powering transmitters (Tx's) and receivers (Rx's) but can also be used for main drive power. However, their cost is higher than lead acids but as they will stand up to 1000 charging cycles this is offset; lead acids give nowhere near this working life. Their voltage is only 1.2V per cell as against a nominal 2V for the lead/acid type. As more units will be required to make up the same voltage this involves extra weight but this is unlikely to cause trouble in most scale work. If used for main drive their discharge rate will be higher than when used for radio work and hence the temperature rise of the cell will be larger and needs to be catered for. In other words do not cram in the cells without adequate ventilation.

All this is straightforward. What is different, however, is the charging conditions. Some nicads are fully sealed and must be charged at a fairly slow rate otherwise internal heat and pressure may build up and burst the cell. However, the vented cylindrical type can be fast-charged, the vent allowing any excess pressure to escape, and this is where complication occurs: before charging can start the cell should be fully discharged. This has to be done by connecting a suitable load across the pack. The unit can then be recharged after calculating the correct charging time. All in all the charging process is much more complicated than when charging lead/acids, and it pays to do the job correctly otherwise damaged or ruined cells are likely to result.

One very important point often overlooked is that model submarines should only be powered by fully sealed cells. Submarines with ordinary lead/acid cells are the perfect recipe for an explosion; the ingredients are all there – hydrogen gas, a by-product of the battery's chemical process, oxygen in the trapped air to make an explosive mixture, and a nice sparking commutator to light the blue touch paper. Many model submarines have exploded but still the message has not been learnt.

PROPELLER SHAFTS

For those that like the easy way out these can be bought finished in a variety of sizes. However, it does seem that many of those available are intended for powerboats, as they are usually far too heavy for scale work. Powerboats, of course, require greater torque, which means an increase in diameter to cater for this, so although they can be used the discerning model maker will probably make his own.

This is essentially a straightforward job, particularly if a lathe is available. The simplest way is to fit a piece of brass or aluminium tube over a length of silver steel. Even so, friction losses are bound to be high as either the shaft or tube, and most probably both of them, will be less than straight and the shaft will tend to bind in the bore. A larger tube giving complete clearance to the shaft is better, the shaft itself running in brass or bronze bearings at either end. These are best flanged but can be made a push-fit, soldered, affixed with cyanoacrylate adhesive, or clenched in as shown in **Fig 225**. The best material for the shaft is undoubtedly stainless steel, fitted into reamered holes in the bushes. If the fit is still tight, slimming down the *shaft* with emery paper is the best way of easing the problem. Care should be taken to ensure that the bushes are pushed in square; this is the main reason for tightness if otherwise the dimensions are correct. Using the lathe as a mandrel press is a good idea: the shaft is held in the three-jaw and the bush pushed in square, with the tailstock. An even more sophisticated method would be to use a mandrel held in the tailstock fitting into the bush bore to hold it axially true.

Waterproofing. If the inboard end of the propeller shaft is above the waterline this should be no problem. However, this is not always possible; the design will just not allow it. If the top end is below the waterline, hydrostatic pressure can, in theory at least, force water into the boat. The classic method of opposing hydraulic pressure is to fit a gland or stuffing box and one is shown (**Fig 225**) for those desiring to do so. This to me is an unnecessary fitment. I have never fitted a stuffing box to any of my models and have never suffered any but the slightest leakage as a consequence. My 'apprenticeship' in working models (before World War II) was largely spent using clockwork as a motive power, and with such low power sources the extra friction caused by glands or stuffing boxes was not permissible, so other methods had to be found.

If the bush face taking the pressure, *ie* the lower end of the tube, is square with the bore and the thrust face of the propeller is also square, no water should get up the tube as the propeller will force itself against the tube bush and thus exclude the water. Only when running astern would there be a gap. If a thrust collar is fitted to the top end of the shaft this will bear on the top tube bush when going astern and thus prevent water entry under these conditions. The total end float of the shaft was set to about 0.002 inches with a feeler gauge, and it was found that once the faces had bedded in no leakage would occur. It is a good idea to put a couple of floors across the hull just where the odd drop of initial leakage falls, to localise the leakage and stop it sloshing around the hull, thus making it easier to sponge out afterwards.

A piece of tube can be soft- or hard-soldered vertically near the top end and, provided the top is clear of the waterline, left open for lubrication purposes (see **Fig 226**). Alternatively a grease nipple can be fitted. Without this fitment the tube needs to be greased or have oil packed on assembly, particularly if the shaft is only silver steel; left to its own devices silver steel rusts very readily. If grease is used, which it can be of course, then avoid using the very viscous types as these will add a lot of drag to the drive, particularly on cold days.

If the model is one where the shaft itself is open between hull and 'A' bracket, the sealing effect described will not work as the propeller will thrust against the 'A' bracket itself and in this case care may be needed to avoid leakage. In full-sized practice the thrust is taken by a thrust bearing of the Michel type, complete with floating thrust pads *inside* the vessel, but this seems an unnecessary complication on average-sized models. With 'open' drives of this type a thrust face can be arranged on the propeller shaft to operate against the 'stuffing' box, thus restoring the conditions described. See **Fig 227**.

PADDLE WHEEL DRIVE

Paddlers make a pleasant change from the more orthodox propeller-driven models. The first problem is to make the wheels themselves, after deciding if the floats should be feathering or not – I think this is really a problem of size, since if the wheel is very small the pivots etc become very weak and liable to damage if any floating debris is encountered.

The main problem then lies in what sort of drive is to be adopted between motor and paddle shaft. With steam there is no problem as the paddle shaft becomes the crank shaft directly driven by the cylinders. Electric drive

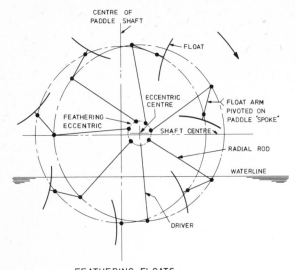

FEATHERING FLOATS

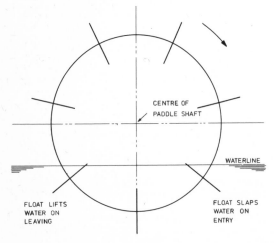

FIXED FLOATS

Fig 230
Diagrammatic arrangement to show the operation of
fixed and feathering type paddle wheels.

does represent more difficulty as the motor
speed relative to the paddle speed is so high.
The problem can be solved in several ways of
course but one way is to set the motor, fitted
with a Pile gearbox, across the hull so the
output shaft lies parallel with the paddle shaft
– see **Figs 216** and **230**. The final reduction of
say 3:1 can be achieved with a chain drive or
one of the new toothed belt drives. These can
be obtained from Hobby's, Knights Hill
Square, London. Pile gearboxes comprise a

number of epicyclic gearbox units that can be
assembled in series; the minimum reduction
using one unit is 3:1 but with all units assembled the total reduction is 360:1 so it should
be easy to arrange a suitable reduction to give
a paddle speed of around 100rpm, which is a
good speed to aim at in the first instance.

Other drives are possible, of course, using
contrate gears and the like, but the modeller
can use his ingenuity on this problem. Perhaps
one further point is that passenger-carrying
paddlers had both paddles locked together –
a Board of Trade requirement. Paddle tugs and
the like, however, had independent paddle
drives which enabled them to turn in their own
length. See **Fig 230**.

A paddle speed of around 100rpm is what
I found satisfactory on my own *Albion*. However, that is free-running speed; in the water
the speed will be somewhat lower than this. In
practice the actual full-scale speed was usually
between 30 and 50rpm but for stern-wheelers
it may be less than that.

COUPLINGS
Much power can be lost in the connection
between motor and propeller shaft, particularly
if the alignment is bad. Probably the best
method is to use a *double* universal coupling
of the HUCO type; even with a poor line-up
the friction losses will then be very low. However, if you use these put a spare one into your
tool kit as they are fairly delicate and pondside
failure can be a nuisance. One point to watch
is that if they are of the type that clamp to the
shaft using grub screws, file a flat on the shaft
to act as a bearing surface for the screws. This
is for two reasons: if the screw slacks off it will
still drive, and secondly any burrs raised by
the grub screw points will not prevent the
coupling from coming off the shaft as they will
lie on the flat (clear of the bore) and not on the
circumference; grub screws fixed directly on
to shafts can be a great nuisance when trying
to disassemble.

Other methods of coupling are lengths of
plastic tubing, (suitable for low power),
springs, bent shaft ends, dogs and slots – the
list is endless and only exhausted when the
ingenuity of the modeller fails. See **Fig 229**.

PROPELLERS
These are fairly difficult to make and often
become the only bought fittings on the model.

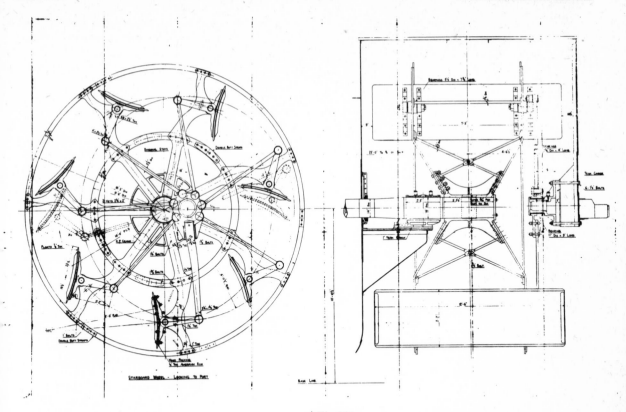

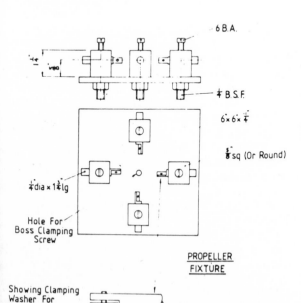

▲Fig 231
Working drawing of a paddle wheel with feathering floats. The diameter of the outer rim is 18ft 3in. The pcd (pitch circle diameter) of the centre of the floats is 14ft. Each float is 12ft 6in long by 3ft 7in wide, and the face of the float has a radius of 7ft. The diameter of the paddle shaft is 14in, increasing to 16in in way of the paddle wheel and its bearing. The centre of the paddle shaft is approximately 3ft 9in above the vessel's load waterline. The centre of the stub shaft on the sponson carrying the eccentric is 1in above and 18in forward of the centre of the paddle shaft.

◀Fig 232
Propeller jig. The dimensions are suitable for average-size propellers.

The range of plastic moulded propellers now available is large and their shape is probably superior to anything that can be produced by the average model shipwright. Most commercially available metal propellers are now fabricated, usually from brass, and the shape, form and set of the blades, etc can leave a lot to be desired. I have known propellers of this type being so misshapen that the blade tips were set at what amounted to a negative angle of attack, thus offsetting any thrust being

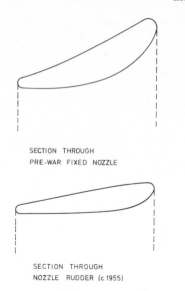

SECTION THROUGH
PRE-WAR FIXED NOZZLE

SECTION THROUGH
NOZZLE RUDDER (c.1955)

Fig 233 ▲
Section through two types of Kort nozzle rings. These show the developments which have taken place over the years. *Prepared from data supplied by the Kort Propulsion Co Ltd*

◀**Fig 234**
A Downton pump.

◀**Fig 235**
Two Deluge pumps.

Fig 236 ▼
Multiple pumps of the plunger type.

developed by the other portions of the blade!

Of course the problem of size, type, pitch, etc can be tackled mathematically, and allowing for a certain degree of applied rule of thumb such calculations can supply the answer. However, I have yet to meet any modellers who actually work out pitch etc in this way. The usual method is to see what others are using, what was used the last time, and then carry out a few tests. The bollard pull tests already described are a good help in this instance; these can be combined with current consumption trials and carried out in the bathroom. In this way the right size and type of propeller can usually be deduced fairly quickly with, among other things, a reasonable battery life.

Following these tests, free-running on the water will almost certainly be a success, although a little adjustment of ballast will probably be required. It is almost impossible to trim a model absolutely satisfactorily in the bath, since the model cannot be sighted as well as when on the pond, and the tendency is to end up a little down by the head or stern. Thus it is advisable to have some of the ballast so arranged that it can be moved around the hull to make these final adjustments. It is also a good idea to standardise on propeller and shaft diameters and the method of fitting. This allows propellers to be swapped about easily between models for preliminary testing and the like.

PROPELLER MANUFACTURE

If you are set on making your own propellers, whether it be as a matter of pride that everything has been made by yourself, or so that you can have the size and type you want rather than accepting what is available, it is not too difficult. Basically the problem is making (usually turning) a boss, making the blades and fitting the components together.

Silver-soldering is to be preferred if the model is to be a working one, but if the blades are fitted, as they should be, into slots cut in the boss, then even soft soldering can be satisfactory. Some sort of fixture is helpful, not only to hold all the parts in the correct relationship for soldering, but to check for angle, pitch, etc. An illustration of such a fixture is seen in **Fig 232**. It can be made universal, to take two, three or four blades, and be large enough for anything likely to be required. Thus it can be used over and over again, and is therefore well worth the time invested in making it.

KORT PROPULSION

The nozzle which has come to be known as the Kort nozzle was discovered by accident. Around 1930 the German authorities, concerned at the erosion of the sides and bottom of canals, asked for a guard to be fitted around the propellers of the large and powerful tugs using these waterways. So a shroud was fitted, and in order to reduce drag it was given a streamlined cross-section to reduce resistance. Not only did the experiment prove successful, but it was noticed also that there was an increase in performance. Subsequently this was investigated, and from the results obtained have been developed the nozzle and nozzle rudder in use today.

In its simplest form the nozzle can be described as a rectangular aerofoil rolled in a ring with the upper part of the wing on the inside. The propeller works within the ring. The technicalities of the subject are beyond the scope of this book, but the outcome of the interaction of the various resulting forces and pressures is an increase in pull while the actual propeller thrust is smaller.

Fig 233 shows a typical cross-section through a ring. Although the illustration is of a nozzle rudder, the fixed nozzle is generally similar, except that the connection to the hull takes the form of a fabricated structure in place of the rudder stock coupling seen in **Fig 221**.

Pumps

Hand-operated pumps of various types were fitted on board sailing ships and other vessels. One of the most popular was the Downton pump. Bucket pumps of the Deluge design are operated by a long lever, the lower end of which can be seen in **Fig 235** where it is cranked to fit into the socket at the top of the rocker arm linked to the plunger. In multiple pumps of the plunger type – those illustrated in **Fig 236** are on board the *Cutty Sark* – the con-

necting rods were coupled to a simple crank-shaft operated by the large handwheel; they were often referred to as flywheel pumps.

Riveted Work

Many modellers are now simulating riveting on their models but care, coupled with some knowledge of what is being represented, is necessary. On all ships the size (diameter) and spacing of rivets is determined by a number of factors such as the thickness of the plates and sections being joined, their location in the ship's structure, and whether this requires watertight or oiltight work, or non-watertight work. For merchant work the required information is to be found in the classification society's rules. Warships are governed by Admiralty requirements, which in the main do not differ widely from merchant practices.

Fig 237(a) shows the form of rivet most commonly used in shipbuilding. The pan head is inside the ship and the point is hammered home into the countersink and left very slightly raised, thus presenting a nearly flush surface. It is not finished in the form of a conical point as in **Fig 237(b)**. The finished diameter of the point is about $1\frac{1}{2}$ times the diameter of the rivet shank. The other type of rivet sometimes seen is that shown in **Fig 237(d)**. It is much used for joining light (thin) metal, such as that for ventilator cowls, and conversely on those parts of the structure which require rivets of large diameter, when the job is done by means of special hydraulic machinery to ensure a tight closure. The place where this can be seen most often is on parts of the superstructure; in the

larger passenger liners particularly, such riveting was very prominent. On bar stems, bar keels and stern frames it was the practice to use rivets with countersunk heads and points as in **Fig 237(c)** the point being finished as in **Fig 237(a)**.

The simulation of rivet points by the application of a suitable medium via a hypodermic syringe with a broken-off needle must be carried out with care and circumspection. On fittings where the visible points, and heads as well where applicable, are of the snap form shown in **Fig 237(d)**, their inclusion can be justified, if properly done. But it is a moot point whether authenticity is enhanced, in many cases, by the addition of shell plating rivet points. In **Fig 248**, which is of a new vessel fitting out, and in some of the other illustrations, the rivet points can be seen quite clearly, but bear in mind that these are mainly close-up photographs. On the other hand they cannot be seen on the plating of the *Fishpool* in **Fig 245**. The builder of the model of the drifter *Ocean Raleigh*, **Fig 243**, has included the riveting, which is quoted as being in accordance with Lloyd's rules for the period (1917). It seems to come down to a question of comparative sizes and scales, and it must be apparent that there is more to the subject than just running a row of dots along the edge of a plate.

Rudders

On older vessels, sail and steam, rudders were usually of the single plate type, the blade being a single plate secured to the rudder stock by forged arms (see **Fig 238**). The thickness of the plate would be $\frac{3}{4}$in to 1in, depending on the

size of the ship. The arms could range from 3in wide and 2in thick tapering to $\frac{3}{4}$in at the blade tip for a 3in diameter stock, to 9in wide and 6in thick tapering to about 1in at the tip for a 14in diameter stock. As the illustration

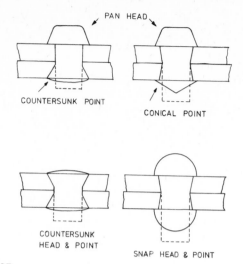

PAN HEAD

COUNTERSUNK POINT

CONICAL POINT

COUNTERSUNK
HEAD & POINT

SNAP HEAD & POINT

Fig 237
Various types of rivet head and point.

shows, the blade was narrow fore and aft and tall. Nowadays single-plate rudders are mainly found on small craft.

The next development was double-plate rudders, where all the supporting structure was sandwiched between two plates. Seen in cross-section from above, the sides of the rudder could be flat, with its shape tapering towards the after edge, or else curved to give a slightly streamlined form (**Fig 239**). Here again it is only the shape in elevation and cross-section that is the concern of the modeller, together of course with the gudgeons and rudder stock.

The rudders seen in **Figs 240** and **241** are of the semi-balanced type, that is, part of the blade is forward of the rudder stock centreline. The stock is attached to the blade by a coupling. This consists of a robust plate, either rectangular or circular, well secured to the top of the blade, often being incorporated in the blade

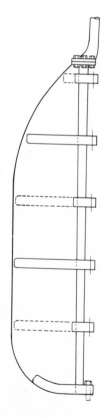

◀Fig 238
Typical arrangement of single-plate rudder, the blade secured to the rudder stock by forged arms.

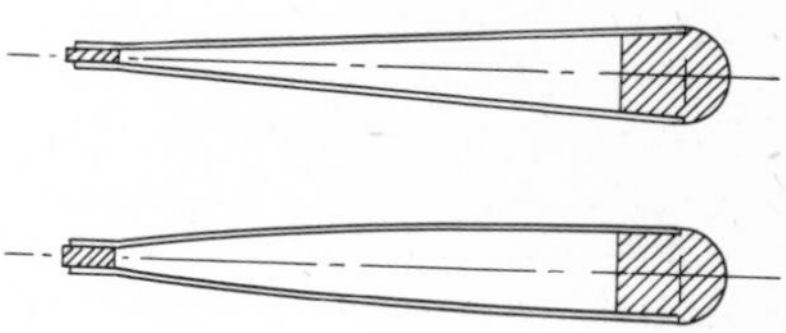

Fig 239 ▶
Section through blade of double-plate rudder showing general shape of flat and streamlined side plates.

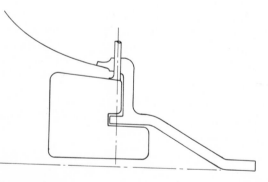

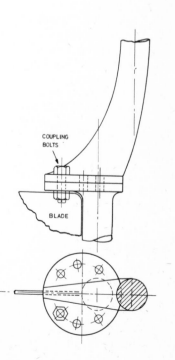

COUPLING
BOLTS

BLADE

Fig 240 ▲
Semi-balanced rudder. This design was much used for twin-screw vessels.

Fig 241 ▶
Horizontal type of rudder stock coupling.

forging or casting, with a plate of similar size on the lower end of the stock, the two being fastened together by heavy fitted bolts and nuts. The coupling was either horizontal or vertical. See **Fig 241** and **242**.

The diameter of the stock is based by the classification society rules on the blade area, the position of the centre of gravity of that area from the centre of the stock, and the speed of the vessel. The area of the blade is usually based on the area of the longitudinal middle line plane of the ship (to all intents and purposes the LBP × mean draught) divided by a variable factor. Values of this factor are quoted as lying between 37 and 50 for different types of warships, 60 for many passenger and cargo ships, and around 30 for small vessels requiring good and rapid manoeuvrability.

Multiple rudders are fitted to many types of shallow-draught craft, and twin rudders to a wide variety of vessels large and small, including the tanker *Batillus*, at the time of its completion in 1976 the largest ship in the world, 554,662 tonnes deadweight and 414.22m (1359ft) long overall.

To facilitate manoeuvering in restricted waterways some vessels, such as ferries, also have a bow rudder. This is designed to come within the line of the stem and is shaped to fair in with the hull lines in that area, with minimal clearance between the edge of the blade and the opening in the hull.

The amount of movement in rudders is normally limited to about 35° to either side of the fore and aft centreline of the ship. For hand-operated gear, stops are fitted to prevent the quadrant or tiller arm exceeding the approved angle. In mechanical gear the necessary limits are built into the machinery.

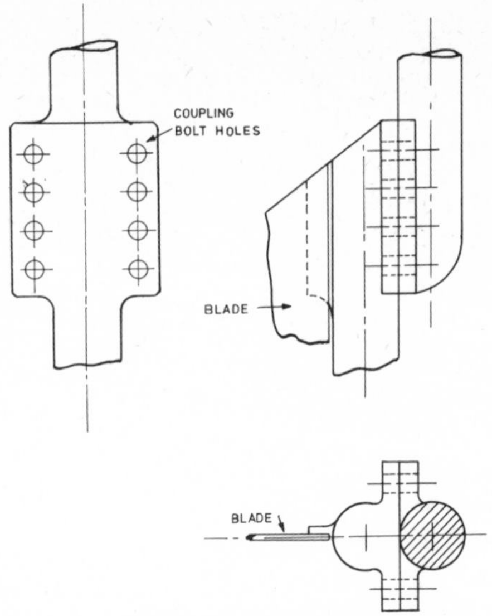

Fig 242
Vertical type of rudder stock coupling.

There is one other type of rudder which ought to be mentioned, the Kort rudder or steerable nozzle, a development of the Kort nozzle. An example of this is seen in **Fig 221**, and some notes about the Kort system will be found in the Propulsion section. Whereas the original nozzle was a ring fixed to the hull in way of the propeller, the steerable nozzle is a complete ring, attached to the rudder stock in the usual way and having a pintle on the underside into the heel of the stern frame. On the after part of the ring there is a vertical fin, rather like part of a rudder blade. Because of its efficiency the angular movement of the ring unit is limited to 25° to either side of the fore and aft centreline of the ship.

Shell Plating

'Shell plating' is the term used to denote the iron or steel plates which form the outer 'skin' of a ship's hull. There is no doubt that the inclusion of this plating on a hull of a model of a riveted ship adds to its appearance, finish and authenticity. This is well illustrated by the model of the drifter *Ocean Raleigh*, 1/48 scale,

by professional modelmaker M Darch, of Salcombe, Devon (**Fig 243**). Just how apparent this plating can be is seen in the photograph of the Harrison liner *Custodian* (**Fig 31**). Conversely its omission, accompanied as often as not by a high gloss finish on a very smooth hull surface, mars what is otherwise a good model.

Fig 243
The steam drifter *Ocean Raleigh*, 1/48 scale, 24in long, showing the realism imparted by the inclusion of the shell plating on the hull. *M Darch*

Fig 244
Butt joint symbol.

Fig 245▶
The bow of the steamer *Fishpool* showing the shell plates flanged and riveted to the stem bar. The strakes of plating and the plate end laps are very prominent. *Author's Collection*

The plate line body plan, **Fig 210**, shows the run of the strakes of plating and their extent, while the position of the plates in each strake, together with their thickness, and at times the size of the plate from which they are to be cut, is found on the shell expansion plan, **Fig 209**. Remember that this plan does not show the true shape of a plate. This can be obtained by marking out the run of each strake and the position of each plate on the model and tracing the outline of a plate on to tracing paper held against the model. When the paper is flattened out it will show the expanded shape of that plate. This method is not applicable when a

Fig 246
There is much of interest to the modeller in this
photograph of the launch of the 115,250 tons
deadweight Shell tanker *Nacella*, with a length of 870ft
and beam of 138ft. The 'ripple' effect on the shell
plating is particularly noticeable, as are the welded
seams. The run of the strakes and panel construction
are clearly visible, and note the presence of a stealer
plate in the second strake above the port fore poppet,
just below the white painted letters 'WB' on the hull
and running up to the bulb on the forefoot. The latter
is a good example of one of the many shapes of
bulbous bow, the figures in the foreground giving a
good impression of its size.

There are a couple of other interesting points worth
noticing: the width of the standing ways and the
relatively small size of the fore poppets, with the keel
blocks in between the ways, and the heavy wire ropes
shackled to lugs on the shell plating and connected
with the heaps of drag chains lying against the side
wall of the berth. The light lines holding up these
wires will snap as soon as the weight first comes on the
drags. Other light lines connect with the fore poppets
to secure them when they float free after the vessel has
entered the water. *Conway Picture Library*

Fig 247
The curved stem of the four-masted barque *Olivebank*.
Note the stowage of the anchor with its fixed stock.

Fig 248
An example of a rolled-plate stem which tapers down to join on to a solid bar stem. This photograph was taken in 1948 while the *Karanja* was still being fitted out prior to being handed over to the owners, the British India Steam Navigation Co Ltd; the rivet points are visible both on the stem plate and the adjacent shell plating. *Conway Picture Library*

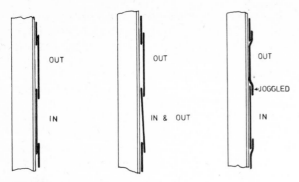

Fig 249
Different methods of arranging the strakes of shell plating.

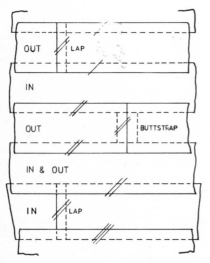

Fig 250
Diagrammatic arrangement of shell seams, end lap and butt. The diagonal strokes indicate the number of rows of rivets.

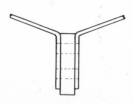

Fig 251
Flanging of shell plates to bar stem or bar keel.

plate has a lot of curvature. The example of a shell expansion plan in **Fig 209**, though for a small tug, is typical, and the information shown is characteristic of that found on such plans.

On riveted ships the long sides of the plates were overlapped and referred to as seams, and the ends were either lapped or else butted, in which latter case they were joined by a covering plate, known as a buttstrap, fitted internally. Laps and seams were either plain or joggled, and strakes either 'in' or 'out', or sometimes 'in and out', as shown in **Fig 249**. On a shell expansion plan the customary method of indicating the strakes of plating is shown in **Fig 250**. Remember that these plans are drawn as if looking at the ship from the outside. The visible, or sight, edge of a plate is indicated by a solid line, the hidden edge by a broken line. Where two plates are butted, the butt or meeting point is shown by a full line and the internal buttstrap by a broken line each side of the full one, their distance apart indicating the width of the buttstrap. Short diagonal strokes across a seam or butt are used to indicate the number of rows of rivets, while a butt joint is also indicated by the symbol given in **Fig 244**. The width of each seam is shown, but unless the edges of the outer strakes are joggled this does not really concern the modeller.

On welded hulls the shell plates are butted on all edges, only the slightly raised surface of the weld being visible. Whilst this should result in a fairly smooth surface, the shell plating invariably has a marked ripple appearance, or concavity, between the frames, as in **Fig 246**.

Before the introduction of the soft-nose, or rolled-plate, stem the shell plating was flanged and riveted to the stem bar, as in **Fig 251**. In section this could range from about 6in × 1¾in in a 200ft vessel to something like 12in × 4½in in a passenger liner. The bar was usually carried above the level of the forecastle or weather deck, where a bulwark or short plate, often referred to as a spirket plate, was attached to it, as in **Fig 245**. Where a vessel had a curved stem, like that of the four-masted barque *Olivebank* shown in **Fig 247**, the bar ran round to join the bow structure under the figurehead. A soft-nose plate stem incorporating a short bulwark can be seen in **Fig 248**.

Where a vessel had a flat plate keel and a bar stem, either the foot of the stem bar was forged into the shape of the hull in the region of the after end of the rise of the forefoot, with the forward end of the forward keel plate lapped on to it, or the forward keel plate(s) was shaped into a tapering trough to accept the end of the stem bar. In ships with a bar keel in place of a flat plate keel the bottom plate on each side, *ie* the garboard strake, was flanged to the bar and riveted to it, as in **Fig 251**. This bar was more or less an extension of the stem bar, to which it was scarphed, but was some 15 per cent greater in cross-section.

The strakes of plating on a model can be represented by using material such as cartridge paper, old litho plates and gummed paper. If the seams are joggled, remember to check their width. Butts can be represented by a shallow score to simulate the indent made by the caulking tool. The extent and the thickness of the shell plates were governed by several factors. These included the size, type and service of the vessel, the requirements of the classification society and of the owner, the position of the plate on the hull, and in the early days of iron and steel production the actual size of plates which the rolling mills could turn out. The thickness can range from $\frac{1}{4}$in for small craft to over 1in for vessels up to about 500ft length, depending on their size. The only way to ascertain the correct scantlings is to see the shell expansion plan of the prototype, or to get hold of one for a very similar class of ship.

Sources of Information

Shipowners, if approached in the right way, are often sympathetic towards the model-maker, and so too at times are shipbuilders, though they will generally require an owner's permission before supplying plans of a recent ship. Nowadays, too, they will almost certainly make a charge for any prints provided. With so many shipyards having closed down over the past hundred years a very large number of invaluable records have been irretrievably lost (destroyed is the word that ought to be used), and it is only very recently that steps have been taken to try to ensure that such records are preserved when yards go out of business and close down. Although much has been lost, much is still available. The National Maritime Museum at Greenwich, for example, has a collection of many thousands of ship plans, covering vessels of all types and many nationalities from about 1700 onwards. Similar institutions elsewhere in this country and overseas also have plans collections. It is usually possible to obtain prints of the majority of the plans held; however, these are not cheap, and delivery can be protracted. The special plans for model-makers are marketed by a number of commercial organisations and individuals, and the names and addresses of a number of these will be found elsewhere in this book. As mentioned earlier, technical journals are a useful source of plans of steamers and small craft, and the principal ones are also listed elsewhere.

Many museums possess very comprehensive photographic libraries, as well as art collections covering the years before the advent of the camera. Other sources of photographs are the Naval Records branches, the Ministry of Defence, the commercial firms specialising in ship photography and, to a more limited extent, the picture agencies and the newspaper picture libraries. The classified advertisements in such periodicals as *Sea Breezes* and *Ships Monthly*, to mention but two, are useful guides to the smaller firms and individuals selling ship photographs. Similar magazines exist in most European and major overseas countries. Some of the technical journals referred to earlier are no longer published, but back volumes of these, and of back issues of the current ones, can be found in the specialist reference libraries, and also in the libraries of the appropriate technical societies. In most cases they can be viewed by appointment, though it may be necessary to indicate beforehand the precise issues which are required. It is usually possible to order photocopies of the relevant articles.

Books can be of considerable help, either by way of the illustrations which they contain or their general content, or by providing statistical or technical data. Works can be found on just about every aspect of the ship – its history, design, construction, powering, working and appearance. There are volumes on ship models and on building ship models. Their diversity and numbers are very great, and some of those which are of interest and use to the beginner are included in the bibliography.

Much useful information can be gained from a visit to docks and harbours for a good look at the ships lying there. They may not be of the type being modelled, but just being able to see them, to look at the shape and construction of the hull, to examine deck fittings and superstructure detail, the cargo handling gear and the rigging is an invaluable experience. If you can use a camera (but make sure that photography is permitted in the area) then you will be able to compile a useful record for future reference. In some places there are ships which have been preserved for posterity, and a visit to these is always a very worthwhile experience.

There are quite a number of clubs and societies which cater for the interests of the ship modeller, and if it is possible to join one then do so. The interests of the members cover a wide field, and a great deal of help and advice is always available, so a beginner could well be saved much frustration, and possibly avoid making costly and irremedial mistakes through the timely help of fellow-members. All of which is, unfortunately, of no benefit to the many people who, through force of circumstance and domicile have to carry on by themselves, aided only by what they can learn from books, magazines and, perhaps, correspondence with fellow-enthusiasts.

Photographs such as that depicted in **Fig 252** are invaluable to a modelmaker for the amount of varied detail which they contain, and they will repay careful study. This particular one, which is of the foredeck of the British Railways' cross channel vessel *Maid of Orleans*, contains in that compact area examples of quite a number of the fittings referred to in this book. A fairly comprehensive run down of some of the salient features will make this point clear.

The first item of interest is the bulwark at the head of the stem which, unusually, has been cut down to allow the fitting of two single fairlead sheaves of the type shown in **Fig 101**. On deck abaft the jackstaff is a watertight hatch having a cover secured by toggle clips. The fairleads, of the three-roller type, are mounted on plate seats fitted over the waterway, as in **Fig 98**. The sheerstrake is carried above the edge of the deck in the usual way, and the guard rail stanchions have been attached to it

(**Fig 110**). The wood capping rail has been carried along the top edge of the bulwark. There is a wide waterway, wherein have been placed a number of Fyffe-type ventilators (see **Fig 298**). The bollards are of the standard pattern shown in **Fig 53**, and appear to be about 10–11in in diameter. Guide sheaves of the kind shown in **Fig 101** are set on strong supports attached to the breakwater, the construction of which should be noted. The two mechanical ventilating units are similar to those in **Fig 291**, but they have some additional fittings. A margin plank about 5in wide has been fitted in way of the breakwater, bollards and base of the windlass. Note how the deck planks, also about 5in wide, have been joggled into the one in way of the after pair of bollards. The electrically powered windlass has a drive to the forward capstan. The stud-link anchor cable can be seen in the cable stoppers set immediately abaft the hawsepipe openings in the deck. Just visible, too, are the cable relieving chains (with the devil's claws hooked on to each cable) and the rigging screws, each of which is shackled on to a lug on the windlass. A point to notice on the windlass warping ends, and also on the capstan barrels, is the fitting of flat bar strips to increase the grip on any rope being used. The after capstan is also electrically driven, and the control unit can be seen in the centre of the breakwater, with a stanchion carrying a deck light and a hanger for the ship's bell immediately forward of it.

These are the salient features of this photograph. A similar mass of useful data can be gained from photographs of other parts of a vessel, examples of which are to be seen among the illustrations in this book.

Fig 252
The forward deck of the British Railways cross-channel vessel *Maid of Orleans*. This ship was completed in 1949 by Wm Denny & Brothers Ltd, Dumbarton. The photograph shows the ship leaving Folkestone on its inaugural run to Boulogne on 22 June 1949. Plans of this vessel are in the Denny Collection in the National Maritime Museum, Greenwich, London. *Conway Picture Library*

Fig 253
The wheel of a sailing vessel, in this instance that of the steel ship *Grace Harwar*. The size of the wheel can be easily appreciated. The mechanism is within the cover. Note the helmsman's grating, and the construction of the cabin skylight. *Conway Picture Library*

Fig 254
A typical teak steering wheel for hand gear, with a strong cast pedestal frame supporting the spindle; the gypsy is within the box cover and the deckhouse.

Fig 255
A metal steering wheel and its pedestal, the latter incorporating a rudder tell-tale on the flat top. *S Lowry*

Fig 256
A typical guide sheave used in conjunction with rod and chain steering gear. The sheave is shaped to allow the links of the chain to lie in their natural position as they pass through, that is, the chain cannot twist. Note also the bulwark stanchion and the lugs riveted to the bulwark to take the shackles of the rigging screws of the mast shrouds. The waterway has been cemented.

Steering Gear

Leaving aside the purely mechanical aspects of fitting a working model with an operable rudder, in the main the only items of a ship's steering gear likely to be encountered by the modeller are the wheel and its immediate means of support and, in the case of hand gear, the rods, chains and sheaves, and any channels in which the rods and chains may run. All the mechanical parts of a vessel's steering gear are either below deck or hidden by a cover of some sort.

Many of the smaller craft favoured by modelmakers had hand gear and hence a wheel of quite robust proportions and construction. These wheels, usually made of teak, are fine pieces of work, and much of the detail can be seen in the photograph. The spokes are in one piece from handgrip to central hub. This hub is a casting, with square tapering sockets to take the squared ends of the spokes. It is bored and keywayed to take the end of the spindle of the steering gypsy, the securing nut being

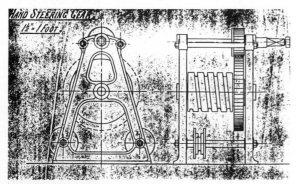

Fig 257
Side and end elevation of a gypsy for hand steering gear. As the chain comes off the barrel it is led round the sheave and so to the side of the wheelhouse. These sheaves are free to travel along the shafts on which they are mounted. The steering wheel is fitted to the (in this case square) end of the top shaft.

covered by the (brass) dome at the centre of the wheel. Shaped and moulded distance pieces between the spokes form the rim, on each face of which there is a brass band of flat rectangular sections. The spoke which lay at the top when the rudder was set amidships was often fitted with a metal cap on the tip of the handgrip, a useful guide if no rudder tell-tale was present. The wheels of powered steering gear were either less in diameter, or made of metal, as in **Fig 255**.

Some details of rod and chain gear can be seen in the photographs. In the wheelhouse would be a gypsy, usually quite a simple affair on the lines of that shown in **Fig 257**. The chain was led from the barrel of the gypsy, which was grooved to take four or five turns of chain, out through either side of the wheelhouse and aft to the rudder tiller arm or quadrant. Its path was chosen to avoid as many obstacles as possible without at the same time taking too many sharp bends. Where there was a straight run rods would be used. At bends, a sheave would be fitted and secured to the structure and a length of chain of just more than sufficient length to accommodate the movement from hard over to hard over would be incorporated in the run. The tiller arm or quadrant was invariably covered by boards or a protective grating, suitable supported. A typical sheave fitting is shown in **Fig 256**.

On sailing ships the wheel and steering mechanism were sited almost directly over the top of the rudder stock; on many, large double steering wheels were fitted.

Despite the reliability of power-operated steering mechanisms, ships were, and are, fitted with emergency steering gear. This was often of the hand type, and the wheel was invariably sited on the poop, or right aft on the main deck if there was no poop.

Superstructures and Deckhouses

In general terms the word superstructures, or the other much-used word upperworks, is taken to refer to those parts of the ship's struc-

ture which lie above the principal deck, though where the classification societies are concerned it does have a more specific definition in relation

Fig 258▶
The box-like form of the older type cargo ship's structure. Note the bridge wing shelters, or cabs as they are often called, and the awning rafters over the navigating bridge. In the foreground can be seen some of the wooden covers for the hatches, the two black 'discs' on each being the recessed handgrips. This photograph was taken while the *Mountpark* was fitting out at Greenock in 1938 for J & J Denholm Ltd, Glasgow.

▲Fig 259
A modern bridge structure, with forward sloping windows to the wheelhouse, the starboard steaming light incorporated in the end of the bridge wing with the screen painted black, the array of navigational aids on the top of the wheelhouse and the mast, the latter with D/F loop, radar scanners, aerials, signal gaff and the two masthead lamps. The boat is bright orange in colour with a dark green cover, and the lifebuoy bright yellow in this case. The under deck stiffening can be seen. The swinging-arm type boat davits are interesting, for davits of this pattern were first fitted on the Hamburg America liner *Imperator* in 1913, and on her two sister-ships, according to available records.

Fig 260▶
This shows the heavy stanchions or deck supports in way of gravity davit trackways, with lighter ones in between, all well bracketed at the top to the curtain plate of the deck over, and at the bottom to the side plating. The lighter type stanchions would also be fitted along the deck clear of the trackways, at about the same spacing. In the picture those to the left have been set back from the edge of the deck to provide stowage space for the accommodation ladder. The ship is the *Port Napier*, of the Port Line, preparing for her maiden voyage in 1947. *Conway Picture Library*

to the determination of a vessel's scantlings.

On larger vessels this superstructure can appear quite complex, but this impression may be due to the presence of so many fittings. When the arrangement plans are studied it will be seen that it is really a series of boxes of various shapes and sizes placed either on top of each other with a deck in between, or side by side; the outboard edges and ends of the deck may be open or may be closed either by a screen or by the side or end of a house.

The shape of each house is lifted from the plans, but the way in which they will be made must depend upon the modeller, the scale of the model, and the materials to be used. There are points to be borne in mind when building

deckhouses, for example the sheer of the deck in the case of long houses, and the camber of the decks for all houses, for the ends must have both the top and bottom edges shaped to that curve. Except in the case of very small scale models it is better to make the houses hollow since this makes the cutting of the camber and the sheer on the ends and sides of houses much easier. One method of forming the openings for the doors, windows and sidelights (portholes) is to face the sides and ends of the block with bristol board or plastic card in which the various openings have been cut. Those for the ports and windows will have to be glazed before the card is bonded to the house, the necessary framing being added afterwards. In the case

of houses having panelled sides and ends this can also be added afterwards, using wood shavings or very thin strips of veneer or other material. On many older vessels the upper edge of a deckhouse, whether of wood or steel construction, was finished with a heavy wood moulding, some examples of which can be seen in **Figs 261** and **262**. This was a prominent feature of the period and must not be omitted.

A look at these mouldings will show that the shape is composed of several concave and convex curves and a few straight or flat sections. For small-scale models the moulding can be made by the drawplate method, much used in the production of dowels. All that is needed is to make a hole in the drawplate having the

Fig 261▶
One of the wooden deckhouses on the RRS *Discovery*, giving some idea of general construction, including that of the panelled door. Note the rigol over the door, the grab rail, the height of the bottom of the door above the deck, and the tread strips on the deck. The patchy appearance of the exterior is due to weathering, and in time this will all be cleaned off and the surface refurbished.

Fig 262▼
Top edge moulding of a deckhouse. Although the house here is of wood construction, the moulding is typical of that on many steel houses. Sometimes the corner is made round instead of square as here.

Fig 263
Although the wheelhouse is steel, wood has been used for the frames and framework of the wheelhouse windows of this steam drifter. Note the wood capping rail beneath the windows on top of the steelwork. On the screen of the port steaming light the chock and the way the base of the screen is cut away for visibility from a low viewpoint are clearly seen.

cross-section of the moulding. This is accomplished with the aid of drills and needle files. In fact a whole range of moulding sections can be added: quadrant, half-round, convex, square and rectangular. As with making bamboo dowels, a strip of suitable wood is prepared just fractionally larger in cross-section than the overall dimensions of the moulding to be made, and one end is tapered down over about $\frac{1}{2}$in length so that it will pass easily through the hole. With the drawplate held firmly in a vice, and with the hole just clear of the jaws (too far away and the plate might possibly bend), the tapered end is passed through the hole and gripped firmly by a pair of strong pliers, and the strip is pulled steadily through the hole without stopping.

Much can be learned about the make-up of superstructures and deckhouses by looking at photographs. Such is the variety of arrangements that it has only been possible to include a few typical examples, the salient features of which are covered by the captions. Further

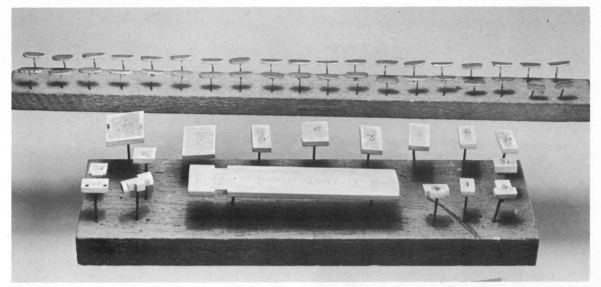

Fig 264
Some, but not all, of the deckhouses for a 1/1200 scale
model of the Cunard liner *Carinthia* (1927); there are a
couple of long ones not shown here. Behind are the
lifeboats for the same model, all made by the pointed-
stick method described in the book. Actually the ship
carried 34 boats, but it is always best to make a few
spares.

Fig 265
Another form of deckhouse, the steel engine and boiler
casing of a steam drifter. Note the access door and
other fittings, and also the small skylight under the
forefoot of the ship's boat. The rod and chain element
of the steering gear can be seen running in the channel
trough from the side of the wheelhouse to the after end
of the casing at deck level, where it passes under a
sheave to run aft along the deck to the stern.

examples will be found among the other illustrations. **Fig 5**, for example, shows some
simple, clean deckhouses, while in contrast **Fig
264** is of most, but not all (there are two more
long ones), of the deckhouses for a 1/1200 scale
model of the Cunard liner *Carinthia* (1927).
Fig 283 gives a good idea of the type of panelled
houses found on many of the liners built in the
latter part of the last century.

Reference was made earlier to overhanging
decks. These are the decks over the superstructure houses which are carried out to the line
of the ship's side as in **Fig 260**. The edge of
the deck is covered by a narrow vertical plate

generally referred to as a curtain plate. The
deck is supported by stanchions, usually of
T-bar or angle section – the scantlings of these
depending upon their spacing – secured at
either end to the adjacent steelwork by
triangular-shaped brackets. With the advent
of gravity davits it became the practice to fit
below each trackway a stanchion of considerably increased size, taking the form of a plate
up to about 18in wide, bracketed at top and
bottom and suitably stiffened on the inboard
side; see again **Fig 260**. Lighter stanchions
were fitted between the heavier ones. This
stiffening of the edge of an overhanging deck

◀Fig 266
A simple deckhouse of the type often referred to as a masthouse. The derrick heel fittings have been placed on the top at the corners, and the whole structure is quite light because the derricks have only a capacity of some 3–5 tons. Note the stowage of the two spare propellers; one right-hand and one left-hand unit indicate that it is a twin-screw ship. Heavy cleats are fitted to the deckhouse to take the free ends of the various rigging lines and tackles.

Fig 267 ▼
A deckhouse used as a platform for cargo winches, a common practice since it keeps these pieces of equipment out of the way, leaving the deck space available for other purposes. Note the conical tops to the derrick supports, here used as ventilators.

◀Fig 268
Good examples of wood companion, skylight and small after deckhouse, showing panelling and other uses of mouldings.

◀Fig 269
A small wood companionway with a pair of doors and a sliding top cover. The cover is secured by a hasp and padlock to the doors to prevent unauthorised entry.

Fig 270
Engine-room skylights and casing, one of the many ▶ forms these can take. Note the long leaf to each of the hinges. Sometimes the edge of the lid is flanged to fit over the frame to prevent the entry of water, and sometimes a flat bar frame, or an angle bar frame, is fitted on the underside of the lid, as here, to go over that on the casing.

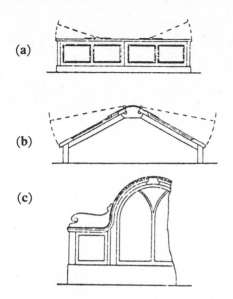

Fig 271
Various types of skylight. (a) flat-roof; (b) sloping-roof;
(c) dome-roof.

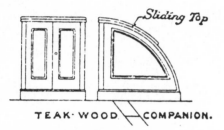

Fig 272
Wood companion with sliding top and two hinged
doors.

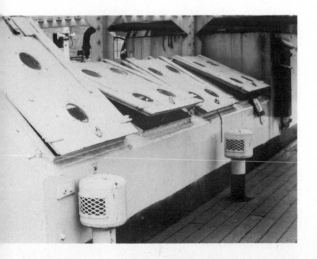

was continued athwartships as well, as was the
fitting of supporting stanchions. These overhanging decks provided promenade or open
deck spaces, protected on the outboard side by
rails or bulwarks. On some ships part of this
space would be given full protection from the
elements by being plated in along the vessel's
side to the full 'tween deck height, light being
provided by large glass windows. A model of
such a ship should be built in a similar way,
except that it may be easier to cut the window
openings in the screen material and glaze them
before fixing it in position. To make this open
area solid and represent the windows by
painted rectangles (except possibly in the case
of some miniatures) is, and looks, all wrong.
The curved, sometimes highly curved, structures found on many of the modern liners as
well as some cargo vessels, can present some
problems in reproduction, and are one of the
instances where the method of moulding plastic
sheet over a former can make the job a lot
easier.

Tankers

Oil tankers are not a type of ship which holds
much interest for modelmakers. Quite apart
from the functional aspect of their appearance,
the complex array of pipelines with their supports, the fore and aft gangway, the oiltight
hatches, the numerous valves and other fittings
which occupy most of the deck space forward
of the superstructure must act as a deterrent.
Although the illustrations are of large or very
large vessels, the situation is very similar on
the smaller ships. The after end is little different for the modelmaker than that of any
average merchant ship, though on larger vessels
the fore end equipment may be slightly more
complex.

Timbers

Such is the variety of timbers now available
that the selection of one or more suitable for
a ship model could appear to present something

◀**Fig 273**
The *Universe Ireland* at the time of her completion in 1968 was the largest ship in the world, having a deadweight capacity of 331,825 tonnes and an overall length of 1132.78ft (345.3m). There is nothing complicated about the superstructure or any of the fittings at the after end. In fact this photograph shows quite a number of interesting features, such as the combined mooring winch and windlass for the stern anchor, with two more mooring winches nearby, and the various outlets at the top of the twin funnels. *Conway Picture Library*

Fig 274 ▼
The complexity of the deck fittings is well seen in this photograph of the *Universe Ireland* running trials in Japan just prior to delivery to her owners. The stern view photograph was taken two months later at the end of her maiden voyage to Bantry Bay, Ireland, and it is interesting to note that in that two months some minor fittings as well as the boat davits have had the colour changed from black to white. *Conway Picture Library*

Fig 275
Some details of the fore and aft gangway and the crossover pipes and valves on a 45,000 tons deadweight tanker. *Author's Collection*

of a problem to those who have just taken up the pastime. However, the experience of others has shown that there are a number of timbers which are well suited for the job. Some details of these and other timbers are given in the accompanying list.

When considering the matter of which wood to use, there are a number of points to be borne in mind. First and foremost it must be well seasoned: to use an unseasoned wood can only lead to trouble. It should be a hardish wood which will work easily without rapid blunting of the tools (which should be kept sharp all the time as a matter of course), have a straight grain that is not too open, be able to retain sharp edges, and not be prone to splitting. The colour should not be too pronounced – it should be neutral in fact – and it should be able to accept paint and glue readily. Some timbers do not do so because of their oily or resinous characteristics.

Although they have been included in the following list, there are some timbers which are suitable only for some aspects of ship-modelling. Among these are oak, beech, teak and mahogany. Some of the more readily obtainable firs and pines (deals), which have not been included because they have varying grain and many knots, can, however, be used for plugs and cores for hulls. Balsa has little or no place in most aspects of scale ship modelling. Obechi, though a popular wood, is one which quickly blunts the cutting tools, and the need to fill its prominent and open grain is another disadvantage.

Holly, box and a number of other woods can only be obtained in small, or comparatively small sections; they are very useful for small fittings and small models. Jelutong, Yellow Poplar, Western Red Cedar, British Columbia Pine, and some of the other pines if carefully selected, can be used for 'bread-and-butter' hulls and solid block hulls, but Parana Pine, though readily available in temptingly wide planks, should be avoided as it splits readily and is not too stable.

Lime is undoubtedly the best all-round wood for the ship modeller, and it has the added advantage of being available in large as well as small sizes. Apple and pear have proved very useful for many special purposes, as have hornbeam, sycamore and satin walnut. Sitka spruce and degame are ideal for masts.

But whatever is said about timber, the final choice as often as not for many modellers is dictated by availability and price. Many of the timbers listed are not cheap to buy. Much is said about old furniture and other wooden objects being sources of supply, and they should not be decried for it is possible to obtain good seasoned material by this means. Do not neglect such mundane items as old tool chests or boxes, even old kitchen equipment, while many 'tourist souvenirs' often contain useful supplies of bamboo or other hardwoods. In fact once you start looking around, the possible sources of supply are surprising.

Apple (*Malus sylvestris*). A pale to medium pinkish-brown hardwood, fine and even in texture. It is about the best wood for bending, is very resistant to splitting, and turns and carves well.

Balsa (*Ochroma pyramidale*). A straight-grained, coarse textured, white to pinkish-white hardwood which is, in fact very soft, very light in weight, with a tendency to crumble at the edges. Very sharp tools are needed to work it, and it also has very poor nail- and screw-holding qualities, though it glues well. It does have certain uses in some branches of ship modelling, but cannot be considered a general-purpose wood.

Beech (*Fagus sylvatica*). White or pale brown in colour with a distinctive fleck, this hardwood is straight-grained and of good texture. It bends and turns well, but it can be rather brittle, and has a tendency to move in conditions of varying humidity.

Boxwood (*Buxus sempervirens*). This is the true boxwood, though the name boxwood is used for a number of similar woods. It is a very fine textured hardwood, excellent for turning and carving, but requires very sharp tools. From the modelmakers' point of view its strong distinctive yellow colour is sometimes found to be something of a drawback. It is not too easy to obtain, particularly in pieces of any size, and it is expensive. Maraicabo Boxwood (*Gossypiospermum praecox*) or Zapatero is not a true box botanically, but it has the qualities of that timber. It is paler in colour, not quite so hard, and tends to split more easily. Other closely related boxwoods are *B. macowani*, or Cape Box, and *B. balearica*, or Balearic Boxwood. *Gonioma kamassi*, or Kynsna Boxwood, though not a member of the true boxwood family, makes a good substitute. It is light yellow to brown in colour and works and finishes well.

Cedar. The true cedars, Atlantic or Atlas, Deodar and Lebanon (*Cedrus atlantica, C. deodar, C. libani*) are light brown coloured softwoods which work well, though *C. deodar* has a high oil content and an unpleasant smell. Many timbers referred to as cedars come from different families and are not true cedars, but in their way have a number of similar characteristics and properties.

Holly (*Ilex aquifolium*). This is a white to grey-white hardwood. Its close grain is straight, but can be irregular in which case it may create some difficulties in working. Nevertheless it is ideal for carving and for making small fittings, and it finishes well. Sharp tools are necessary.

Hornbeam (*Carpinus betulus*). A dense, fine-textured, white hardwood. The grain can be irregular at times. It turns well, takes a very good finish, and can be cut to very small scantlings.

Jelutong (*Dyera costulata*). A white to straw-coloured softwood noted for its fine, even texture and straight grain. It cuts easily and carves to give fine detail with excellent retention of edges. It has virtually replaced yellow pine (*Pinus strobus*) as the wood used by pattern-makers. Small latex-trace horizontal cavities will almost certainly be found at times when cutting into the wood. These are a feature of this timber.

Lancewood (*Oxandra lanceolata*). A pale creamy hardwood, very evenly textured and with a straight grain. The heartwood is dark, so preference is given to the pale creamy sapwood. It is ideal for masts and spars, but it is difficult to obtain. Much of what is called lancewood today is in fact degame (*Calycophyllum candidissimum*), another type of lancewood known as lemonwood in America; it has almost identical characteristics and is a quite satisfactory substitute.

Larch (*Larix europa*). A pale to medium brown softwood with pronounced growth rings. A hard, tough wood, it is the traditional timber for boat planking.

Lime (*Tilia vulgaris*). In America the timber of *T. americana* closely resembles European lime and is known as basswood; basswood is also the name given in some places to the wood of *Liliodendron tulipifera* or American Whitewood (Yellow Poplar, *qv*). It is a pale, almost white softwood with a straight grain and a fine and uniform texture. It is an ideal wood for carving, for cutting to very small scantlings, and has the ability to retain very sharp edges, and to bend; it finishes with a very smooth surface. In all it is perhaps the best all-round wood for a ship modeller.

Mahogany (*Swietenia macrophylla*). This is the American mahogany and is designated Honduras, Brazilian, Peruvian, etc from the country of its origin. A medium to deep red-brown coloured hardwood, it works easily, though it has a tendency to be brittle, and takes a superb finish. Having too pronounced and open a grain for many modelling purposes, it nevertheless has a place on large scale models of such vessels as open pleasure launches.

Maple. In America *Acer saccharum* is known as Rock Maple or Hard Maple and *A. saccharinum* as Soft Maple. Their properties, apart from certain more technical attributes, are much the same as those of sycamore.

Oak (*Quercus robur*). This is the traditional English oak, long the principal timber used in the construction of ships in this country. However, its coarse texture and prominent markings make it unsuitable for many aspects of ship modelling.

Obechi (*Triplochiton scleroxylon*). Although classified as a hardwood it is very light in weight, and has a pale straw colour. It works and finishes well when very sharp tools are used, but end grain surfaces have a tendency to crumble when being cut. The texture is coarse, and care is needed when using a filler.

Pear (*Pyrus communis*). This is a pale brown hardwood which can be used unpainted to represent mahogany. It is hard to split, finer in texture than apple and with a straight grain in

good pieces; it takes a fine finish and turns well. It has a slight blunting effect on tools, but cuts well.

Pine. One of the leading reference books lists 17 timbers with the name 'pine', but of these only 12 are true pines. A softwood which is generally easy to work, the characteristics of the different types vary considerably, making some of little use to modelmakers. Those that are of use are Western White Pine (*Pinus monticola*) and British Columbian Pine or Douglas Fir (*Pseudotsuga taxifolia*).

Plywoods. Contrary to what is often thought, good quality waterproof or resin-bonded plywoods do have a number of uses in ship modelling. Some care should be exercised when selecting such material.

Satin Walnut (*Liquidambar styraciflua*). Better known as American Red Gum, and classified as a hardwood. Actually Satin Walnut is the name given to the brown to reddish-brown heartwood of the tree, while the white sapwood is referred to as Hazel Pine. Both have a close texture, irregular grain and a silky surface.

Satinwood (*Fagara flava*). This is the West Indian satinwood, which is generally considered better than the similar related woods from other areas. In colour this softwood ranges from cream to golden yellow, and it has a bright, satiny sheen when finished. It has a fine uniform texture, but an irregular grain; nevertheless, it turns and finishes well. There is a slight chance that the fine dust created when working this wood may cause a slight irritation of the skin.

Spruce. Varieties are Canadian or White Spruce (*Picea glauca*) and Sitka or Silver Spruce (*P. sitchensis*). It is a softwood, creamy white to pale yellow in colour, fine and uniform in texture. It has a straight grain, thus making it very useful for masts and spars. It works and finishes well. In Europe it is sometimes called Whitewood (*qv*).

Sycamore (*Acer pseudoplatanus*). This *acer* is called maple in Europe, being of the same genus as the trees providing the maple. It is a pale coloured hardwood, usually straight-grained, though at times some samples are found with a wavy grain. It has a fine, even texture, cuts cleanly and takes a good finish. Sharp tools are needed, and it is a wood that is used quite widely by many modelmakers.

Teak (*Tectona grandis*). Another hardwood much used for shipbuilding. It is light golden brown in colour, with darker streaks. Though the grain is straight it is also coarse, which makes it unsuitable for all but very specialised modelmaking purposes, and its abrasive nature is very hard on tool edges. Apart from its lack of suitability for most model work it is an outstanding timber. Quite a number of woods are called teak, but the only genuine teak, *T. grandis,* is that which comes from Burma.

Walnut (*Juglans regia*). This is the European walnut, and *J. nigra* is the American walnut. The former is grey-brown with almost black streaks, while the latter is a uniform dark purple-brown. Somewhat coarse and open-grained from the modelmaker's point of view, it is a decorative hardwood and as such does have some limited uses in ship models. It is easy to work and turns well.

Western Red Cedar (*Thuja plicata*). A very straight grained, non-resinous, fine-textured softwood, varying in colour from pale pinkish-brown to dark brown. It works easily and can take a good finish. It is advisable to use only brass or copper screws for fastenings.

Whitebeam (*Sorbus aria*). This and rowan (*S. aucuparia*), being closely related to the apple, make useful substitutes for that wood. It is a tough, hard wood which, though it soon blunts cutting tools, turns and carves well and takes an excellent finish.

Whitewood (*Picea abies*). In Europe the wood of this tree is known as European Whitewood or Baltic Whitewood, and also as White Deal. It is a typical softwood, white to yellow-brown in colour, and it works well.

Yellow Pine (*Pinus strobus*). This pale yellow to light brown softwood with its fine even texture and straight grain is now very hard to acquire and very expensive. It was the mainstay of the patternmaker's industry for many years, and has now been replaced by jelutong (*qv*). In America it is known as Eastern White Pine.

Yellow Poplar (*Liriodendron tulipifera*). The American Whitewood. This softwood varies in colour from the white of the sapwood to the pale brown of the heartwood. It is straight-grained, with a fine even texture, and takes a smooth finish, but it does not bend easily.

Yew (*Taxus baccata*). Almost as hard as oak, though it is classed as a softwood. It is red-brown in colour with fairly visible growth rings. The texture is fine and even and the grain usually straight; it is a wood that does not bend easily.

Towhooks, Towing Gear

Tugs must, without doubt, be one of the most popular of ship prototypes for modelmakers. At the same time it is surprising how often the plans of such vessels supplied for modellers lack precise detail of the most essential piece of the tug's equipment, the towhook.

The designs for hooks vary widely to suit the many requirements of the different types of tug and the work it has to do. Many of the large tugs are fitted with towing winches, which are more suited to the nature of the work which they are called upon to perform.

Although modelmakers in the main do manage to produce reasonably true to type hooks, in spite of the aforementioned lack of detail, the one point on which many models lose points lies with the spring fitted to the hook. These are very solid, robust items, the diameter of the material of the spring depending on the load it is required to absorb. For example, a hook for a small 300bhp Thames barge towing tug is fitted with two springs each 11in long × 3in outside diameter, and the spring material is of $\frac{3}{4}$in diameter. With something like eleven coils in the length the gap between coils is little more than $\frac{1}{4}$in; it is able to take a load of some 3 tons or so. On ship- and barge-towing tugs the hook itself is usually of one of the two shapes illustrated. The manner in which it is mounted varies a great deal. In many instances it is fitted directly on to a casing; in others it is fitted with some form of spring shock-absorbing mechanism, and so mounted that it can swivel horizontally, and also lift in an upward direction. All hooks are fitted with some form of quick-release gear, hand-operated on the smaller tugs but mechanically operated on large tugs, either locally or

Fig 276
Two towhooks on a 1/24 scale model of the steam tug *George V* by Ken Watts. One is a spring towhook and the other a fixed hook. Both are shackled to a heavy round bar, on which they can move sideways, and the shackles also allow upward movement. Under the mid-point of each can be seen the strong support with a convex bar on its upper surface.

Fig 277
The two fixed hooks of the steam tug *Challenge*, showing how they are secured to the casing. On the further hook the quick-release arm has been tripped to show how the hook falls down to allow the towrope to pull free immediately. On the other hook it can be seen in the working position, with towrope in place.

from the wheelhouse. Details of the hand-operated gear can be seen in the illustrations. It is customary to provide some form of support, of robust construction, under hooks to take the weight, with a piece of half-round bar on top to act as a rubbing surface for the hook as it swivels.

Whereas on most tugs the hook is fitted somewhere just abaft midships, modellers will notice that on the type of tug referred to as a water tractor, because of its Voith Schneider method of propulsion, it has been found possible to place the hook right aft. The way these vessels move and manoeuvre is very different from that of the conventional tug.

Ventilators

The cowl ventilator shown in **Fig 287** is the commonest type found on board ship. It can range in size from some 6in in diameter (this is the diameter of the stem, not the cowl) to the massive 6ft 3in of those fitted to the first *Mauretania* – perhaps the most well-known cowl ventilators of all time. **Fig 282** shows a group of the smaller-size ventilators, and a couple of large ones can be seen in **Fig 284**. Over the years there has been some alteration

Fig 278
A spring towhook, showing the heavy coil spring, the material of which is square in cross-section. Note the closeness of the individual coils. When the pull comes on the hook, the hook and the body (the rectangular 'box' surrounding the spring) move aft, compressing the spring, the total amount of compression possible being shown by the length of the slot seen in the side of the body. The body slides along the heavy, square-section eyebolt which runs through the length of the spring, the eye being connected to a shackle (bottom left corner of photo) with the rectangular plate seen at the far end of the spring being secured to the end of the eyebolt. *S Lowry*

Fig 279
The action of this spring towhook is somewhat different from that of the hook shown in the photograph of the steam tug *George V*. As the pull comes on the hook the two cams open at the top and close at the bottom as the hook moves aft, thus compressing the spring and absorbing the shock. On the quick-release gear, there should be a pin through the hole at the top of the hook, to prevent the gear being released accidentally. To release the towrope this pin is removed, and the L-shaped handle knocked forward to bring its ringed end off the tip of the hook. This frees the lever on which this L-shaped lever is pivoted, and which in turn is holding the towhook in position. With the lock on the hook freed, the pull on the towrope causes the hook to pivot downwards and aft, thus releasing the towrope.

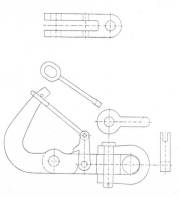

Fig 280
Arrangement of the 'Liverpool'-type towhook. The scantlings of the hook are made to suit its particular application.

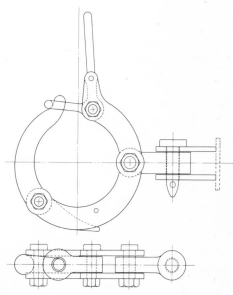

Fig 281
Arrangement of a circular-type towhook.

Fig 282▶
Some examples of the smaller size of cowl ventilators.
Fyffe-type ventilators can be seen just inside the rails.
The ship is the Lamport & Holt cargo vessel *Delius*
(1937).

Fig 283▼
A photograph showing the prominent rims of the
earlier type of cowl ventilator, a particularly interesting
shot for it shows the well-known Union liner *Scot*,
built by Denny of Dumbarton in 1891, in drydock at
Belfast for lengthening by 54ft by Harland & Wolff
Ltd in 1896. *Conway Picture Library*

in the shape of the cowl, the prominent flange
or rim seen in **Figs 283** and **288** and the bulbous
back to the cowl in **Fig 289** having disappeared.
The shape of cowl shown in **Fig 290** is found
on many foreign-built vessels.

The next most frequently seen type of ventilator has what is customarily referred to as
a 'mushroom top', and this top can take a
number of different forms, as can be seen in
Figs 166 and **284**, while **Fig 291** gives some
further details. This form of top can also be
seen on derrick posts (samson posts) used as
ventilators.

Mechanical ventilation equipment take
many forms, but it consists essentially of a
motor driving a fan set within a casing with,
for supply fans, an inlet for fresh air, and
trunking leading to distribution points within
the vessel. **Fig 285**, though of a small unit,
gives a good idea of the basic layout. The motor
is mounted on deck and the fan is in the circular
casing to which the motor is attached. **Fig 286**
shows another arrangement, while further
details of typical units can be seen in **Figs
292–294**. Because each installation has to be

built to suit the application and its position on
board ship, it is not really possible to include
any form of standard design. Certainly those
companies concerned with their construction
will have a series of standard motor and fan
units which they incorporate into the required
trunking and inlet/exhaust heads. The units
shown in the diagrams are intended to give the
modeller some idea of their composition. The
dimensions shown on the various diagrams are
correct for the units depicted, all of which are
of actual installations, but the sizes will differ
for other vessels. A good general arrangement
plan should offer some guidance to the appropriate layout and to the overall dimensions.

Fig 295 shows another type of ventilator
head, and this one, too, can be seen on the top
of derrick posts which act as ventilators. **Figs
296** and **297** are of small supply and exhaust
vents, and again the diameter of the stem will
be such as to suit the application. Examples of
the Fyffe ventilator shown in **Fig 298** can also
be seen inside the guard rails in **Fig 282**, while
the torpedo ventilator shown in **Fig 301** is
usually found on the side of deckhouses, as in

Fig 284 ▶
Typical mushroom ventilators and cowl ventilators.
The diameter of the large cowl ventilator in the
background is 42in for the stem and 75in for the cowl.
The ship is the *Beaverdell*, built by Lithgows Ltd, Port
Glasgow, in 1946 for the Canadian Pacific Railway Co
Ltd

Fig 285 ▼
Typical mechanical ventilation arrangement, showing
how the motor is connected to the fan casing. The ship
is the *Beaverdell*.

Fig 166. The goose- or swan-neck ventilator
illustrated in **Fig 299** can be found in various
forms and sizes on board ship. Certain regulations govern the height above deck of the
opening and the attachments which have to go
thereon.

The ways and means which modelmakers
have devised for producing cowl ventilators are
many and varied, ranging from moulding in
plastic wood, bending over the heads of large
nails, utilising (smokers') pipes, carving in
wood and so on. Quite apart from anything
else the presence of several different sizes, in
both height and diameter, on any one ship
limits ideas of mass production. The scale of
the model has a considerable bearing on the
means of fabrication. The builder of miniature
models can make use of fine wire, entomolog-
ical and other pins, with their heads turned
over close to the shank and the convex top filed
away, for the smaller ventilators. For the larger
ones the cowl can be made by cutting in half
a mustard or turnip seed, taking out the pith
and leave a hemispherical 'bowl', which is then
glued to a piece of dowel of appropriate diam-

Fig 286
Another example of mechanical ventilation, showing
how the vent trunk is supported by brackets to the
deck. The ship is the *Winchester*, built by Denny of
Dumbarton in 1947 for the Southern Railway
Company.

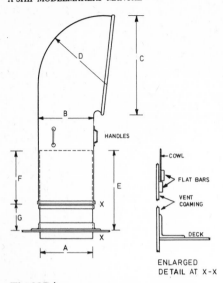

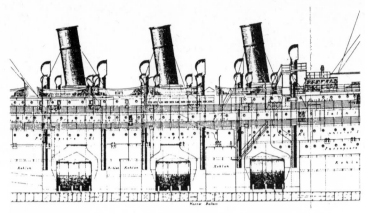

Fig 287 ▲
Cowl ventilator, with spigot (E) fastened to deck plating by an angle bar ring. A is the internal diameter of the spigot, and is the stated 'size' of the ventilator (9in, 24in, etc). B is A $+\frac{3}{4}$in approx to give free fit on the spigot. C varies from 1.8A to 2A. Radius D is 1.25A. The height E of the spigot is governed by classification society rules. F can vary between 6in and 2ft or more, depending on the requirement.

Fig 288 ▼
Two of the older shapes of cowl ventilator. That on the right was often seen on German North Atlantic liners and other vessels of the latter part of the last century. See also **Fig 289**.

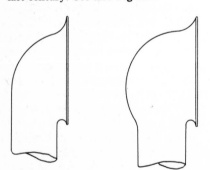

Fig 289 ▲
Part elevation of the Hamburg-America Line's *Furst Bismarck* (1891), showing the bulbous-back cowls illustrated in **Fig 288**.

Fig 290 ▶
Front elevation of the type of cowl found on many foreign-built ships.

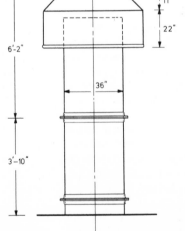

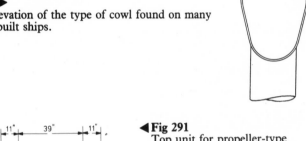

◀ Fig 291
Top unit for propeller-type exhaust fan. The 'propeller' is contained within the main part of the trunk.

eter representing the stem. Since there is quite a variation in the size of the individual seeds in any one packet, it is possible to select one of the correct diameter. Paint, carefully applied, can be used to smooth off and fill in the joint between husk and dowel.

The arrival of plastic or polystyrene card, and polystyrene extrusions, rod or tube, has made the production of cowl ventilators much easier. Rod of suitable diameter, and it is available in a considerable range of sizes, can be used for the stem, the end being trimmed off at an angle to suit the shape of the cowl. The cowl can be made by plug-moulding polystyrene card, which is available in sheets having an approximate size of 13in × 8$\frac{3}{4}$in

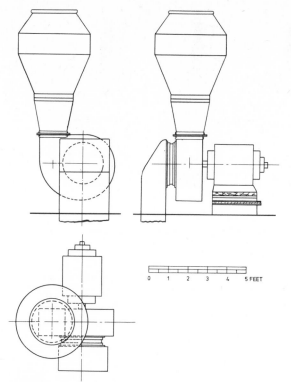

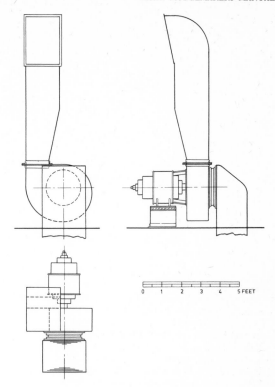

Fig 292
Arrangement for a mechanical exhaust fan; the motor
can be seen to the right in the right-hand elevation.
The top of the conical unit is open, though covered
with a wire mesh.

Fig 293
Another arrangement for an exhaust fan. The opening
in the top of the trunk would be covered with wire
mesh.

(335 × 220mm), and in thicknesses from
0.005in to 0.10in (about 0.012 to 2.5mm). The
technique of plug-moulding was described by
Roger Chesneau in *Model Shipwright* 33 (p66)
and the essential part of his article is reproduced here:

'The theory [of plug moulding] is simple: a
section of polystyrene card is warmed until it
becomes soft, and then a plug is thrust into the
softened portion which, when cool, assumes
the shape of the plug. In practice, there are a
number of fairly severe limitations involved in
the process – which, however, tend to become
less of a problem as one familiarises oneself
with it.

'The essential equipment required for
heat-moulding plastic card consists of nothing
more than a sheet of ⅛in balsa, a block of balsa
(the dimensions of which will be determined
by the size of the moulding to be produced),
a heat source such as a cooker ring, grill or
even an electric fire, and perhaps a length of

dowelling. The size of the plastic card used
will also vary according to the moulding
required; items requiring some measure of
structural strength will, of course, call for a
thicker card, and deeply drawn mouldings will
also demand a heavier gauge, for reasons which
will become apparent shortly. The usual
modelling tools will be needed, plus a few
drawing pins.

'. . . For the sake of example it can be
imagined that a 4.5in gunhouse is to be produced. The balsa block is first carved and
sanded to the correct size and shape, ignoring
all surface excrescences; once the required proportions have been achieved it is then necessary
to reduce the overall dimensions of the shape
to allow for the thickness of the plastic card
shell which will be moulded around it. A piece
of dowelling is then attached to the underside
to act as a handle. The plug – the so-called
'male' mould – is now complete.

'In order to exercise some control over the

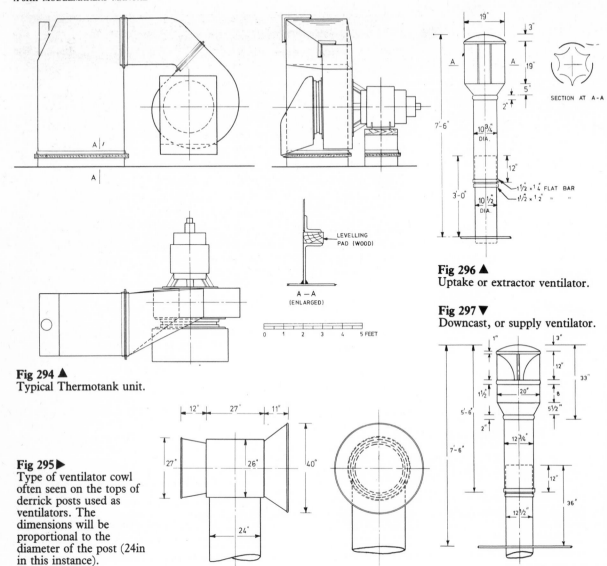

Fig 294 ▲
Typical Thermotank unit.

Fig 295 ▶
Type of ventilator cowl often seen on the tops of derrick posts used as ventilators. The dimensions will be proportional to the diameter of the post (24in in this instance).

SECTION AT A-A

LEVELLING PAD (WOOD)

A — A
(ENLARGED)

Fig 296 ▲
Uptake or extractor ventilator.

Fig 297 ▼
Downcast, or supply ventilator.

moulding process it is now necessary to produce a receptacle that will act both as a framework on which to mount the plastic card and as a template through which the plug may be guided. This 'female' mould is simply an aperture in the balsa sheet large enough for the plug to pass through, allowing an even clearance (again, the thickness of the card) all round; the sheet should be large enough to withstand the pressure to which it will be subjected during the moulding process, and the area of wood on one side should be generous enough to allow it to be held over the chosen heat source. The edges of the aperture should also be smoothed off to avoid any chance of 'snagging'.

'The plastic card – large enough to give a good $\frac{1}{2}$in to $\frac{3}{4}$in overlap all round the hole – is next pinned securely to the female mould, and the whole is held over the heat source, plastic card uppermost, until the card directly over the hole becomes soft. The mould is then withdrawn and the male plug pressed firmly through the receiving mould. When cool the plastic is unpinned and the excess trimmed away.

'. . . It is unlikely that the modeller attempting to plug-mould polystyrene sheet for the first time will get a satisfactory result. The principal difficulty is choosing the correct time to withdraw the female mould from the heat

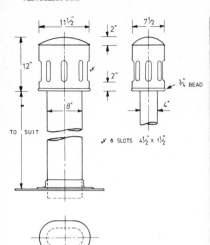

Fig 298 ▲
Fyffe ventilator.

Fig 299 ▼
A swan-neck, or gooseneck, ventilator.

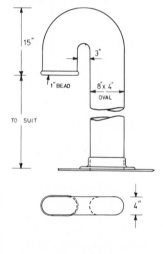

Fig 300 ▲
Alternative types of swan-neck ventilators. Note the two wood bungs for sealing the open ends of the ventilators.

Fig 301 ▼
Detail of a torpedo ventilator.

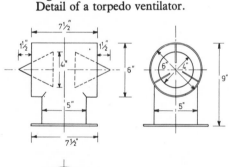

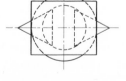

Fig 302 ▼
Plug moulding cowls. Top: dowel turned to size of cowl. Middle: female mould. Bottom: plastic sheet after moulding and before being trimmed. Right: dowel for cowls with deep flanged rim.

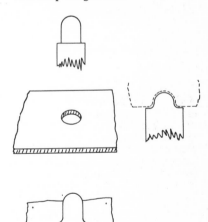

source and here, quite frankly, there is no substitute for experience. However, the moulds can be used again and again and plastic card is still relatively inexpensive.

''Webbing' is one side-effect which frequently manifests itself, and this occurs generally because the female mould is too large for its male counterpart; in this case a new female mould must be prepared. If the plastic is heated too much, stretching may be uneven, resulting in areas of thinness over the moulding. If a

particularly deep draw is required the walls of the moulding may end up so weak as to render the product unusable; thicker card will therefore be necessary. ('Undercutting' is not of course possible in any form of plug-moulding; where complex shapes are to be moulded, therefore, the item will have to be considered as two halves, or even several individual components, and treated accordingly.)'

The plug for a ventilator cowl can be made simply by rounding the end of a piece of dowel turned to the correct internal diameter (**Fig 302**). For cowls of the type shown in **Fig 288** the end of the dowel will have to be made to the shape shown in **Fig 302** and the edges of the female mould shaped to match the plug. Any beading round the rim of a cowl can be made of plastic rod, or stretched sprue, of the right diameter. By winding a length of this round the dowel plug a ring of the exact diameter, or shape, of the cowl will result, which can be secured in place with a touch of liquid cement.

If a larger and more robust mould is required this can be made from such material as car body filler. When putting it into a suitable receptacle choose one which will allow the top surface to be smoothed off. In this method the male plug initially will have to be made to the full external size of the cowl. After preparing the filler material, thoroughly wax the plug (candlewax is ideal) and press firmly into the soft mould and leave it to set. On withdrawing the plug reduce its overall size by the thickness of the plastic sheet to be used. In addition, round off the edges of the mould to reduce drag on the sheet. Some modellers, after thoroughly waxing the plug and the mould,

find it advisable to give the mould an initial warming before laying the plastic card in place to be heated. Once the card is sufficiently soft, the whole set-up is removed from the heat source – a cooker grill is ideal – and the plug firmly pressed home. After waiting a few moments plug and moulded sheet can be removed. A firm, level working surface will be found advantageous for this work. On larger scale models the top of the stem inside the cowl should be hollowed out: anyone peering into the vent should be able to see the way for the air to pass down to the decks below!

Plastic rod can be used to make mushroom ventilators, either by the use of discs, cut from rod of the right diameter, bonded to that used for the stem, or by heating the end of the stem rod to produce a lump which can be shaped, when cool, to form the desired ventilator top. Rod can also be used for the swan-neck ventilators and, if flattened to an oval section, for Fyffe ventilators.

All the ventilators mentioned are those found most frequently on board ship, but the modeller must not be surprised to encounter some other forms from time to time.

Fig 303
A typical arrangement of a small-capacity water tank.

Water Tanks

Tanks of all sizes, some cylindrical, some rectangular, were mounted on deck and on the tops of houses, being required for a number of shipboard services. The seating arrangement was usually on the lines of that shown in the illustration. In the majority of cases the associated pipework was on a more comprehensive scale than that shown in **Fig 303**.

Windlass

Fig 304 shows a type of windlass fitted to many of the smaller wood-built sailing ships. An examination of plans and photographs of such vessels shows that this was a fairly standard

Fig 304 ▲
The wood windlass on the schooner *Maud Mary*, photographed in Glasgow Docks about 1937–38.

Fig 305 ▼
The construction and operating mechanism of this sailing barge windlass can be seen clearly. Crank handles fit on to the squared end of the shaft through the small pinion (top left). The barge is the *Cambria*, one of the vessels in the Historic Ships Collection in St Katharine's Dock, London.

Fig 306 ▲
The pawl bitt from the fore side, showing the connecting rods from the crosshead to the traveller. This traveller is held to the purchase ratchet rim by the turned ends of the side members of the traveller. Inside the traveller are pawls which engage the teeth of the ratchet. As the operating lever is depressed, the whole traveller slides along the rim. On raising the lever the internal pawls at once engage with the ratchet, thus locking the traveller to the purchase rim. As the lever is raised higher the windlass barrel is turned. At the top of the stroke the brake pawls prevent back-run of the barrel, and as the lever is once more depressed the traveller moves back round the rim, ready for the next stroke. The same takes place on the other side of the bitt with the other traveller. This windlass is on the *Kathleen & May*.

◀Fig 307
The operating gear of a hand windlass. At the top are the crosshead and its bracket; the handles fit into the rectangular opening at each end of the crosshead. The two vertical rods connect to the purchase mechanism. Below the curved cross-beam are the brake pawls, attached to the after face of the pawl bitt and engaging with the central ratchet on the barrel. Either side of this are the purchase ratchets. Just above the cross-beam is the bracket for the ship's bell.

Fig 312▶
Small steam windlass with warping drums on extended shaft. This windlass can be operated by hand if required by means of the handles on the ends of the upper shaft carrying the small pinion. The vessel is the steam tug *Challenge*, one of the vessels in the Historic Ships Collection in St Katharine's Dock, London.

◀Fig 308
A typical hand-spike operated windlass. The model is of the Cowes (Isle of Wight) ketch *Bee*, built in 1801. The model was built by Alastair Brown to a scale of ½in = 1ft (1/24).

Fig 309▼
The construction of a steam windlass is shown here. The handwheel at the top operates the linkage to engage the cable-lifting mechanism. The brake band is tightened or slackened by the handle to the left of the cable where it is entering the chain pipe. The white object at the bottom centre is part of the chequered steel plating covering the steam supply pipe. The windlass was manufactured by Emerson Walker Ltd

◀Fig 310
Fore end of a steam windlass similar to that shown in **Fig 309**. In this the brake-operating gear is on top, and that for the sliding pinions on the warping drum shaft adjacent to the cylinders. The connecting rods from the pistons connect with the short shaft at the bottom front. *P N Thomas*

◀Fig 311
This is an electrically driven windlass by Clarke Chapman Ltd, (CPR *Beaverglen*), the drive from the motor on the deck below connecting with gearing to the shaft seen between the cable and the rigging screw. Note the detail of the linkage for the brake mechanism, and the shape of the warping drum.

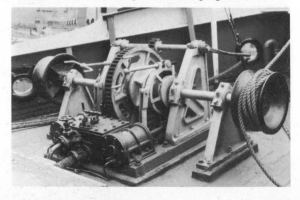

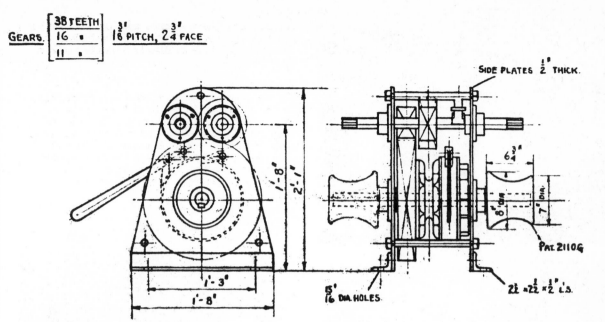

Fig 313 ▲
Arrangement of small, hand-operated anchor windlass, suitable for a chain cable of about ¾in diameter. The operating handles are fitted on the ends of the shafts at the top of the windlass. The handle to the left of the drawing is the brake handle.

Fig 314 ▼
Anchor cable capstans, showing very clearly the constructional details of both capstans and their seating arrangements. At the right foreground is a good example of a mooring capstan. *Clarke Chapman Marine*

Fig 315
A good example of an electro-hydraulically driven automatic mooring winch/windlass installation. Other interesting details in this photograph include the construction of the bulwarks, the twin roller fairleads, Panama-type fairleads and the watertight access hatch; note the height of the latter's coamings. *Clarke Chapman Marine*

form of construction, with but minor variations. More detail of the operating mechanism can be seen in **Figs 306** and **307**. The operating levers or handles, one each side, fitted into the crosshead, which can be seen on the top of the pawl bitt.

Another example of a wood windlass can be seen in **Fig 305**. This one is worked by means of crank handles fitted on to the squared ends of the short shaft carrying the small pinion near the top of the bitts. Thames sailing barges were among the type of craft fitted with this windlass.

An even simpler type of windlass can be seen in **Fig 308**. This was worked by means of long hand-spike levers inserted into the square holes seen in the whelps. Back-run was prevented by means of the pawl and ratchet seen in the middle of the barrel.

The construction of a typical powered windlass can be seen in **Fig 309**. The main element is the cable lifter which is shaped to take and hold firmly yet freely the links of the chain. Mounted on a horizontal shaft, the rest of the mechanism is there to provide the means of turning this shaft, but warping drums are usually fitted to make use of the power available. Whilst the principle has remained the same the design has been adapted over the years to suit the different kinds of prime mover which have become available, and different manufacturers have developed their own ways of installing the various pieces of essential ancillary equipment.

The windlass seen in the above-mentioned photograph is steam-driven. The piston connecting rods couple to the short horizontal shaft seen just above the base. On this shaft is a small pinion which meshes with a large one on the long shaft carrying the warping drums (for more details of these drums see **Fig 311**. On this long shaft are two small sliding pinions, each of which can be moved along independently to engage with a large pinion fitted to the shaft carrying the cable lifter. This operation is carried out by means of the handwheels seen at the top of the windlass, which operate the pivoted linking arm. Note that each lifter and its pinion are on separate shafts, to allow independent operation. Alongside each lifter is a brake drum, the band of which is tightened or slackened by the handle and screw mechanism seen over the top of the drum in **Figs 310** and **311**, whilst an alternative arrangement can be seen in **Fig 309**. **Fig 317** shows the general arrangement of a windlass.

As noted above, this is a steam windlass. The layout for an electrically operated one is similar, the driving motor being fitted on the

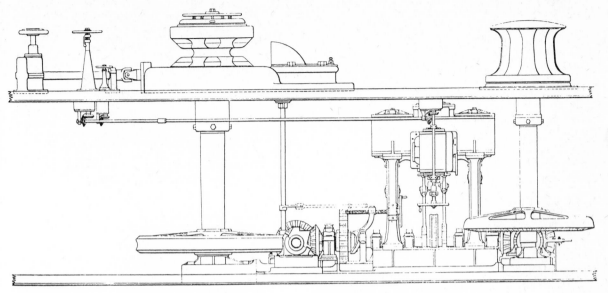

Fig 316▲
Sectional elevation showing arrangement of anchor
capstan and mooring capstan. Though this is for a
vessel of an earlier period than that shown elsewhere,
the layout has not varied much over the years – except
for the motive power.

Fig 317 ▼
General arrangement of a steam windlass for handling a
$2\frac{5}{16}$in diameter stud link cable.

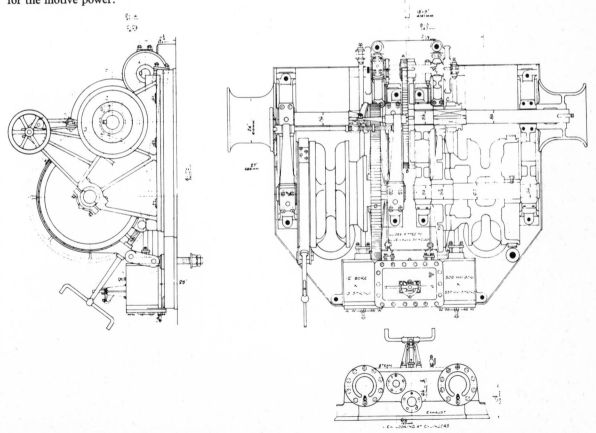

Fig 318 ▶
The (refurbished) dolly winch on the three-masted schooner *Kathleen & May*. Note the squared end of the shaft to take the operating crank handle.

Fig 319 ▼
The shaft bearings and the pawl and ratchet gear of the dolly winch on the *Kathleen & May*.

Fig 320 ▼
The brail winch on a sailing barge. Crank handles can be fitted on the squared ends of each of the three shafts seen at the top of the frame. The barge is the *Cambria*.

Fig 321 ▼
A leeboard winch on a sailing barge, with the addition of a warping drum. The operating crank handle goes on one of the two square-ended shafts at the top of the frame. The heavy rope lying across the top of the winch is not connected with its operation. The barge is the *Cambria*.

Fig 322▶

This photograph of a Jarvis brace winch was taken on board a four-masted barque in Glasgow about 1937. The winch was used to swing the three lower yards. It consists of six tapering drums, of identical shape, mounted in pairs on three shafts, and operated by handles fitted to the fourth shaft (seen above the centre pair of drums), which is geared to all three drum shafts. The drums are built up of iron or steel bars, scored to ensure that the braces wind on evenly. In use, as the brace from one end of a yard is wound on to its drum the corresponding brace to the other end of the yard is paid out from its drum. The tapering drums account for the difference in travel of the opposite braces on a yard. In fitting the braces to the drums, they are secured to the small end and wound on until the centre is reached, when they are led to their respective yards; the yards must be squared across the ship when carrying out this operation. The winch is, of course, fitted with the usual ratchet, pawl and brake mechanism.

after part of the base in the position occupied by the steam cylinder assembly. This can be seen in **Fig 252**. Sometimes, as is the case for the windlass seen in **Fig 311**, the motor is placed on the deck below, the drive being by a vertical shaft connecting with a set of gears engaging the shaft carrying the warping drums. As the cable leaves the holder when heaving in, it passes through a chain pipe incorporated in the base down to the chain locker.

The size of a windlass is usually denoted by the diameter of the chain cable which it is designed to lift.

A steam windlass of the type shown in **Fig 312** was often fitted to smaller craft such as this steam tug. When necessary it could be operated by hand. Vessels which rarely had cause to use an anchor, like small tugs and similar service and commercial craft operating in river and estuarial waters, and which moored to a quayside when not in use, were fitted with a hand windlass of the kind shown in **Fig 313**.

On many large passenger liners, and on some cross-channel ships, the anchor cable is handled by a special capstan instead of a windlass. This is rather like the cable lifter of a windlass mounted horizontally and connected to operating machinery sited on the deck below. A good idea of the general layout of this method can be seen in **Fig 314**, while **Fig 316** shows more details of the arrangement. Mooring capstans are normally incorporated in the arrangement to replace the warping drums on a windlass.

Winches

Winches for several different purposes can be found on board ship: for handling cargo, for mooring, for lowering the boats, for handling baggage and stores, for hauling nets and handling lines on fishing vessels, for towing purposes on tugs, and so on.

For cargo-handling they range from the simple handy billy, or dolly winch, found on many small sailing vessels (**Figs 318** and **319**) to the steam winch (**Figs 323** and **332**) and to the electric and hydraulically powered units of today (**Figs 324–329** and **333–337**). The large cargo-carrying sailing ships were fitted with brace or halliard winches and crab winches to facilitate the working of the ship, while on the smaller craft such as the Thames sailing barge brails and leeboards were handled by winches of the type shown in **Figs 320** and **321**. The basic design of the trawl winch, the lynch-pin of a trawler's outfit, has altered little other than in size and in the type of power unit as the vessels got bigger (see **Figs 330** and **331**).

The ever-increasing size of oil tankers and bulk carriers, and the development of the spe-

Fig 324 ▼

A useful view of a Scott winch generally similar to their Standard winch shown in the diagrams. The construction of the deck seat to which the winch is bolted is clearly seen. Note the wood chock between the seat and the winch baseplate. This photograph also shows the construction of the derrick heel fitting and the way the swivel block is attached. Note how the vertical steel ladder on the derrick post is secured by short lugs. On the right of the picture can be seen a good example of a pedestal fairlead. This one incorporates a single horn at the top. A margin plank has been fitted round the area occupied by the winch, with the deck planks butted against it. The space within the margin planks has been filled with cement or other similar compound. *Laurence Scott & Electromotors Ltd*

Fig 323 ▲

An early-pattern steam winch. There is another cylinder in the same position on the far side of the winch.

◄Fig 325
The Scott standard DC winch. This is the deckhouse type, with the controls (the two black handles) clearly visible above the folding step. The pedal of the foot brake lever can be seen to the right of the folded step. Note the bare steel deck below the winch, with a steel flat bar saveall surround projecting at least 3in above the deck planking. There is a margin plank all round the area, with an additional one each side into which the ends of the deck planks are joggled; this can just be seen at the bottom left of the picture. *Laurence Scott & Electromotors Ltd*

Fig 326 ▼
A pair of Scott 'Corrector' type winches, of the self-contained type. There are several other points of interest in this photograph: the construction of the hatch coamings, the watertight hatch for access to the hold, the steel ladder in the foreground with its chequered plate treads, and behind it the stool for the heel fitting of the 80-ton heavy lift derrick (the heel fitting itself is obscured by the lead block). *Laurence Scott & Electromotors Ltd*

cialised craft required for the offshore oil industry, has been accompanied by a whole range of new designs of winches. Such is their speciality that it has not been found possible to include details of them in this section.

The dolly winch, as can be seen from the illustrations, is quite simple to construct, the main members being either of wood or, in some designs, of cast iron, in which case they can be cut out of brass sheet or plastic card. The barrels and warping ends are of wood, and can be turned, wire being used for the shafts and the crank handles, and suitable clock gear-wheels utilised for the large and small pinions.

The constructional problems become more involved when a steam winch is required. As with many other fittings, whilst the basic design or working principle remains the same, every manufacturer had his own interpretation and designs. From the photographs it can be seen

◄Fig 327
Front view of a Scott self-contained 'Corrector' winch, left-hand type. The topping winch is set at an angle to suit the lead of the wire.

Note the tubular guard rails, where the rails are welded to the stanchions (no balls). *Laurence Scott & Electromotors Ltd*

Fig 328►
This Scott self-contained Standard 'Selector' winch is coupled to one of the maker's topping winches, details which can be seen in **Fig 339**. In the curved corner of the bulwark stands the winch control pedestal; this is shown also in **Fig 338**. Note the two footrungs at the bottom of the derrick post on the inboard side, with the vertical steel ladder immediately above them.

Another point of interest is the construction of the support on the derrick post for the derrick heel fitting and lead block attachment. The topping block in this instance is bolted to a welded lug at the head of the derrick. *Laurence Scott & Electromotors Ltd*

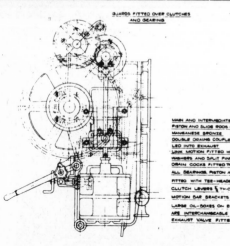

◄Fig 329
This shows clearly the construction of a warping winch. The power unit is a Scott self-contained 'Corrector' winch, and the warping ends are fitted on extended shafts, suitably supported on their inboard side. The shafts have protective covers fitted over them between winch and supporting pedestal; this is not a universal practice. Warping winches are more usually found at the after end of a ship, rather than on the forecastle as here. Other points of interest are the construction on the breakwater, the windlass (showing the chain pipes for the 2¼in cable), the pedestal fairleads (or warping guides), the derrick crutches on the mast, and the rails round the opening in the deck for the steel ladder (the treads of which each comprise three close spaces round steel bars, probably about ¾in in diameter). The ship is the Blue Funnel Line *Centaur* (1964). *Laurence Scott & Electromotors Ltd*

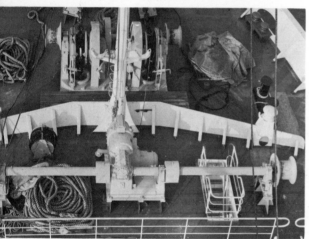

GUARDS FITTED OVER CLUTCHES AND GEARING

MAIN AND INTERMEDIATE WHEELS IN HALVES
PISTON AND SLIDE RODS OF FORGED
MANGANESE BRONZE
DOUBLE DRAINS COUPLED UP AND
LED INTO EXHAUST
LINK MOTION FITTED WITH HEADED PINS
WASHERS AND SPLIT PINS
DRAIN COCKS FITTED TO SLIDE VALVE CHAMBERS
ALL BEARINGS, PISTON AND SLIDE ROD GLANDS
FITTED WITH TEE-HEADED BOLTS
CLUTCH LEVERS ⅝ THICK
MOTION BAR BRACKETS FITTED WITH DOWEL PINS
LARGE OIL-BOXES ON ECCENTRIC STRAPS WHICH
ARE INTERCHANGEABLE
EXHAUST VALVE FITTED

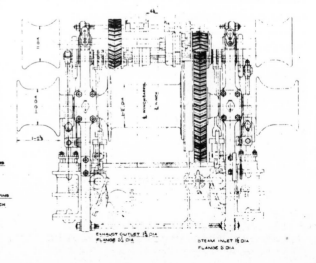

EXHAUST OUTLET 1½ DIA
FLANGE 5¼ DIA

STEAM INLET 1½ DIA
FLANGE 5 DIA

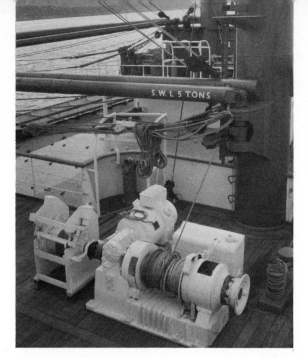

Fig 330 ▼
Many details of the arrangement of a trawl winch can be seen in this photograph of the electrically driven winch fitted to the diesel-electric all-freezer stern trawler *Ross Valiant* (1964). In front of each winding drum is the automatic warp-reeving gear trolley; the one on the port side has the warp running through it, and that on the starboard side can be seen with the warp end swivel lying between the rollers. These trolleys move transversely across the width of the drum to ensure an even lay of wire on the drum. The outer handwheel port and starboard operates the screwdown band brake on each drum, whilst the two inner ones operate similar brakes on the inner warping drums. On the outboard end of each main shaft is a double-waisted warping end. The power unit is situated at the centre of the winch, the necessary gearing and clutches to the main shaft being under the protective covers. The two winding drums can be operated independently. This is a large trawl winch, but the basic design is much the same for all trawl winches, whatever the power unit; most do not have the two inner warping drums. *Laurence Scott & Electromotors Ltd*

that, in contrast to the electric winches, the steam winch is a somewhat complicated item to reproduce at a small scale. To do the job properly the detailed drawings of the winch are required, or at least of one of the same period and similar design. **Fig 332** is an arrangement of a steam winch (*c*1948) having a 5-ton lifting capacity; it gives a very good idea of the general layout. As is often the case with winches of this type, this one has four warping drums.

Electrically driven winches, on the other hand, are a great deal less complicated from the modelmaker's point of view, as can be seen from the drawings and photographs. Although the illustrations are principally of the products of one manufacturer, they can be considered as typical, in a general way, of the majority of electric winches used for cargo-handling. A winch of the type shown in **Fig 342** was often fitted to smaller ships, where its compact design

Fig 331 ▶
More details of the construction of a trawl winch, of the smaller size, can be seen in this photograph. It shows the starboard half of the winch. It was fitted to a conventional type of distant-water trawler awaiting demolition in the late 1970s.

◀Fig 332
Arrangement of a horizontal steam winch, 5-ton capacity. As with many steam winches, this one has four warping ends. *By courtesy of Clarke Chapman Ltd*

was advantageous if deck space was at a premium. **Fig 343** is of a design of winch which could be used for several purposes, such as handling mooring lines, hoisting baggage, or lowering a ship's boats.

The size of a winch varied according to its purpose and the load it was required to lift. In addition, it was often adapted for special purposes, such as having the warping drums fitted on extended shafts to act as a special mooring winch, as in **Figs 329** and **340**. It could be coupled to heavy-duty geared barrels when used in conjunction with heavy lift derricks, or connected to another special winch – a topping winch – which controlled the outreach of the derrick, as in **Figs 328** and **339**.

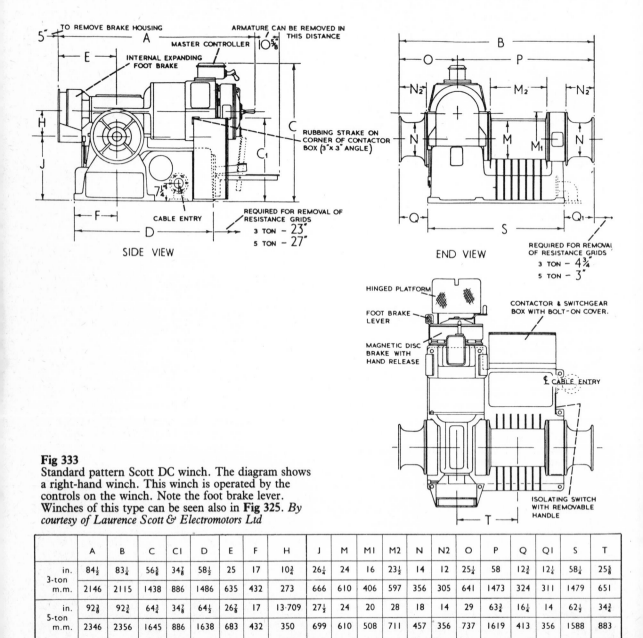

Fig 333
Standard pattern Scott DC winch. The diagram shows a right-hand winch. This winch is operated by the controls on the winch. Note the foot brake lever. Winches of this type can be seen also in **Fig 325**. *By courtesy of Laurence Scott & Electromotors Ltd*

		A	B	C	CI	D	E	F	H	J	M	MI	M2	N	N2	O	P	Q	QI	S	T
3-ton	in.	$84\frac{1}{2}$	$83\frac{1}{4}$	$56\frac{5}{8}$	$34\frac{7}{8}$	$58\frac{1}{2}$	25	17	$10\frac{3}{4}$	$26\frac{1}{4}$	24	16	$23\frac{1}{2}$	14	12	$25\frac{1}{4}$	58	$12\frac{3}{4}$	$12\frac{1}{4}$	$58\frac{1}{4}$	$25\frac{5}{8}$
	m.m.	2146	2115	1438	886	1486	635	432	273	666	610	406	597	356	305	641	1473	324	311	1479	651
5-ton	in.	$92\frac{3}{8}$	$92\frac{3}{4}$	$64\frac{3}{4}$	$34\frac{7}{8}$	$64\frac{1}{2}$	$26\frac{7}{8}$	17	13·709	$27\frac{1}{2}$	24	20	28	18	14	29	$63\frac{3}{4}$	$16\frac{1}{4}$	14	$62\frac{1}{2}$	$34\frac{3}{4}$
	m.m.	2346	2356	1645	886	1638	683	432	350	699	610	508	711	457	356	737	1619	413	356	1588	883

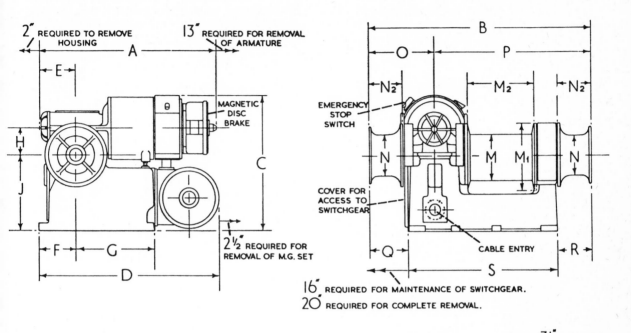

Fig 334
Self-contained Scott 'Corrector' type winch. The diagram shows a right-hand winch. This winch is controlled from a pedestal of the type shown in **Fig 338.** *By courtesy of Laurence Scott & Electromotors Ltd*

SIZE		A	B	C	D	E	F	G	H	J	M	M1	M2	N	N2	O	P	Q	R	S	T
3-ton	in.	$62\frac{1}{8}$	$78\frac{3}{8}$	47	$63\frac{1}{2}$	$13\frac{1}{2}$	$13\frac{1}{4}$	$27\frac{3}{4}$	$9\frac{1}{4}$	$26\frac{1}{4}$	16	$23\frac{1}{2}$	24	14	12	$22\frac{5}{8}$	$55\frac{3}{4}$	$13\frac{3}{8}$	12	53	$23\frac{1}{2}$
	mm.	1578	1991	1194	1613	343	337	705	235	667	406	597	610	356	305	575	1416	340	305	1346	597
5-ton	in.	73	$88\frac{1}{2}$	52	73	$16\frac{5}{8}$	16	$34\frac{1}{2}$	12·282	$26\frac{1}{4}$	20	28	24	18	14	$26\frac{3}{4}$	$61\frac{3}{4}$	$15\frac{1}{2}$	14	59	$25\frac{3}{4}$
	mm.	1854	2247	1321	1854	422	406	875	312	667	508	711	610	457	356	679	1568	394	356	1498	654
7-ton	in.	$81\frac{1}{2}$	92	58	86	18	$20\frac{1}{2}$	42	$16\frac{1}{2}$	$26\frac{1}{4}$	20	28	24	18	14	$27\frac{1}{2}$	64	$14\frac{1}{2}$	14	63	27
	mm.	2070	2337	1473	2184	457	521	1067	419	667	508	711	610	457	356	698	1626	368	356	1600	686

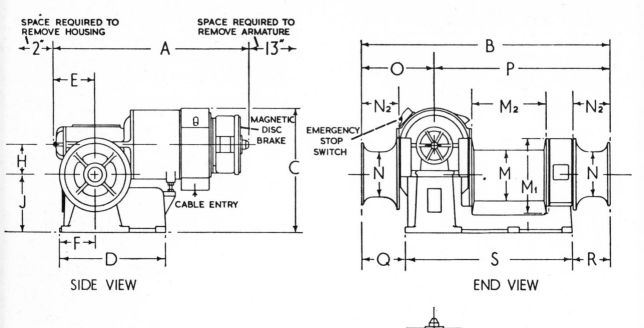

SIDE VIEW

END VIEW

Fig 335
Another version of the Scott 'Corrector' winch, known as the deckhouse type since much of the electrical equipment is fitted in an adjacent deckhouse and not on the winch itself as in the self-contained type. The winch is controlled from a pedestal of the type shown in **Fig 338**. *By courtesy of Laurence Scott & Electromotors Ltd*

SIZE		A	B	C	D	E	F	H	J	M	M1	M2	N	N2	O	P	Q	R	S	T
3-ton	in.	$62\frac{1}{8}$	$78\frac{3}{8}$	$38\frac{3}{4}$	$34\frac{1}{4}$	$13\frac{1}{2}$	$11\frac{3}{4}$	$9\frac{1}{4}$	18	16	$23\frac{1}{2}$	24	14	12	$22\frac{5}{8}$	$55\frac{3}{4}$	$13\frac{1}{8}$	$12\frac{1}{4}$	53	$23\frac{1}{2}$
	mm.	1578	1991	984	870	343	298	235	457	406	597	610	356	305	573	1416	333	311	1346	597
5-ton	in.	73	$88\frac{3}{4}$	$47\frac{1}{2}$	44	$16\frac{5}{8}$	14	12·282	22	20	28	24	18	14	27	$61\frac{3}{4}$	$15\frac{1}{2}$	14	$59\frac{1}{4}$	$25\frac{1}{4}$
	mm.	1854	2254	1207	1118	422	355 6	312	559	508	711	610	457	356	686	1568	394	356	1505	654
7-ton	in.	$81\frac{1}{2}$	92	$55\frac{1}{2}$	54	18	18	$16\frac{1}{2}$	24	20	28	24	18	14	$27\frac{1}{2}$	64	$14\frac{1}{2}$	14	63	27
	mm.	2070	2337	1410	1372	457	457	419	610	508	711	610	457	356	698	1626	368	356	1600	686

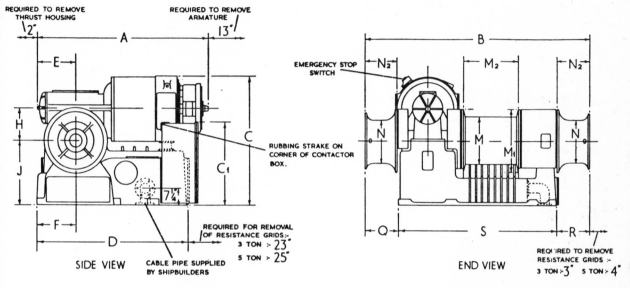

Fig 336
Scott standard 'Selector' winch, self-contained type.
Control is from a pedestal of the type shown in **Fig
338**. Note the ribbed casing below the winch barrel. A
winch of this type can also be seen in **Fig 328**. *By
courtesy of Laurence Scott & Electromotors Ltd*

SIZE		A	B	C	CI	D	E	F	H	J	M	MI	M2	N	N2	Q	R	S	T
3-ton	in.	62	89	48	$34\frac{7}{8}$	$58\frac{1}{2}$	$13\frac{1}{2}$	17	$9\frac{1}{4}$	$26\frac{1}{4}$	16	$23\frac{1}{2}$	24	14	12	$11\frac{1}{4}$	$12\frac{1}{4}$	$65\frac{1}{2}$	$25\frac{5}{8}$
	mm.	1575	2261	1219	886	1486	343	432	235	667	406	597	610	356	305	286	311	1664	651
5-ton	in.	73	$96\frac{1}{4}$	$53\frac{1}{2}$	$34\frac{7}{8}$	$64\frac{1}{2}$	$16\frac{5}{8}$	17	12.282	$27\frac{1}{2}$	20	28	24	18	14	$13\frac{3}{4}$	14	$68\frac{1}{2}$	$27\frac{1}{4}$
	mm.	1854	2445	1359	886	1638	422	432	312	699	508	711	610	457	356	349	356	1740	692

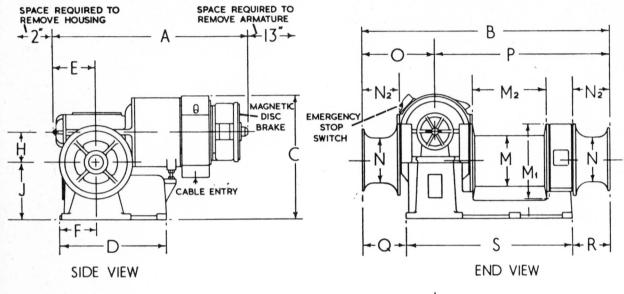

SIDE VIEW   END VIEW

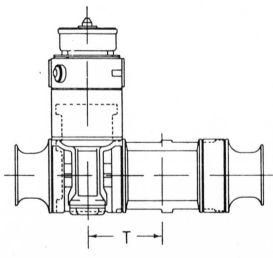

Fig 337
The deckhouse version of the Scott standard 'Selector'
winch. *By courtesy of Laurence Scott & Electromotors Ltd*

SIZE		A	B	C	D	E	F	H	J	M	M1	M2	N	N2	O	P	Q	R	S	T
3-ton	in.	$62\frac{1}{8}$	$78\frac{3}{8}$	$38\frac{3}{4}$	$34\frac{1}{4}$	$13\frac{1}{2}$	$11\frac{3}{4}$	$9\frac{1}{4}$	18	16	$23\frac{1}{2}$	24	14	12	$22\frac{5}{8}$	$55\frac{3}{4}$	$13\frac{1}{8}$	$12\frac{1}{4}$	53	$23\frac{1}{2}$
	mm.	1578	1991	984	870	343	298	235	457	406	597	610	356	305	574·6	1416	333	311	1346	597
5-ton	in.	73	$88\frac{3}{4}$	$47\frac{1}{2}$	44	$16\frac{5}{8}$	14	12·282	22	20	28	24	18	14	27	$61\frac{3}{4}$	15	14	$59\frac{1}{4}$	$25\frac{3}{4}$
	mm.	1854	2254	1207	1118	422	356	312	559	508	711	610	457	356	686	1668	394	356	1505	654

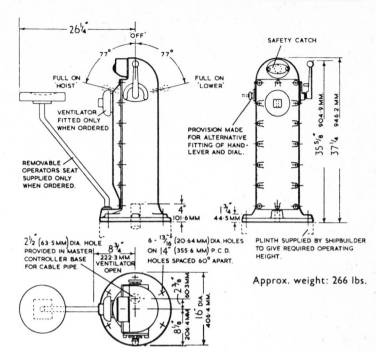

Fig 338 ▶
The approximate dimensions of the control pedestal for both deckhouse and self-contained winches. One of these pedestals can be seen in **Fig 328**. *By courtesy of Laurence Scott & Electromotors Ltd*

Fig 339 ▼
Scott topping winch. The dimensions shown are suitable for either a 3-ton or 5-ton capacity unit. A winch of this type can also be seen in **Fig 328**, coupled to a standard 'Selector' winch. *By courtesy of Laurence Scott & Electromotors Ltd*

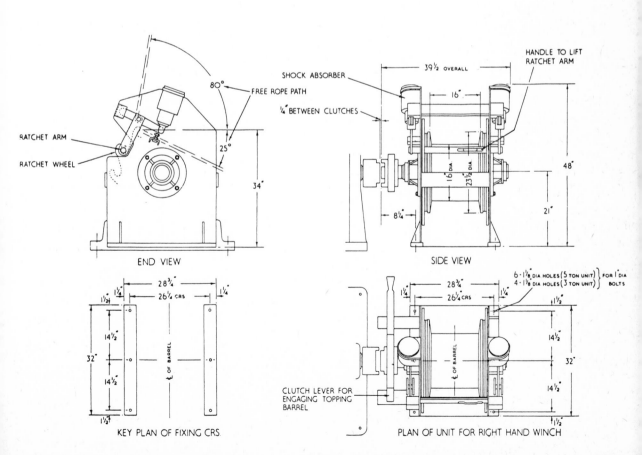

END VIEW

SIDE VIEW

KEY PLAN OF FIXING CRS.

PLAN OF UNIT FOR RIGHT HAND WINCH

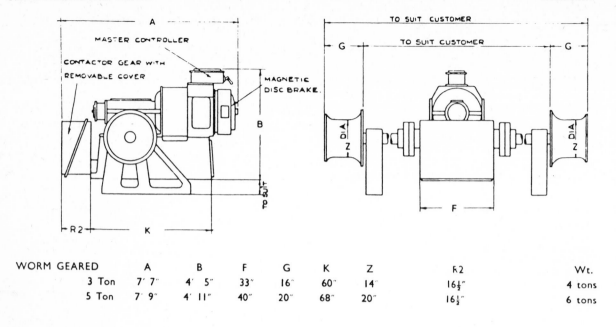

WORM GEARED	A	B	F	G	K	Z	R2	Wt.
3 Ton	7′ 7″	4′ 5″	33″	16″	60″	14″	16½″	4 tons
5 Ton	7′ 9″	4′ 11″	40″	20″	68″	20″	16½″	6 tons

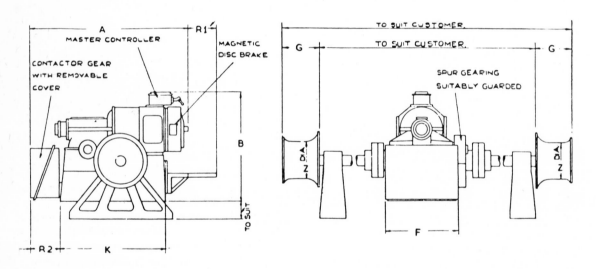

WORM and SPUR GEARED	A	B	F	G	K	Z	R2	Wt.
3 Ton	7′ 2½″	4′ 11	40″	20″	57½″	20″	16½″	5¾ tons
5 Ton	8′ 1	5′ 10	42″	25″	65½″	26	16½″	8½ tons

Fig 340
Typical arrangement of a warping winch. The distance of the warping drums from the winch will depend on the layout of the ship. A winch of this type can be seen in **Fig 329**. Note that the controls for the winch are mounted on the motor. *By courtesy of Laurence Scott & Electromotors*

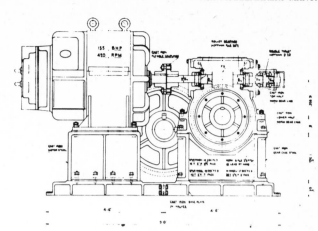

Fig 341
General arrangement of a large
warping winch having a 14-ton
capacity. Electrically driven, it was
made about 1946. *By courtesy of
Napier Bros*

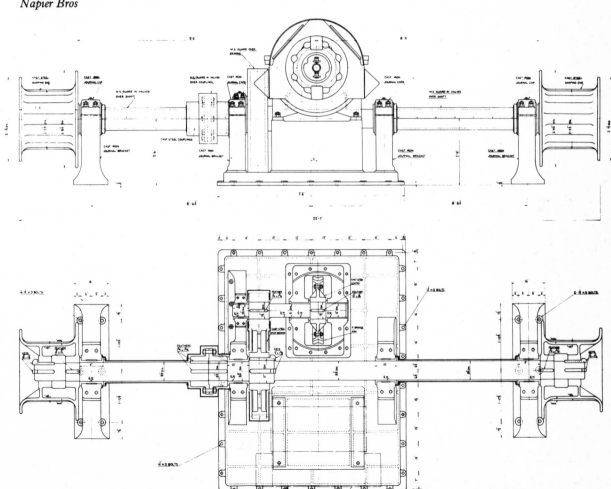

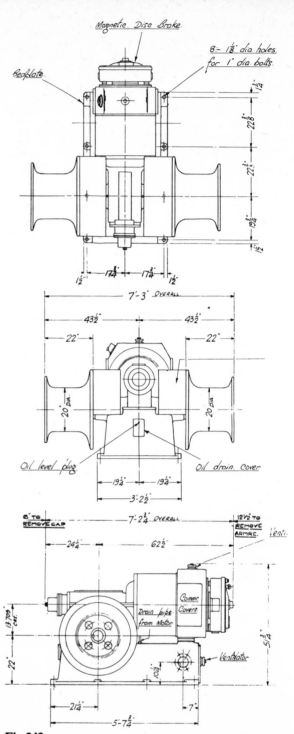

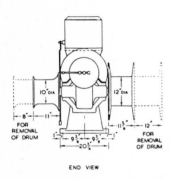

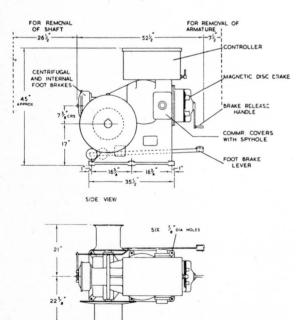

Fig 342
Plan of the Scott coaster winch. This has a warping drum one side and a rope drum on the other side. *By courtesy of Laurence Scott & Electromotors Ltd*

Fig 343
Arrangement of the Scott mooring winch. Note that there is no rope storage barrel on this winch. This is a 5-ton capacity winch. Lighter versions of this pattern of winch can be used for handling baggage. Another use for the heavier capacity models is in connection with lowering the ship's boats. *By courtesy of Laurence Scott & Electromotors Ltd*

Bibliography and Sources

The following is of necessity but a limited selection of the great range of source material available to the ship modeller across the world. Some may feel that worthwhile titles, institutions and sources have been omitted, which should have been included. This is probably so, but unfortunately it is a situation which arises whenever an exercise of this nature has to be carried out.

A number of the titles shown are out of print, but loan copies of most can usually be obtained through the public library services. At times they can be found in the lists of the specialist dealers in new and secondhand maritime books. Back volumes of the technical journals can be consulted in the libraries of those museums which carry copies, and at times (and then by appointment) in the private libraries of some of the technical societies. **Note:** An asterisk (★) against a date of publication indicates that there have been several further editions or reprints since the book was first published. R indicates a reprint.

SHIP MODELLING

Bates, A L: *Western Rivers Steamboat Cyclopaedium* (1968 Hustle Press, Leonia, New Jersey, USA)

Battson, R K: *The Shipmodeller's Workshop* (1947 Percival Marshall, London)

Bowen J L: *Waterline Ship Models* (1972 Conway, London)

Campbell, G F: *The Neophyte Shipmodeller's Jackstay* (1962 Model Shipways, Bogota, New Jersey, USA)

Chesneau, R: *Scale Models in Plastic* (1979 Conway, London)

Coker, C: *Building Warship Models* (1974 Coker Craft, Charleston, USA)

Craine, Lt Cdr J H: *Ship Modelling Hints & Tips* (1948, R1973 Conway, London)

Edson, M: *Ship Modeller's Shop Notes* (1979 Nautical Research Guild Inc, 6413 Dahlonega Rd, Washington DC 20016, USA)

Fox Smith, C: *Ship Models* (1951, R1972 Conway, London)

Freeston, E C: *The Construction of Model Open Boats* (1975 Conway, London)

Grimwood, V R: *American Ship Models &*

How to Build Them (1942 Norton, New York, USA)

Hambleton, F C: *Famous Paddle Steamers* (1948, R1977 Argus Books, Watford)

Hobbs, E W: *Model Power Boats* (1929 Cassell, London)

Lewis, J C: *A Ship Modeller's Logbook* (1950) Percival Marshall, London)

McKee, E: *Clenched Lap or Clinker* (1972 National Maritime Museum, London)

McNarry, D: *Shipbuilding in Miniature* (1955 Percival Marshall, London)

McNarry, D: *Ship Models in Miniature* (1975 David & Charles, Newton Abbott)

Musciano, W: *Building & Operating Model Ships* (1976 Hale, London)

Purves, A: *Flags for Marine Artists & Modellers* (1950 Percival Marshall, London)

Reeve, B & Thomas, P: *Scale Model Ships* (1951 Sidgwick & Jackson, London)

Rogers, R C: *Painting & Lining Models* (1973 Argus Books, Watford)

Safford, E L: *Model Radio Control*

Smeed, V: *Boat Modelling* (1964 Argus Books, Watford)

Smeed, V: *Power Boat Models* (1977 Argus Books, Watford)

Smeed, V: *The World of Model Ships* (1979 Argus Books)

Trollope, A D: *Power Driven Ship Models* (1959 Percival Marshall, London)

Underhill, H A: *Plank on Frame Models* (2 vols. 1958, R1974 Brown, Son & Ferguson, Glasgow)

Underhill, H A: *Masting & Rigging the Clipper Ship & the Ocean Carrier* (1946, R1978 Brown, Son & Ferguson, Glasgow)

Underhill, H A: *Deepwater Sail* (1952 Brown, Son & Ferguson, Glasgow)

Veenstra, A: *Handbook of Ship Modelling* (1981 Argus Books, Watford)

Warring, R: *Radio Controlled Model Boats* (1981 Argus Books, Watford)

Warring, R: *The New Glass Fibre Book* (1980) Argus Books, Watford)

Wingrove, G A: *The Techniques of Ship Modelling* (1974 Argus Books, Watford)

— *Model Boat Propellers* (1972, R1980 Argus Books, Watford)

— *Manual of Ship Making* (1947 Popular Science, New York)

SHIP CONSTRUCTION

Abell, Sir Westcott: *The Shipwright's Trade* (1948, R1981 Conway, London)

Barnaby, K C: *Basic Naval Architecture* (1949)

Baxter, B: *Naval Architecture* (1976 Hodder & Stoughton, London)

Biles, Sir J W: *Design & Construction of Ships* (2 vols. c1910)

Caldwell, A: *Screw Tug Design* (1946 Hutchinson, London) Revised edition by J N Wood under title *Caldwell's Screw Tug Design* (1980 Hutchinson, London)

Hardy, A C: *From Slip to Sea* (1926)

Hardy, A C: *Merchant Ship Types* (1924 Chapman & Hall, London)

Hogg, R S: *Naval Architecture & Ship Construction* (1942* Munro, Glasgow)

Holmes, Sir George V: *Ancient & Modern Ships: Part I Wooden Sailing Ships; Part II Steamships* (1900 & 1906 HMSO, London)

Holmes, Campbell: *Practical Shipbuilding* (2 vols. 1916)

Hughes, C W: *Handbook of Ship Calculations, Construction & Operations* (1942 New York)

Kemp, J & Young, P: *Ship Construction Sketches & Notes* (1958* Stanford Maritime, London)

Macrow, C & Woollard, L: *Naval Architects & Shipbuilder's Pocket Book* (1900*)

Munro Smith, R: *Design & Construction of Small Craft* (1924 London)

Munro Smith, R: *Merchant Ship Design* (19? Hutchinson, London)

Nicol, G: *Ship Construction & Calculations* (1909* Brown, Glasgow)

Paasch, H: *From Keel to Truck* (1885 Antwerp)

Paasch, H: *Illustrated Marine Encyclopaedia* (1890 Antwerp, R1980 edited by D MacGregor, Argus Books, Watford)

Pollock, W: *Building Small Ships* (1948)

Pollock, W: *Designs of Small Oil Engined Vessels*

Pollock, W: *Small Vessels*

Pursey, J H: *Merchant Ship Construction* (1942* Brown, Son & Ferguson, Glasgow)

Thearle, S J P: *The Modern Practice of Shipbuilding in Iron & Steel* (2 vols. 1886* Collins, London)

Waine, C V: *Steam Coasters* (1977, Revised Edition 1980 Waine Research, Albrighton)

Walton, T: *Know Your Ship* (1896* Griffin, London)

Walton, T: *Steel Ships* (1901* Griffin, London)

SHIP MODELLING MAGAZINES

Marine Models: Publication in its original form ceased in September 1939; resumed publication after the war for a short period in much reduced format

Model Boats: Monthly. MAP Ltd, PO Box 35, Bridge Street, Hemel Hempstead, Herts HP1 1EE, UK

Model Shipbuilder: Bi-monthly. PO Box 441, Menomonee Falls, WI 53051, USA

Model Ships & Power Boats: Published from January 1948 to December 1956, then incorporated with *Model Engineer*

Ships & Ship Models: Published from September 1931 to September 1939

Model Shipwright: Quarterly from 1972. Conway Maritime Press Ltd, 2 Nelson Road, Greenwich, London SE10 9JB, UK

TECHNICAL JOURNALS

Engineering: (since 1866). Design Council, 28 Haymarket, London SW1 4SU, UK

Hansa: (1864). C Schroeder & Co, Stubbenhuk 10, 2000 Hamburg 11, W Germany

Holland Shipbuilding: (1952). PO Box 277, 3300 AG Dordrecht, Netherlands

Journal de la Marine Marchande: (1919). 190 Boulevard Haussmann, 75008 Paris, France

Le Genie Civil: (France)

Marine Engineering/Log: (1878). Simmonds Boardman Publishing Corporation, 350 Broadway, New York, NY 10013, USA

Marine Week: (1974). IPC Industrial Press, Quadrant House, Sutton, Surrey, UK

Maritime Reporter & Engineering News: (1939). 107 East 31st Street, New York, NY 10016, USA

Motor Ship: (1920). IPC Industrial Press, Quadrant House, Sutton, Surrey, UK

Navires, Portes et Chantiers: (1950). 190 Boulevard Haussmann, 75008 Paris, France

Reed's Special Ships: (1977). Saracen Head Building, 36–37 Cock Lane, London EC1A 9BY, UK

Schiff und Hafen: (1948). PO Box 1347, D-2000 Hamburg 50, W Germany

Shipbuilding & Marine Engineering International: (1958). Whitehall Press, Earl House, Maidstone, Kent, UK

Shipbuilding & Shipping Record: (1913). Now incorporated with *Marine Week*
Shipping World & Shipbuilder: (1883). Marine Publications International Ltd, 42–43 Lower Marsh, London SE1 7RQ, UK
Small Ships: (1977). IPC Industrial Press, Quadrant House, Sutton, Surrey, UK
The Engineer: (1856). Calderwood Street, London SE18 6QN, UK
The Naval Architect: (1971). 10 Upper Belgrave Street, London SW1 8BQ, UK
The Shipbuilder: (1906). Now incorporated with *Shipping World & Shipbuilder*
Vereines Deutscher Ingenieure: (1857). VDI Verlag GmbH, Graf Recke Strasse 84, Postfach 1139, 4000 Dusseldorf, West Germany

PLANS FOR SHIP MODELLERS
Fisher A J, 1002 Etowah Street, Royal Oak, Michigan 48067, USA
Jecobin Ltd, 31 Romans Way, Pyrford, Woking, Surrey GU22 8TR, UK
MacGregor Plans, 99 Lonsdale Road, London SW13 9DA, UK
Maritime Models Greenwich, 7 Nelson Road, London SE10 9JB, UK
MAP Ltd, PO Box 35, Bridge Street, Hemel Hempstead, Herts HP1 1EE, UK
Model Shipbuilder Plans, PO Box 441, Menomonee Falls, WI 53051, USA
Model Shipways Co Inc, 39 West Lee Road, Bogota, New Jersey 07603, USA
Sambrook Marine Plans, 84–86 Broad Street, Teddington, Middlesex, TW11 8QT, UK
Taubman Plans Service, Box 4G, 11 College Drive, Jersey City, NJ 07305, USA
The Dromedary, Ship Modellers Associates, 6324 Belton Road, El Paso, Texas 7991, USA
The Floating Drydock, c/o General Delivery, Kregsville, Pa 18333, USA
Underhill Plans, Bassett-Lowke Ltd, Kingswell Street, Northampton NN1 1PS, UK
Vic Smeed, PO Box 6, Croxley Green, Rickmansworth, Herts WD3 4RE, UK

SHIPBUILDERS' PLANS
These collections do not include material from yards still in operation, except for a few examples of early historical plans.

Danish National Archives, Rigsarkivet, Rigsdagsgarden 9, 1218 Copenhagen, Denmark
Musée de la Marine, Palais de Chaillot, 75116 Paris, France
National Maritime Museum, Greenwich, London SE10 9NF, UK
Smithsonian Institute, Jefferson Drive at 10th Street, Washington DC, 20560, USA
Scottish Record Office, PO Box 36, HM General Register House, Edinburgh EH1 3YY, Scotland, UK
Strathclyde Regional Archives, PO Box 27, City Chambers, Glasgow G2 1DU, UK
The Archives, The University, Glasgow G12 8QQ, UK
Tyne & Wear Archives Dept, Blandford House, West Blandford Street, Newcastle upon Tyne NE1 4JA, UK

SHIP PHOTOGRAPHS
Beken & Son, Cowes, Isle of Wight, UK
Duncan, A, 14 South Hill Road, Gravesend, Kent DA12 1JN, UK
Imperial War Museum, Lambeth, London SE1 6HZ, UK
National Maritime Museum, Photo Section, Greenwich, London SE10 9NF, UK
The Peabody Museum, 161 Essex Street, Salem, Massachusetts 01970, USA
Real Photograph Co, 69 Stanley Road, Broadstairs, Kent, UK
Skyfotos Ltd, Littlestone Road, New Romney, Kent, UK
Steamship Historical Society of America Collection, University of Baltimore, 1420 Maryland Avenue, Baltimore, Maryland 21201, USA
The Mariners' Museum, Newport News, Virginia 23606, USA
Wright & Logan, 20 Queen Street, Portsea, Portsmouth, Hants, UK
The Society for the Preservation of New England Antiquities, 141 Cambridge Street, Boston 14, Massachusetts, USA

GENERAL REFERENCE
Of the titles which follow two are of great interest to ship modellers. *The Denny List* gives in-depth details of the National Maritime Museum's collection of plans at Greenwich of the vessels built by Denny at Dumbarton. The *Modern British Shipbuilding Guide to Historical*

Records lists for the first time information as to the whereabouts of such shipbuilders' plans and records which have survived the many shipyard closures.

Other publications which come into this section are those like *Conway's All the World's Fighting Ships 1860–1905, 1922–1946* (*1947–1982* will be published in Autumn 1982, and *1906–1921* will follow), Talbot Booth's *Merchant Ships*, and the numerous books dealing with passenger liners, coastal vessels and paddle steamers, the histories of shipping companies and specific services. The illustrative material in these books is the principal interest to the modeller. Little has been published, other than in pocket book form or in the transactions of the technical societies, about tugs, trawlers, modern coasters and special service ships. Much useful material has appeared in print in America about the vessels built and operated on that country's rivers, lakes and canals, and around its coasts.

Beaver, P: *The Big Ship* (Brunel's *Great Eastern*. 1969 Evelyn, London)

Braynard, F: *Leviathan* (5 vols. 1972 South Street Seaport Museum, New York, USA)

Braynard, F: *The Big Ship: The Story of the SS United States* (1981, The Mariners' Museum, Newport News, USA)

Ball, A & Wright, D: *Great Britain* (1981 David & Charles, Newton Abbott)

Cairis, N: *Passenger Liners of the World Since 1893* (1979 Bonanza Books, New York, USA)

Corlett, E: *The Iron Ship* (1975 Moonraker Press, Bradford-on-Avon)

Dunn, L: *Famous Liners of the Past* (1964 Adlard Coles, London)

Emmerson, G: *John Scott Russell* (1977 Murray, London)

Gilmer, T: *Working Watercraft* (1972 Patrick Stephens, Cambridge)

Greenhill, B: *Merchant Schooners* (1951. R1968 David & Charles, Newton Abbott)

Greenhill, B & Giffard, A: *Victorian & Edwardian Steamships From Old Photographs* (1979 Batsford, London)

Greenway, A: *A Century of Cross Channel Passenger Ferries* (1981 Ian Allan, Shepperton)

Guthrie, J: *Bizarre Ships of the Nineteenth Century* (1970 Hutchinson, London)

Guthrie, J: *A History of Marine Engineering* (1971 Hutchinson, London)

Hardy, A C: *Seafood Ships*

Hilton, G, Plummer, R, Jobe, J: *The Illustrated History of Paddle Steamers* (1977 Edita Lausanne SA, Switzerland)

Hofman, E: *The Steam Yachts* (1970 Nautical Publishing Co, Lymington, Hants)

Hume, J & Moss, M: *Clyde Shipbuilding From Old Photographs* (1975 Batsford, London)

Kludas, A: *Great Passenger Ships of the World, 1858–1976* (5 vols. 1975–77 Patrick Stephens, Cambridge)

Landstrom, B: *The Ship* (1961 Allen & Unwin, London)

Lyon, D J: *The Denny List* (1975 National Maritime Museum, London)

McDonald, D: *The Clyde Puffer* (1977 David & Charles, Newton Abbott)

Shaum, J & Flayhart, W: *Majesty at Sea* (1981, Patrick Stephens, Cambridge, UK)

Stapleton, N R J: *Steam Picket Boats* (1980 Dalton, Lavenham, Suffolk)

Sea Breezes: Monthly. 202 Cotton Exchange Building, Old Hall Street, Liverpool L63 9LA, UK

Ships Monthly: Monthly. Waterway Productions Ltd, Kottingham House, Dale Street, Burton-on-Trent DE14 3TD, UK

MARITIME MUSEUMS

As well as those shown below there are many other maritime museums, and collections of ship models, large and small, in cities and towns in many countries.

Ålands Sjöfartsmuseum, Mariehamn, Finland

Altonaer Museum, Museumstrasse 23, Hamburg 50, W Germany

Bath Marine Museum, 963 Washington Street, Bath, Maine, USA

Central Maritime Museum, Gdansk, Poland

Central Naval Museum, Pushkin Square, Leningrad, USSR

Danish Maritime Museum, Kronborg Castle, Handels-Og Sofartsmuseet, Paa Kronborg, Helsingør, Denmark

Deutsches Museum, 8000 Munchen 26, Munich, W Germany

Deutsches Schiffahrtsmuseum, Van-Ronzelenstrasse, D-2850, Bremerhaven, W Germany

Dossin Great Lakes Museum, Belle Island Park, Detroit, Michigan, USA

Exeter Maritime Museum, The Quay,
Exeter, Devon, UK
Imperial War Museum, Lambeth, London
SE1 6HZ, UK
Mariners' Museum, Newport News, Virginia
23606, USA
Maritime Museum Prins Hendrik, Burg
s'Jacobsplein 8, Rotterdam, Netherlands
Merseyside County Museums, William
Brown Street, Liverpool, UK
Merseyside Maritime Museum, Pier Head,
Liverpool, UK
Museum of Transport, 25 Albert Drive,
Glasgow G41 2PE, UK
Museo de la Mare, Via San Giorgio N,
Trieste 3, Italy
Museo Storico Navale, Venice, Italy
Museo de Marinha, Praca do Imperie,
Lisbon, Portugal
Museo Maritimo, Puerto de la Paz 1,
Barcelona, Spain
Museo Naval, Montalban 2, Madrid, Spain
Mystic Seaport Museum, Mystic,
Connecticut, USA
National Maritime Museum, Greenwich,
London SE10 9NF, UK
National Maritime Museum, Oslo, Norway
National Scheepvartmuseum, Steenplein 1,
Antwerp, Belgium
Nederlands Historische Scheepvart Museum,
Schuytstraat 57, Amsterdam, Netherlands
Peabody Museum, 161 Essex Street, Salem,
Massachusetts, USA
Rijksmuseum, Hobbemastraat 21,
Amsterdam 2, Netherlands
Royal Scottish Museum, Chambers Street,
Edinburgh, Scotland, UK

Science Museum, Exhibition Road, South
Kensington, London SW7, UK
Smithsonian Institution, Constitution
Avenue, Washington DC, USA
South Street Seaport Museum, 203 Front
Street, New York, NY 10038, USA
Sjöfartsmuseet, Goteborg V, Sweden
Vancouver Maritime Museum, Cyprus
Street, Vancouver 9, British Columbia,
Canada
Many museums publish handbooks and other
material about or in connection with their
exhibits, as well as photographs, and these can
be invaluable sources of information.

SOCIETY JOURNALS
Das Logbuch: Arbeitskreis Historischer
Schiffbau eV, Postfach 176, Heidesheim, W
Germany
The Mariner's Mirror: Society for Nautical
Research, The National Maritime Museum,
Greenwich, London SE10 9NF, UK
Nautical Research Journal: Nautical Research
Guild Inc, 6413 Dahlonega Road,
Washington DC 20016, USA
The American Neptune: The Peabody
Museum, Salem, Massachusetts 01970, USA
Also such works as the *Transactions* of the Royal
Institution of Naval Architects (UK), Institute
of Engineers and Shipbuilders in Scotland
(UK), the North East Institute of Engineers
and Shipbuilders (UK), the Society of Naval
Architects and Marine Engineers (America),
and the Institute of Marine Engineers. Though
technical, these contain useful information on
all aspects of ship design and construction.

List of illustrations/Index

Because the Catalogue section of this book is in alphabetical order an index is not really necessary. However, the following alphabetical list of illustrations can be used to find more specific details within the main entries. **Note:** *the references are figure numbers, not page numbers.*